CANADIAN GOVERNMENT AND POLITICS IN COMPARATIVE PERSPECTIVE

Second Edition

Earl H. Fry

Associate Professor of Political Science
and Coordinator, Canadian Studies Program
David M. Kennedy International Center
Brigham Young University

UNIVERSITY
PRESS OF
AMERICA

LANHAM • NEW YORK • LONDON

JL
61
.F79
1984 / 52,801

All University Press of America books are produced on acid-free
paper which exceeds the minimum standards set by the National
Historical Publications and Records Commission.

To Elaine, Chris, Lisa, Anna,

Kimberly, and Steven

iii

Acknowledgements

I was awarded in 1983 a Senior Fellowship in Canadian Studies and this generous grant provided the released time and travel funds needed to complete the research for this book. I am grateful to Richard Seaborn, Brian Long, Norman London, and Harold Hickman for encouraging my research and teaching efforts in the field of Canadian Studies and commend the Association for Canadian Studies in the United States (ACSUS) for sponsoring scholarly conferences which have provided some of the concepts and insights to be found in this book.

Special thanks are also extended to Ken Stiles, George Mierisch, Susan Hubbard, Kent Francis, and Allen Morrison for their research endeavors and to David Elton of the University of Lethbridge for helping to administer a special questionnaire in Canada. Marilyn Webb and her very efficient staff in Brigham Young University's Faculty Support Center did an excellent job in preparing the manuscript and Wendy Butler, Donna Parkinson, and the able staff in the David M. Kennedy International Center were very helpful in the preparation of special tables and charts.

I would also like to thank my wife Elaine and my children Chris, Lisa, Anna, Kimberly, and Steven for their patience, perseverance, and unwavering support at home.

Finally, I am very grateful for the students who have enrolled in my Canadian Politics, Canadian Foreign Policy, and North American Heritage courses at Brigham Young University and would like to thank them for offering valuable suggestions for the revision of the original manuscript.

CONTENTS

Preface

This book is intended for a reading audience which knows very little about Canada and Canadian government and politics. Based on the responses to a special questionnaire prepared by the author and other survey results, it is clear that this audience should include about 99.8 percent of all Americans and non-Canadians and a fair number of Canadians as well.

Americans have long considered that Canada is the best friend of the United States, but their knowledge of Canada, Canadians, and why this friendship exists between the two North American nations is extremely limited. For example, one hundred American university students were asked by the author to identify some of the prominent features to be found in Canadian society in general and the Canadian political system in particular. Eleven percent of these students could correctly identify Canada's capital city, 10 percent could come close to guessing Canada's current population, 11 percent knew when Canada's present constitution officially became the law of the land, 1 percent could name the premier of Canada's major French-speaking province, and no one at all had any idea when Canada's confederation was formed.

The first chapter of the book provides an introduction to Canadian society and looks at some of the stereotyped images of Canada conjured up by many Americans and other non-Canadians. This chapter is appropriately entitled "Canadian Society in Comparative Perspective: A Brief Look at How the MacKenzie Brothers Survive and Prosper in the Great White North." The second chapter highlights Canada's historical development and the third chapter examines Canada's constitutional framework. The fourth chapter discusses Canadian federalism and the role of Quebec in the contemporary federal system. The fifth chapter deals with political socialization, elections, and political parties, and the sixth chapter analyzes Canada's governmental institutions and how public policy is made at the national level. The last chapter is devoted to Canada's role in the world and the special challenges which it faces in having a superpower as a neighbor.

The book is written by an American professor who has had several years of experience doing research on Canada and who has directed two Canadian Studies programs in the United States. Features of Canadian society are frequently compared and contrasted with those to be found in other advanced industrial societies, especially the United States and some of the nations of Western Europe. This technique has been used in order to provide non-Canadian readers with some familiar frames of reference, and it also permits the reader to consider what might be some of the comparative strengths and weaknesses of Canada's political and governmental systems.

In summary, the book uses "plain English" to provide a general introduction to Canadian government and politics. Once having finished this volume, the reader should be in good shape to tackle much more sophisticated and specialized Canadian political science textbooks.

CANADIAN SOCIETY IN COMPARATIVE PERSPECTIVE:
A BRIEF LOOK AT HOW THE MACKENZIE BROTHERS
SURVIVE AND PROSPER IN THE GREAT WHITE NORTH

An Introduction to Politics and Political Science

The purpose of this study is to make the workings of the Canadian political system at least somewhat understandable to those who know very little either about Canada or political science. In addition, the Canadian political system will be viewed in comparative perspective. In other words, features prominent in the Canadian system will be compared with other political systems, particularly the American system, and similarities and differences will be identified and examined.

A concerted effort will also be made to keep the use of political "jargon" at a minimum. Over 50 years ago, Lawrence Lowell was reportedly asked at what point would the study of politics evolve into a science. His answer was not until it had acquired "a vocabulary totally unintelligible to the normal well-educated layman."[1] Unfortunately, the study of politics has indeed achieved the status of a science along the lines which Lowell predicted. In effect, many writers in the field of political science are seriously afflicted with the disease known as "academese," meaning that their writing is often stilted, pompous, and unclear. Hopefully, this comparative study of Canadian politics and government will steer clear of the academese syndrome and will thus be more comprehensible to the normal well-educated person.

Nevertheless, a few key terms often used in political science must be understood by the student new to the field. A political system, as defined by Robert Dahl, is "any persistent pattern of human relationships that involves, to a significant extent, control, influence, power or authority."[2] Dahl goes on to define the government as "an entity" that successfully upholds a claim to the exclusive regulation of the legitimate use of physical force in enforcing its rules within a given territorial area."[3] The state is "the political system made up of the residents of that territorial area and the government of the area."[4] In other words, there may be various political systems within a nation, both in the private and public spheres. For example, a large company such as General Motors has its own distinct political system, with the president of the company being able to exercise some control, influence, power, or authority over lower echelon employees at GM. On the other hand, Joe and Jane Citizen, who accept the state system as being legitimate (conforming to recognized principles and standards), would allow a representative of the state system, a police officer, to give them a ticket on a public highway, whereas they would refuse to allow the president of GM to pull them over and to give them a ticket for driving a Ford instead of a Chevrolet. Therefore, the state system normally monopolizes power in certain key areas, power which would not be available to other political systems in the private and public sectors.

Ironically, many people who recognize the right of the state to exercise authority over them in various spheres are completely turned off by the notion of politics, identifying this term with corruption, nepotism, and highhandedness. Nonetheless, the activities which occur in most modern state systems dramatically affect the individual from the cradle to the grave. As Karl Deutsch points out, one year before the French Revolution of 1789, the French king collected eight percent of the GNP (the gross national product or the sum of all the goods and services produced).[5] A century later, the French Third Republic government was still collecting eight percent. But today, it is not uncommon for Western governments to collect forty or fifty percent of the GNP, with figures being even higher in communist nations. Thus, the sphere of governmental control and influence has dramatically increased and in the nuclear era, the state may well determine the survival or destruction of not only its own citizens, but people living in other countries as well. Consequently, it would seem to be prudent for Joe and Jane Citizen and their compatriots to keep abreast of what is going on not only in their own nation, but in other nations as well, and to take an active part in trying to influence governmental decisions which will affect their personal lives.

2

Canada and the Consociational Dimension

Canada is an industrially advanced society, joining a very exclusive "club" of nations which includes several major Western European countries, the Soviet Union, Japan, Australia, New Zealand, and the United States (Table I:1 provides a map of Canada and Table I:2 compares Canada with some of the other advanced industrial societies). Canada also has a democratic political system with an essentially capitalistic economic structure. A democracy is a political system "in which the opportunity to participate in decisions is widely shared among all adult citizens," as contrasted to a dictatorship which is a political system "in which the opportunity to participate in decisions is restricted to a few."[6] Capitalism is an economic system "in which most major economic activities are performed by privately owned and controlled firms," as compared to a socialist economic system "in which most major activities are performed by agencies owned by the government or society."[7]

In his discussion of Western democratic systems, Gabriel Almond classifies Canada as an "Anglo-American" political system.[8] Yet Canada differs from the other Anglo-American systems because of its two founding peoples legacy and the presence of a large, cohesive French-speaking minority. Arend Lijphart has therefore classified Canada as a "consociational democracy" which is fragmented into subcultures (basically the French and English subcultures) but which is nonetheless democratically stable.[9]

Other consociational nations include Belgium, the Netherlands, Switzerland, and Austria. The Netherlands, for example, has significant Catholic, Protestant, and liberal-secular subcultures in which it is quite possible for a person to be educated from kindergarten through college, marry, and then choose a profession without interacting substantially with any of the other subcultures. These Dutch subcultures are thus highly compartmentalized, or segregated from one another, but the leaders of each group cooperate in the political sphere in order to insure governmental stability and harmony in the nation as a whole. In the late 1970s, as many as 14 parties were represented in the Dutch parliament and five of these parties participated in the governing coalition. In spite of

3

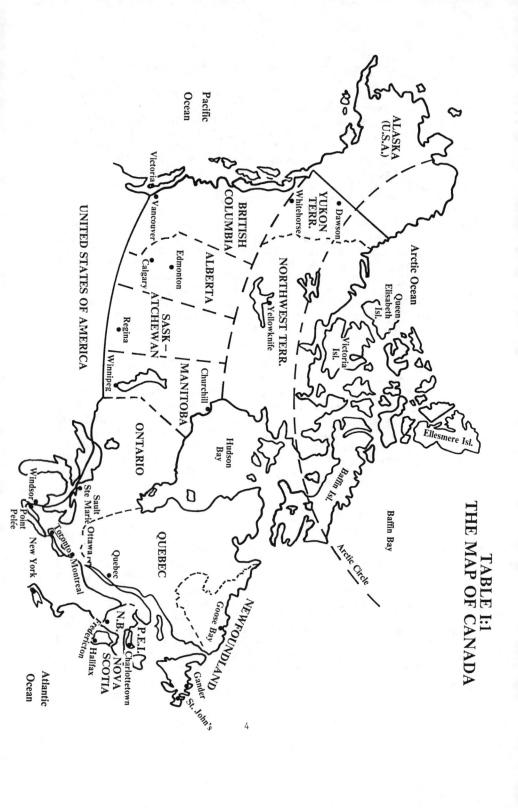

TABLE I:1
THE MAP OF CANADA

4

TABLE I:2

COMPARISON OF SELECTED ADVANCED INDUSTRIAL SOCIETIES

	Canada	U.S.A.	U.K.	France	W. Germany	U.S.S.R.
Population (1982 estimates in thousands)	24,469	232,295	56,095	54,174	61,697	269,867
Surface Area (Km^2)	9,971,500	9,371,829	243,978	551,670	248,640	22,402,200
Density (population per Km^2)	2	25	230	98	248	12
Crude Steel Production (1980-millions of short tons)	17.5	111.8	12.5	25.5	48.3	163.1
Per Capita Gross National Product (1980-$U.S.)	10,130	11,360	7,920	11,730	13,590	4,550
Gross Domestic Product (1980-millions of $U.S.)	253,350	2,587,100	522,850	651,890	819,140	*

Sources: The World Factbook, 1982 and the 1982 Commodity Year Book.

5

this extremely high number of political movements, the Dutch have traditionally enjoyed a very stable democratic system.

Lijphart insists that for success to be achieved by a consociational democracy such as Canada's, in which there is often little interaction between French Canadian and English Canadian groups, the leaders (or "elites") of the two major subcultures must (1) have the ability to accommodate the divergent demands of their subcultures, (2) be able to transcend traditional points of difference and join in fruitful discussions with each other, (3) be committed to preserving the political system and improving its stability and cohesiveness, and (4) clearly understand the perils of political fragmentation.[10] As will be discussed in a later chapter, recent events which have transpired in Quebec have now placed in question the willingness of the Canadian subcultures to fulfill these four preconditions for national unity.

American Perceptions of the Northern Neighbor

Canadians generally have a much greater awareness of features of American society than Americans do of Canadian society. The Canadians are better informed because they (1) are inundated with American television programs, books, magazines, and other purveyors of American cultural values, and (2) recognize that actions carried out by the United States might dramatically affect their own way of life, thus prompting them to keep somewhat abreast of what is occurring in the neighboring superpower. Conversely, Canada is rarely mentioned in American schools or by the mass media. For example, in terms of quality, the New York Times is generally considered to be the number one newspaper in the United States and takes great pride in its international news coverage. Moreover, the state of New York shares a common border with Canada and because of this close geographic linkage, New Yorkers might be expected to have a greater interest in Canadian public affairs than say British or Egyptian affairs. However, a survey of the 1981 New York Times index shows that more articles, editorials, and letters were written about Great Britain (284), Egypt (206), El Salvador (412), Iran (approximately 900), Northern Ireland (approximately 300), and the Soviet Union (approximately 370), than Canada (172).

6

The American news media concentrate on spectacular events, particularly violent, hostile, tragic, or bizarre occurrences which will easily attract the attention of their readers or viewers. Canada is rather staid and predictable in comparison to many hotspots around the world and thus rarely receives media attention unless a province is trying to secede or the wife of the prime minister decides to walk out on her famous spouse. Thus Americans know very little about this nation to the north which is one of the most peaceful, civilized countries in the world and which has maintained very close and harmonious relations with the United States for well over a century and a half. Moreover, Americans have nonchalantly taken for granted the longstanding good relations between the two countries without ever learning the basic reasons for this enduring friendship.

To ascertain your own knowledge level about Canada, complete the following quiz.

1. What is the capital city of Canada? (11%)

2. Who is Canada's prime minister? (74%)

3. Which political party does Canada's prime minister represent? (10%)

4. How is Canada's prime minister selected? (23%)

5. Name four of Canada's provinces. (43%)

6. Which city is considered as Canada's major commercial, communications, and banking center? (22%)

7. Which province produces the great bulk of Canada's oil and natural gas? (27%)

8. Who is the current premier of Canada's major French-speaking province? (1%)

9. What is Canada's current population? (10%)

10. Over the past three years, are there any issues which have provoked significant disagreements between the governments of Canada and the United States? If your answer is yes, identify one of these issues. (20%)

11. Who is Canada's head of state? (10%)

12. Identify the two chambers which comprise Canada's parliament. (2%)

13. When did Canada's present constitution officially become the law of the land? (11%)

14. When was the Canadian confederation formed? (0%)

15. Which province recently held a referendum to decide whether or not it wanted to remain a part of Canada? (53%)

The answers to these questions are found in the footnote section at the end of this chapter.[11] This quiz was administered in the fall of 1982 to 100 undergraduate students enrolled in political science courses at universities in the United States. The numbers placed in parentheses after each question indicate the percentage of correct answers. In other words, only 11 percent of American university students could correctly identify the capital city of Canada, 43 percent could name four Canadian provinces, 1 percent could identify Quebec's premier, and 10 percent could come relatively close to guessing Canada's population. A quiz utilizing parallel questions about the United States was also administered in the autumn of 1982 to 100 undergraduate students enrolled in political science courses at universities in Canada. The questions and correct responses to this quiz are found in the footnotes.[12] To say the least, the Canadian students have a much greater knowledge level about the United States than the American students have about Canada. Indeed, all of the Canadians could correctly identify America's capital city, 85 percent could name ten American states, 31 percent could identify the governor of America's most populous state, and 41 percent could come close to pinpointing the population of the United States.

Although certainly not conducted with any
scientific rigor, interviews gathered by a Canadian
author who toured the United States during the 1970s do
offer some valuable impressionistic insights into
American perceptions of the northern neighbor. All of
the Americans who were interviewed from coast to coast
were asked what they thought of Canada or Canadians.
Some of the older ones conjured up the image of Nelson
Eddy and Jeanette MacDonald riding off in the Canadian
sunset singing amorous words of praise to each other.
As one Texas housewife stated, "Mountains, I think of
mountains and people singing."[13] Some other Americans
nurtured the Sergeant Preston "Far North" image. A law
student from Washington, D.C. stated that she thought
of "Canadians going to work every day, walking across
the tundra."[14] Some associated Canada with the
harboring of American draft resisters during the
Vietnam era. A pensioner from Nebraska contended that
Canadians "took in draft dodgers, yeller-bellies, and
that weren't right."[15] And finally, a hardware clerk
in Virginia insisted that much could be learned about
the Canadian character by observing a favorite Canadian
pastime, curling:

> They got a game up there, you ever hear of
> it, called curling? You have this big stone
> and you throw it down the ice, like bowling,
> really more like lawn bowling, and these
> other people standing around have brooms and
> they brush the living hell out of the ice and
> that's the way it's played. I saw it on the
> television one time. It's practically a
> national sport the way the guy explained it,
> and he said they used to play it with jam
> pots. What the hell? They say you can tell
> a lot about people by the sport, you know,
> they reflect what they feel in the sports
> they pick. Well, all I got to say is every
> time I think of Canada I think of these poor,
> dumb nuts flailing away with a broom while a
> rock goes whizzing by.[16]

For many American sports fans, curling is not the
first thing to come to mind when thinking about Canada.
Rather, Canada connotes images of hockey games with
frequent brawls, football games which permit only three
downs to achieve a first down and which are played on
110-yard fields, and bilingual baseball where a strike
is "une prise" and a home run is "un coup de circuit."

For many younger Americans, Canada in the 1980s brings to mind the antics of Bob and Doug MacKenzie, a couple of hosers from the "Great White North." The image of Canada portrayed by the MacKenzie brothers is one of perpetually bitter winters in which down home folks sit around wearing earmuffs and drinking beer in order to pass the time away.

Even though Americans are usually quite ignorant of what is going on north of the border, they evince greater trust in Canada than any other nation (as is illustrated in Table I:3). The two nations share close to a 4,000 mile-long border along the 49th parallel and a 1,500 mile-long border between Alaska and the Yukon. The percentage of trade with each other far exceeds that of any other two nations in the world. There are also more than 70 million crossings at the Canada-U.S. border each year. In addition, Northwestern Canada is located approximately 600 miles from Soviet territory, making Canada the only nation in the world directly situated between the two superpowers and underlining the strategic importance of friendly relations between the two North American nations. In effect, the great number of Canadian-American interactions and Canada's strategic importance to the United States would seem to warrant a much greater interest among Americans concerning what transpires north of the 49th parallel.

Canada's Peaceful, Affluent Society

Although much attention will be given in this study to existing and potential problems in Canada, the overall condition of Canadian society should be kept in proper perspective. Canadians are a highly prosperous people, having an average income at least 20 times higher than that of people in the Third World. There is virtual cradle to grave security in Canada and the people have little fear of major civil strife or even of localized criminal activities. For example, there were 493 homicides committed throughout Canada in 1980 as compared to 1,903 in New York City alone in that same year. Canada is also one of the world's major "breadbaskets" because of its high production of grains and other edible materials. It is also richly endowed with many other important natural resources.

10

TABLE I:3

How Americans Rate Other Nations*

	Highly Favorable	Mildly Favorable	Mildly Unfavorable	Highly Unfavorable	Don't Know
Canada	75%	20%	1%	1%	3%
Australia	49	42	3	1	5
Brazil	21	60	11	2	6
Israel	28	50	13	5	4
Japan	30	54	9	3	4
Soviet Union	6	17	27	47	3
West Germany	33	48	11	4	4

*The survey was conducted in July 1980.

Source: Survey Research Consultants International, Index to International Public Opinion, 1980-1981 (Westport, Conn.: Greenwood Press, 1982).

Canadians on the whole are also a highly governable people who enjoy free elections and a peaceful, orderly transition of power at all governmental levels. Americans might take these political features for granted, as do many Canadians, but for a good portion of the world's people free elections and an orderly transition of power based on bona fide electoral results are an unknown luxury.

The Canadian political system has thus been quite proficient in helping to fulfill the basic demands of its population. In fact, a definite linkage does exist between the performance of the governmental system and what Abraham Maslow has referred to as the "hierarchy" of human needs which, if fulfilled, will provide the potential for full human development. Maslow asserts that the first need which must be satiated for all humans is physiological, the need for food, water, shelter, etc. Once this need is reasonably satisfied, a person then seeks safety, order, dependability, and predictability in his environment. The third need is for love, affection, and belongingness; the fourth is for esteem; and the last is for self-actualization or self-fulfillment.[17] The following illustration shows the importance of satisfying these basic needs:

> Let us say that person A has lived for several weeks in a dangerous jungle, in which he has managed to stay alive by finding occasional food and water. Person B not only stays alive but also has a rifle and a hidden cave with a closable entrance. Person C has all of these and two more men with him as well. Person D has the food, the gun, the allies, the cave, and in addition, has with him his best-loved friend. Finally, Person E, in the same jungle, has all of these, and in addition is the well-respected leader of his band. For the sake of brevity we may call these men, respectively, the merely surviving, the safe, the belonging, the loved, and the respected.[18]

As Ronald Manzer has suggested, the "political goods" of a state governmental system are integrally linked to the five hierarchical needs in terms of welfare, security, fraternity, equality, and liberty respectively.[19] Unfortunately, many governmental systems in the world have been unable to contribute to

12

the fulfillment of some of these needs, with an
appreciable number not even being able to cope with the
physiological needs of their citizens. Although
opinions would differ depending on one's political
orientation, many Canadians would nonetheless agree
that their political system has performed
satisfactorily in helping to satisfy the basic needs of
the general populace. In essence, Canada is a highly
prosperous, civilized, peaceful society in which many
people in the world would undoubtedly desire to live.

Basic Geophysical Characteristics of Canada

Extending from the Atlantic to the Pacific and
from the American border to the Arctic, Canada is the
second largest country in the world after the USSR and
is more expansive than all of Europe. This vast nation
is populated by only 24 million people, about one-tenth
the size of the United States and somewhat larger than
the population of California. The average number of
people living in a square kilometer in Canada is only
two, as compared to 24 in the United States (see Table
I:4 for an overview of the Canadian provinces and
territories).

Very rigorous physical features are predominant in
Canada with over one-half of the nation being affected
by permafrost (permanently frozen ground). The average
temperature in January is a frigid -18°C, as compared
to an average of 0°C in the United States. Although
appreciably larger than the United States and long
respected as a major supplier of food for the world,
Canada possesses about four percent of the world's
arable land, as compared to America's 23.5 percent. In
addition, Central Canada is divided from the prairie
regions by the Great Lakes and by a 1,000 mile-long
shield of ancient rock formations which affords far
from conducive conditions for human habitation. The
sea also separates Newfoundland from the mainland, the
Appalachians separate the Maritime provinces from
Quebec, and the Rockies separate Alberta from British
Columbia. All of these natural barriers have at one
time or another proved to be formidable obstacles
standing in the path of Canadian expansion.

On the other side of the ledger, Canada possesses
a veritable cornucopia of natural resources and for the
moment has adequate reserves in such materials as iron

TABLE I:4

An Overview of the Canadian Provinces and Territories

Province	Capital	Entry Into Confederation	Population (1981)	% Overall Population	Seats in House of Commons (1983)
Alberta	Edmonton	1905	2,237,724	9.2	21
British Columbia	Victoria	1871	2,744,467	11.3	28
Manitoba	Winnipeg	1870	1,026,241	4.2	14
New Brunswick	Fredericton	1867	696,403	2.9	10
Newfoundland	St. John's	1949	567,681	2.3	7
Nova Scotia	Halifax	1867	847,442	3.5	11
Ontario	Toronto	1867	8,625,107	35.4	95
Price Edward Island	Charlottetown	1873	122,506	0.5	4
Quebec	Quebec City	1867	6,438,403	26.5	75
Saskatchewan	Regina	1905	968,313	4.0	14
Northwest Territories	Yellowknife	*	45,741	0.2	2
Yukon	Whitehorse	*	23,153	0.1	1

ore, uranium, coal, nickel, oil, natural gas, and forest products. It can also lay claim to one of the world's last frontiers. Approximately 90 percent of all Canadians live within 200 miles of the American border, leaving the vast northern expanses which are rich in certain natural resources virtually uninhabited. For example, the Northwest Territories, which are administered by the Canadian federal government, encompass an area of 1,305,000 square miles but are populated by only 45,000 people. In comparison, Alaska, which has often been referred to as America's last frontier, has 412,000 people living in an area of 586,000 square miles, less than half the size of the Northwest Territories.

Canada is a montage of geographical features spiced with a widely varied ethnic composition. It has many wilderness expanses, but it is also highly urbanized and industrially advanced. To say the least, the stereotyped Great White North image of Canada conjured up by many Americans is a gross misperception of contemporary Canadian society.

NOTES

[1]Quoted in S. E. Finer, <u>Comparative Government</u> (New York: Basic Books, 1971), p. 3.

[2]Robert A. Dahl, <u>Modern Political Analysis</u>, 3rd ed. (Englewood Cliffs, N.J.: Prentice-Hall, 1976), p. 3.

[3]Ibid., p. 10.

[4]Ibid.

[5]Karl W. Deutsch, <u>Politics and Government</u>, 2nd ed. (Boston: Houghton Mifflin, 1974), p. 3.

[6]Dahl, p. 5.

[7]Ibid.

[8]Gabriel A. Almond, "Comparative Political Systems," <u>Journal of Politics</u>, 18 (August 1956): 391-409.

[9]Arend Lijphart, "Consociational Democracy," <u>World Politics</u>, 21 (January 1969):207-225.

[10]Ibid., p. 216.

[11]The answers to these questions, as of June 1983, were as follows:
        (1)   Ottawa.
        (2)   Pierre Trudeau.
        (3)   Liberal Party.
        (4)   The prime minister is quite simply the leader of the party which generally has the largest representation of seats in the House of Commons.
To explain this selection process in greater detail, a politician is first selected by a party convention as the leader of the party. If at the next general election the party receives the most seats in the House of Commons, the party will generally be asked to form a new government and the leader of the party will become the new prime minister. The party leader runs in a local constituency for a seat in the House of Commons just like any other parliamentary candidate in Canada or similar to a candidate for the House of Representatives in the United States. Voters in the United States do vote for candidates for the American

presidency, or more precisely, for a slate of electors committed to support a specific candidate in the Electoral College. In contrast, the Canadian electorate as a whole does not vote directly for candidates to fill the office of prime minister.

(5) Any four from the following list of ten provinces would be acceptable: Alberta, British Columbia, Manitoba, New Brunswick, Newfoundland, Nova Scotia, Ontario, Prince Edward Island, Quebec, and Saskatchewan.

(6) Toronto.

(7) Alberta.

(8) René Lévesque.

(9) 24 million. Any answer ranging from 20 to 28 million would be considered as correct.

(10) Yes. Issues provoking significant disagreement between Canada and the United States include acid rain, fishing regulations, foreign investment policies, and trade policies.

(11) Queen Elizabeth II.

(12) The House of Commons and the Senate.

(13) 1982.

(14) 1867.

(15) Quebec.

[12]The following quiz was administered to university students in Canada. The numbers in the parentheses indicate the percentage of correct answers.

1. What is the capital city of the United States? Washington, D.C. (100%)

2. Who is the President of the United States? Ronald Reagan. (98%)

3. Which political party does the President of the United States represent? Republican Party. (86%)

4. How is the President of the United States selected? The major candidates for the presidency are selected at party conventions and the American electorate votes for a slate of electors committed to support a specific candidate in the Electoral College. (6%)

5. List ten of the states in the United States. Alabama, Alaska, Arizona, Arkansas, California, Colorado, Connecticut, Delaware, Florida, Georgia, Hawaii, Idaho, Illinois, Indiana, Iowa, Kansas, Kentucky, Louisiana, Maine, Maryland, Massachusetts, Michigan, Minnesota, Mississippi, Missouri, Montana, Nebraska, Nevada, New Hampshire, New

17

Jersey, New Mexico, New York, North Carolina, North Dakota, Ohio, Oklahoma, Oregon, Pennsylvania, Rhode Island, South Carolina, South Dakota, Tennessee, Texas, Utah, Vermont, Virginia, Washington, West Virginia, Wisconsin, Wyoming. (85%)

6. Which city is considered as the United States' major commercial and banking center? New York City. (87%)

7. Which state in the United States produces more oil and natural gas than any other state? Texas. (85%)

8. Who is the current governor of the most populous state in the United States? George Deukmejian of California. (31%)

9. What is the present population of the United States? 232 million. Any answer ranging from 210 to 250 million would be considered as correct. (41%)

10. Over the past three years, have there been any policies pursued by the U.S. government which have provoked significant disagreements with the government in Ottawa? If your answer is yes, identify one of these policies. Yes. Issues provoking significant disagreement include acid rain, fishing regulations, foreign investment policies, and trade policies. (58%)

11. Who is the current Secretary of State in the United States? George Shultz. (16%)

12. Identify the two chambers which comprise the Congress of the United States. The House of Representatives and the Senate. (30%)

13. When did the present constitution of the United States officially become the law of the land? 1789. (4%)

14. When was the Declaration of Independence proclaimed? 1776. (67%)

15. People from which island are currently debating whether or not they should seek to become a state within the United States? Puerto Rico. (43%)

[13]Walter Stewart, As They See Us (Toronto: McClelland and Stewart, 1976).

[14]Ibid.

[15]Ibid.

[16]Ibid.

[17]Abraham Maslow, _Motivation and Personality_, 1st ed. (New York: Harper, 1954), Chapter 5.

[18]Quoted in Ronald Manzer, _Canada: A Socio-Political Report_ (Toronto: McGraw-Hill Ryerson, 1974), p. 6. Original citation found in Maslow, _Motivation_, p. 115.

[19]Ibid., p. 7.

II

THE CANADIAN HERITAGE: ANOTHER
ATTEMPT TO MAKE OLD EVENTS
LOOK RELEVANT TODAY

French Canada

The Creation, Evolution, and Demise of New France

French links to the New World may be traced back
to Jacques Cartier who made a series of exploratory
voyages to North America beginning in 1534. As was
common for explorations of that period, neither
Cartier nor his sponsor, the King of France, were
terribly interested in new land. Rather, the main
motivation for the trip was gold, silver, or any other
precious metal on which they could lay their hands.
For example, Cartier's premier voyage to the New World
was inspired by rumors of a mineral-rich Kingdom of
the Indians known as Saguenay.

Cartier never discovered the legendary kingdom,
but his explorations up the St. Lawrence and into
other regions prompted French officials to at least
consider the establishment of a permanent settlement
in the New World. Unfortunately, extremely cold
weather and the lack of logistical support ruined the
efforts of Cartier and his compatriots to set up just
such a settlement in 1541.

Over 60 years later, permanent settlements were
finally established in Acadia and in the area of
present-day Quebec City. Samuel de Champlain, often
referred to as the "Father of Canada," was the instrumental force in the founding of many of these settlements in the vast wilderness area then known as Nova
Francia or New France.

Jolliet, Marquette, La Salle and other explorers
paved the way for the building of additional villages
in New France, but the interest of the French government in Canadian affairs was sporadic at best. A
trading conglomerate known as the Canada Company was
granted initial authority by the government to
colonize the continent. In 1627, the French crown

replaced the Canada Company and transferred extensive powers over New France to the Company of the Hundred Associates. Finally in 1663, New France became an official colony of the mother country with almost all governmental authority remaining in France and no provision being made for representative rule. French officials who were assigned to the new colony and who remained directly answerable for their actions to the crown included a governor, an intendant, and a bishop. The governor represented the monarch in New France and was responsible for enforcing the law and defending the colony. The bishop was the representative of the church and supervised the activities of the parishes, hospitals, and schools. The intendant was an administrator who watched over the day-to-day affairs of the colony and took charge of trading activities as well as the recruitment of new colonists. At the time, New France had a sparse population of 3,000 French settlers.

In the meantime, English settlements were cropping up all over North America and the French populace was soon vastly outnumbered by settlers of English descent. At the time of the official British takeover of New France in 1763, there were 70,000 inhabitants in New France and 1,500,000 in English North America. Certainly by 1750, the handwriting was already on the wall indicating that the English would soon seize the New World possessions of France. The lack of monetary and military support and the absence of a vigorous policy to encourage French citizens to migrate to the New World (only 10,000 French citizens migrated to New France from 1608 until 1763) eventually cost the French government dearly. In effect, the continuous intrigues and wars in Europe which preoccupied France, as well as disastrous fiscal policies pursued by Louis XIV and other French leaders, all acted to seal the fate of the colony across the ocean. When asked to come to the aid of the beleaguered colony at a time when France was fighting a continental war with Great Britain, Louis XV arrogantly remarked that "when the house is on fire, one doesn't bother about the stables."

The social system which prevailed in New France and the free-wheeling nature of some of its inhabitants also contributed to the demise of the colony. Up until 1663, New France was controlled by fur trading monopolies whose first concern was with reaping profits rather than with setting up new townships and tilling the land. When some of the land was finally used for farming purposes, the seigneurial system was transplanted from Old France to the new colony. Seigneurialism was a semi-feudal social system in which a seigneur, a form of colonial land agent, directed the affairs of the habitants, the tillers of the land. The habitants were undoubtedly better off materially than the serfs of the feudal age, but they were nonetheless forced to mill their products in facilities owned by the landed gentry and were required to make payments in kind to the seigneurs and to satisfy the corvée--periodic labor obligations to the landowners. Such a system did little to inspire improved farming techniques and there were few incentives available for those habitants who wanted to get ahead and still remain as tillers of the soil.

A special breed of French Canadian, known as the coureur de bois, occupied a special niche in the early colonial period. The coureur de bois, a combination trapper-explorer-mountainman who was the forerunner of the Jim Bridger-Jeremiah Johnson prototype, spent most of his time in the wilderness and had little use for the seigneurial system, France, or most anything that smacked of civilization. The coureur de bois remains deeply ingrained in Canadian folklore, as well he should, but his nomadic lifestyle did little to foster the establishment of much-needed permanent settlements which might have helped New France to keep pace with the English expansion in the New World.

French mercantilist policy also forbade the growth of indigenous economic activity in the Western Hemisphere colony. Part of the rationale for this policy was to insure that the colonists continued to purchase most of their goods from French enterprises. In the long run, however, this policy thwarted the efforts of those who believed that New France had to develop its own urbanized middle class and had to foster some industrialization in order to fend off English expansionism. In addition, French authorities did little to encourage the growth of a sense of community among the colonists, as is aptly illustrated by the fact that there was not one printing press in all of French Canada during the course of its existence.

23

The Jesuits became a major missionary force in New France as early as 1625 and the Catholic Church played an integral role in the governing of the colony at both the national and local levels. As mentioned earlier, tripartite authority over New France was vested in the hands of a governor, an intendant (a precursor to the French prefect who represents the central government in each of France's metropolitan and overseas departments), and a bishop. At the local level, the parish priest usually chaired the council which oversaw the activities of the parish region. Many of the priests at the grassroots level were sensitive to the needs of the people and recognized the shortcomings of the colonial administration. On the other hand, the top church hierarchy was directly answerable to the secular authority of the crown and was thus more concerned with the overall objectives of France than with the particular needs of the New World colonists.

French failures in the periodic wars against England, the crown's haphazard concern for colonial affairs, and the growth in the number and in the power of English North American colonists all combined to bring down New France. At the conclusion of the Seven Years' War, which was highlighted in the New World by the English victory on the Plains of Abraham and the fall of Quebec in 1759, France was required to forfeit its North American possessions to England. As a consequence, Canada finally came under the control of one unified colonial administration.

The Quest for Survivance

French Canada From 1763 Until Confederation

Some of the French Canadians were undoubtedly bitter about the English takeover in 1763, but many had gradually divorced themselves from France as the years passed and considered themselves as Canadiens rather than as French citizens. Though they retained their allegiance to the French language, religion, and civil code, these French Canadians were not overly concerned with the transfer of administrations, believing that their daily lifestyles would remain relatively unaffected by the changes at the national level. Moreover, some might have even welcomed the new regime as a panacea for some of the inegalitarian social customs which had been perpetuated by the French colonial system.

The English were at least somewhat aware of the feelings of the French Canadians and through the passage of the Quebec Act of 1774 vowed to honor the retention of the Catholic religion and the French civil code. The empathy shown by the English and the minimal intrusion into the daily routines of the French Canadians help to explain the indifference shown by many of French descent toward the American Revolution. Even though the revolutionaries asked for French Canadian support and France eventually became an ally of the American insurgents, the French connection was very weak in 1776 and the French Canadians could perceive little difference in being directed by English-speaking Britons or English-speaking Americans. With few exceptions, the French Canadians just wanted to be left alone to do their own thing--care for their families, till their land, and cherish whatever meager possessions they might have gathered together over the years.

The already tenuous connection with France was further weakened as a result of the French Revolution of 1789. The French Canadians were a highly traditional people who felt a deep repugnance and distrust for the liberal-secular values of the French revolutionaries. Even in 1837, when Louis Joseph Papineau spearheaded the Rouge movement and demanded the establishment of representative government, many of the tradition-oriented French Canadians opposed Papineau because of his liberal, anti-clerical ideas.

The Constitution Act of 1791 officially divided Canada into two distinct territories, one predominantly French-speaking and the other English-speaking. The two territories were eventually brought together again under one government with the implementation of the Act of Union in 1840, but the French Canadians were still allowed to use their French civil code instead of the English common law tenets. Finally in 1867, the French region, which had periodically been referred to as Lower Canada or Canada East, was incorporated into the new Canadian confederation as the province of Quebec. Thus, in spite of the recommendations of Lord Durham and certain other English notables who favored the "anglicization of French Canada," Quebec entered the

25

new federal nation with French Canadian traditions fairly well intact.

Quebec Since Confederation

Throughout the 19th and well into the 20th century, Quebec remained a highly traditional society based on agricultural production. The birthrate among French Canadians through most of this period was extremely high, which is perhaps not too surprising when one takes into account the religious beliefs, agrarian character, and desire of the French Canadians to survive as a distinctive people on a continent dominated by an English-speaking populace. However, some of the sons and daughters of this highly prolific people were either forced off the land or prompted to seek employment in Quebec's urban areas. Job opportunities were scarce in the cities, however, and a French Canadian diaspora occurred as thousands were forced to leave the province and either head westward or southward to find industrial jobs in other parts of Canada or the United States.

Some of those who were able to remain in Quebec eventually became quite prominent in the national affairs of the new confederation. Georges-Etienne Cartier was a valuable ally and assistant leader to Sir John A. MacDonald, Canada's first prime minister. Indeed, both MacDonald and Cartier were instrumental in keeping the fragile confederation together during some very turbulent times. Sir Wilfrid Laurier later became Canada's first French Canadian prime minister in 1896 and served until 1911. Two other French Canadians have subsequently held the post of prime minister, Louis S. St. Laurent (1948-1957) and Pierre E. Trudeau (1968-present).

In spite of the distinguished service rendered by a great number of French Canadians on behalf of the confederation, many have nonetheless been embittered by the traditionally strong ties between Canada and Great Britain which have existed since 1867. This resentment finally precipitated an explosive situation in 1917 when the Canadian parliament enacted a mandatory draft law. Many French Canadians refused to honor the draft and some of the major political leaders in the province openly urged the young men to resist conscription. Battles broke out in several areas within the province with scores injured and hundreds jailed. The French Canadians argued that Canada was supporting British imperialist goals in World War I and that the French-speaking population should not be expected to fight for the benefit of the British. A similar episode almost erupted during World War II but a compromise dealing with conscription and overseas service was eventually worked out. This issue represented a major point of schism between French and English-speaking Canadians and even today, the idea of membership in the British-inspired Commonwealth of Nations still rankles some of the more ardent French Canadian nationalists.

Although events since 1960 will be developed in greater detail in a subsequent chapter, brief mention should be made of the important changes in Quebec society over the past two and one-half decades. In 1959, Premier Maurice Duplessis died and his very traditional, boss-oriented regime was toppled several months later after two decades of dominating Quebec politics. The new Lesage administration pushed forward in 1960 with the modernization of Quebec society and coined the phrase, "maître chez nous" (masters in our own houses). The so-called "Quiet Revolution" was thus underway as Quebec quickly modernized and pushed for expanded rights within the confederation. During the 1960s, Quebec also signed several cultural and educational agreements with France and French President Charles de Gaulle visited Montreal in 1967 and uttered his much-publicized phrase, "Vive le Québec libre" (Long live free Quebec).

In 1970, terrorist groups organized under the banner of the FLQ (Front de Libération du Québec--Quebec Liberation Front) carried out a series of bombings, kidnappings, and murders. The FLQ insisted that French Canadians had been treated as second class citizens much too long within the confederation and that Quebec must become a sovereign socialist state through violent means, if necessary. The Ottawa government eventually rushed troops into the area, the FLQ forces were imprisoned or forced into exile, and order was restored.

Quebec's continued participation in the Canadian confederation was once again questioned with the victory of the Parti Québécois in the provincial elections of November, 1976. Through the democratic electoral process, a significant percentage of the Quebec voters opted in 1976 to bring to power a party which had pledged to work for the creation of a new Quebec nation. In 1980, a referendum was held to determine whether or not the Quebec government should be given a mandate by the voters to negotiate a sovereignty-association arrangement (basically political sovereignty and economic association) with the rest of Canada. This referendum issue was defeated decisively by the voters with 59 percent voting no and 41 percent yes. Francophone voters were split almost 50-50 on the issue, whereas non-French-speaking Quebec residents voted overwhelmingly against the proposal. Several political commentators began to write the obituary of the Parti Québécois in the aftermath of the crushing referendum defeat, but the PQ was returned to power in the 1981 provincial elections with a greater majority than had been achieved in 1976. Thus the question still remains open to speculation as to whether New France will eventually be reincarnated in the form of a politically sovereign nation of Quebec.

French Canadians Outside of Quebec Since Confederation

The struggle for survival as a separate French Canadian ethnic group with a distinct culture and language has been felt most keenly by those French-speaking Canadians living outside of Quebec. The French originally colonized the area known as Acadia (now Nova Scotia) in the first decade of the 17th century. This territory soon became a region of major dispute between the French and newly-arrived English settlers and Acadia finally reverted to English jurisdiction with the signing of the 1713 Treaty of Utrecht. Pressure on the French settlers either to accept English customs or to leave the region was extremely high, and many French-speaking citizens were expelled from the colony during the Seven Years' War. A significant number of these refugees finally settled along the eastern coast of the United States and some even traveled as far south as Louisiana. Those French-speaking people that came from Acadia and eventually established roots in Louisiana were nicknamed the "Cajuns."

28

Some of the French Canadians who had settled in Western Canada and who had intermarried with the native population were in the forefront of efforts to resist English Canada's efforts to take over lands west of Ontario. The leader of two of the most noteworthy revolts of the Métis (people of mixed European and Indian descent) was Louis Riel. Fearing the loss of their homesteads, Riel and his followers fomented the Red River Rebellion of 1869 in order to protest Canadian government plans to annex that area into the confederation. This revolt failed and the area under dispute became part of the new province of Manitoba in 1870. Riel fled to the United States but eventually returned in 1884 to lead another Métis revolt further west in Saskatchewan. During the course of this unsuccessful struggle, Riel was captured and later executed, thus becoming a martyr for French Canadians who admired his will to resist English Canadian domination.

Some of the provinces outside of Quebec eventually refused to honor the right of French Canadian children to be educated in French, even though the federal government had given the French-speaking populace certain guarantees and the Quebec provincial government had always protected the right of the English-speaking minority in that province to send its children to English schools. Many of the French Canadians in the other provinces were also forced, by necessity, to speak English in the working place. As a result of these strong pressures to conform to the dominant cultural values, many of the French Canadians living outside of Quebec were eventually assimilated into the English-dominated system.

English Canada

The Pre-Confederation Period

The English monarch staked a claim to Canadian territory soon after John Cabot, an Italian navigator who had been commissioned by Henry VII, sailed along the eastern coast of North America in 1497. Although English settlements were to be established in the early part of the 17th century in what would later be the United States, very little activity took place north of the border for almost 200 years after Cabot's voyage. Finally in 1670, the Hudson's Bay Company was granted a charter by the crown to supervise trade and economic development in a vast area which stretched from Hudson Bay to the Rocky Mountains. The Hudson's Bay Company was to hold on to much of this territory for two centuries.

The great influx of English settlers into the American colonies and eventually areas of Canada soon made the French Canadian settlements fairly much an island in a sea of English-speaking people. The English control over North America was finally consolidated in 1763 but was soon undermined by the efforts of the American revolutionaries to seek independence from the mother country. In 1775, an American expeditionary force invaded Canada and captured Montreal, but the vast majority of Canadians sided with Great Britain and the bulk of the American troops were withdrawn by the end of that year. In 1778, Lafayette proposed a second invasion of Canada but was quickly overruled by Washington and his staff.

Interestingly enough, the American Revolution helped to strengthen the resolve of British settlers in Canada to remain closely allied with Great Britain. Because of persecution suffered south of the border as a result of their anti-revolutionary sentiments, over 40,000 United Empire Loyalists fled to Canada and became vociferous opponents of American revolutionary values. At the time of the revolution, 17,000 people lived in the colony of Nova Scotia, but as a result of the influx of loyalists from America, Nova Scotia's population tripled in the space of just a few years. New Brunswick also became a separate colony in 1784 largely as a result of the large migration of loyalists into the area. Thus the coming of the United Empire Loyalists had a profound impact on Canadian society and these emigrants from south of the border eventually formed the backbone of resistance to the U.S. effort to conquer Canada in 1812.

For many years, Great Britain ruled Canada without making any provisions for the colonial governor or his appointed council to be responsible for their actions to the Canadian people. Finally in 1837 and 1838, over a half century after representative government had been instituted in the United States, organized groups of French-speaking and English-speaking Canadians revolted against the

30

English authorities and demanded more of a say in governmental affairs. The English government soon dispatched Lord Durham to Canada to inspect the situation and make recommendations for change. Durham's report favored the union of Upper and Lower Canada (now Ontario and Quebec) and the establishment of a government responsible to the wishes of the Canadians. The first condition was satisfied immediately with the Act of the Union of 1840, while the second recommendation was enacted much more slowly, culminating in the passage of the British North America Act in 1867.

The Post-Confederation Period and the Links to Great Britain

Even after the confederation was established and Canada became independent in many spheres of governmental activity, the connection between British Canada and Great Britain remained very strong. For example, the Canadian government actively encouraged volunteers at the turn of the century to go to South Africa and fight on the British side in the Boer War. Canada also entered World War I right after Great Britain's entry and approximately three years before the United States became involved in the conflict. The toll of 55,000 Canadian dead during that bitter struggle was appreciably higher than the number of U.S. battlefield casualties. Canada also declared war on the Axis powers soon after the British declaration in 1939 and had been embroiled in the conflict for more than two years before the United States entered the global struggle following the Japanese attack on Pearl Harbor.

Throughout the first half of the 20th century, the parliament and Privy Council of Great Britain continued to play a significant, albeit sporadic, role in Canadian affairs. The British parliament remained the ultimate amending agent of the British North America (BNA) Act and the Privy Council served as the court of last resort for certain judicial matters. Finally in 1949, the Supreme Court of Canada became the court of last appeal for all judicial decisions, and Canada's new constitution enacted in 1982 totally eliminated Great Britain from the constitutional amendment process.

In addition, Canada has undoubtedly become the master of its own policies in both internal and external affairs, particularly after the resolution of certain problems in the 1920s and 1930s. In 1921, the Liberal Party under William Lyon MacKenzie King won the general election but was later implicated in a series of scandals. King asked the governor-general, who is the representative of the British crown in Canada, to dissolve parliament and to schedule new elections. Normally, the governor-general respects the decision of the prime minister in these matters, but in this case, the governor-general refused to dissolve parliament and instead asked another prominent political leader to form a new government. Such a government could not be pieced together, however, and elections were eventually held with the issue of the governor-general's powers being of paramount importance. King's party won the election, clearly underlining the point that the governor-general was not to exercise significant discretionary powers.

At the Imperial Conference of 1926, Canada and several other dominions within the British empire asked for a clarification of their relationship vis-à-vis Great Britain. Certain points were agreed to at this conference and in 1931, the Statute of Westminster was passed and this document affirmed the equality in status of all members of the empire. The Statute proclaimed that Canada and the other dominions would be responsible for their own foreign policies, have the right to pass any legislation which they deemed as necessary for protecting the welfare of their people, and have the prerogative of ignoring any British law which might be construed as detrimental to the interests of their own citizens.

Nonetheless, the British connection is still revered by certain segments of English Canadian society and it was as late as the 1960s before the British Union Jack and "God Save the Queen" were dropped as Canada's official flag and national anthem respectively. Even today, Canada is officially a monarchy, but in a recent poll only 29 percent of Canadians were aware of this.[1] Canada's head of state is the British monarch, but only 15 percent in the same survey were aware of this fact, while 68 percent erroneously considered the prime minister as being head of state.[2] Canadian ignorance in this case is

somewhat understandable because the monarch and his or
her representatives have no significant authority in
Canada and the real policymaking power is concentrated
in the hands of the prime minister and his cabinet.
Thus in spite of the lingering British ties, Canada is
indisputably a sovereign nation and responsible for
its own actions.

The First 110 Years as a Nation

Canada became a largely sovereign nation on
July 1, 1867, partially as a result of the American
Civil War. In fact, the major goals of the founding
fathers of the Canadian confederation were, in effect,
to (1) establish a system of self-government, (2) keep
Canada from being annexed by the United States, and
(3) arrange for the annexation of Western territories
north of the 49th parallel before the United States
laid claim to these areas.

During the early part of the Civil War, Great
Britain closely identified with the Confederate cause
and provided some assistance to the South, including
the granting of permission to construct naval vessels
for the South in English shipyards. Once the war
effort swung heavily in favor of the North, Canadians
justifiably feared that the Union might seize Canada
as retribution for the British support of the South.
This apprehension helped to consolidate the efforts of
Canadian statesmen who favored the creation of a
separate Canadian nation which would be independent
from Great Britain.

In 1864, the 33 assembled delegates at the Quebec
Conference drew up 72 resolutions relating to the
creation of a new Canadian nation. Most of the
recommendations by these "Fathers of Confederation"
were later incorporated into the British North America
(BNA) Act which was passed by the British parliament
in 1867 and which became the basis for the
establishment of the new Canadian confederation.
Charter members of the new confederation included the
provinces of Quebec, Ontario, Nova Scotia, and New
Brunswick. John A. MacDonald became the first prime
minister of the country and guided the infant
political union for almost 20 years (1867-1873,
1878-1891) through a period typified by growing pangs
and significant economic problems. Canada gradually

expanded westward but also incorporated settled areas along the east coast. Manitoba (1870), British Columbia (1871), Prince Edward Island (1873), Alberta (1905), Saskatchewan (1905), and Newfoundland (1949) later joined the original four members of the confederation. Part of the inducement for far western participation in the new nation was a pledge by the Canadian government to construct a transcontinental railroad. This railroad was finally completed in 1885 and required a large infusion of government funds because the physical obstacles which had to be overcome during construction required vast amounts of capital which could not be raised exclusively by Canada's private economic sector.

Although actually losing population in the 1880s and early 1890s because of serious economic troubles, Canada has generally experienced a steady population growth through procreation and immigration. In addition, Canada has enjoyed a fairly steady industrial growth and was able to emerge from World War II physically unscathed and in the midst of full industrial production. This state of affairs after the Second World War compares favorably with the situation in the United States but contrasts markedly with the devastation which plagued much of Europe. Not only did Canada emerge from the war as a major industrial power, but also as a nation well-versed in the uses of nuclear technology. Canada constructed its first nuclear reactor in 1945 and began operating its first nuclear power plant in 1960. In the post-war era, Canada has been a major exporter of nuclear fuels and nuclear technology, but has tried to insure that its technology both at home and abroad is directed solely toward peaceful purposes. Indeed, Canada has refused to develop nuclear weapons even though it has the capability and technological know-how to do so. All in all, Canada's twelve decades of nationhood have been characterized by the avoidance of major civil strife and many Canadians have been fortunate enough to have prospered materially.

A Comparison of Canadian and American Development

The development of Canadian and American societies may be contrasted in several areas. First of all, America's tremendous population superiority (see Table II:1), coupled with certain geophysical and resource advantages, made westward expansion much easier and helped to precipitate an earlier and much more rapid industrial and urban growth. For example, even though the American government provided some lucrative incentives to the companies involved, the construction of the transcontinental railroad was largely carried out by private firms, just as the trans-Alaska pipeline was to be a century later. But because of much more ominous physical barriers as well as a smaller population and economic base, it was considered necessary for the Canadian government to be actively involved in the financing of its transcontinental railroad and several major projects thereafter. Consequently, there has been greater precedence in Canada than in the United States for an active state role in a broad range of economic affairs. On the other hand, the economy of scale which has traditionally favored the United States has allowed it in recent years to play a much more influential, although at times controversial, role in world affairs.

Secondly, America has had a well-publicized revolutionary tradition, whereas Canada actually fostered a "counter-revolutionary" legacy.[3] Through warfare, America split off from Great Britain and proclaimed itself a republic. Canada, on the other hand, continued to accept British leadership and resisted all efforts by American revolutionaries to use force to sever the umbilical cord leading to London. As a result, Canada remains a constitutional monarchy and a member in good standing of the Commonwealth of Nations. It also proved, however, that independence could be achieved through peaceful means without firing a shot, although self-government did not come to Canada until almost a century after the American Revolution. Moreover, Canada has a much younger tradition of representative government than does the United States.

Thirdly, even though the United States abruptly ended what it considered to be a subservient role to Great Britain, it has nevertheless remained a "British" nation. The "melting pot" concept which became a guiding principle in American development helped to insure that British cultural values would permeate almost all sectors of American society and that the English language would eventually be adopted

35

by nearly all the newcomers to America's shores. In sharp contrast, Canada's "two founding peoples" tradition and its unofficial "mosaic" doctrine (respect for the perpetuation of ethnic group values) has seemingly prompted greater tolerance than in the United States for a variety of cultural practices.

TABLE II:1

POPULATION FIGURES FOR CANADA
AND THE UNITED STATES

Canada	Year	United States
161,000[a]	1790	3,929,000
2,436,000	1850	23,192,000
4,325,000	1880	50,156,000
5,371,000	1900	75,995,000
10,377,000	1930	122,775,000
18,238,000	1960	178,464,000
21,516,000	1970	203,212,000
24,469,000	1982	232,195,000

[a]includes only the area then known as "Canada"

Sources: Historical Statistics of Canada, Statistical Abstract of the United States, Census of Canada, 1965-1871, Vol. IV, and periodic Statistics Canada and U.S. Bureau of the Census population reports.

Fourthly, in religious matters, America's development reflected the "mosaic" idea much better than Canada's. The American denominational tradition normally reflected a fair degree of tolerance for religious sects while at the same time frowning upon any close church-state relations or the creation of an "official" state church. In Canada, the Anglican Church has always been a major political force and during one period was granted liberal land and tax concessions by the state authorities. In the French-speaking areas, the Catholic Church has long dominated religious matters and for many generations was predominant in determining Quebec's secular policies at both the local and provincial levels.

Fifthly, westward expansion was a much more civilized affair in Canada with few traces of the "Wild West" mentality which even today seems to permeate some segments of American society. The Royal Canadian Mounted Police (RCMP) was organized in 1873 to keep order in the vast Northwest Territories which had recently been acquired by Canada from the Hudson's Bay Company. The Mounties brought order early to the Western outposts and were much more tolerant of the needs of the native population than many of their counterparts in the United States. Several American Indian tribes, for example, fled to Canada in order to seek sanctuary from the authorities in the United States. As a result of this civilized expansion process, Canada does not have in its folklore the equivalents of a Jesse James, a Billy the Kid, or a Little Big Horn. One might well reflect on which nation should have the most pride concerning its Western heritage.

Sixthly, Canada's membership in the British empire and later in the British Commonwealth helps explain why it pursued a more active role than its southern neighbor in certain aspects of pre-World War II international affairs. In his famous farewell address, George Washington warned the young American nation of the dangers of becoming involved in "entangling alliances" abroad. With few exceptions, Washington's advice was heeded by later generations of policymakers who were content to seek expansion in the Western Hemisphere and leave overseas affairs alone. Thus the United States remained relatively isolationist in its foreign policy for almost 150 years, whereas the British connection gave impetus to a much more cosmopolitan outlook on the part of Canadians. In a negative sense, however, the ties with Great Britain helped persuade the English Canadian majority to become integrally involved in certain overseas conflicts which were vehemently opposed by the French Canadian minority, thus weakening Canadian national unity in the process.

And lastly, Canada has never suffered a major cataclysmic schism comparable to the American Civil War. As a result of this war and an understandable desire to avoid such an outbreak in Canada, the founders of the confederation vigorously pushed for a strong central government and fairly weak provincial governments. The founders perceived that too much authority had been granted to the state governments by the American constitution and that the power of the states had eventually fomented the division between North and South. Ironically, in spite of the intentions of the Fathers of Confederation, the provincial governments today exercise much more authority than their counterparts in the American states and the Parti Québécois in Quebec would be quite pleased to secede from the confederation. Even if secession does occur, however, it should be infinitely more peaceful and orderly than the unsuccessful effort of the Confederacy to break off from the Union in 1860.

TABLE II:2

SIGNIFICANT EVENTS IN CANADIAN HISTORY

c.990   THE VIKINGS EXPLORE THE NORTHERN TIP OF NEWFOUNDLAND. Keep in mind, however, that the native peoples of North America had settled the continent long before the arrival of the white race. The natives were generally nomadic and fairly primitive in terms of life-style, but some tribes were later to become quite sophisticated in their governing processes, particularly the Five Nations of the Iroquois.

1497   JOHN CABOT, AN ITALIAN HIRED BY REPRESENTATIVES OF HENRY VII OF ENGLAND, DISCOVERS A PORTION OF THE CANADIAN ATLANTIC COAST AND DUTIFULLY CLAIMS THE AREA FOR HIS EMPLOYER.

1534   JACQUES CARTIER, A FREE AGENT EXPLORER WHOSE OPTION HAD BEEN PICKED UP BY THE KING OF FRANCE, DISCOVERS THE GULF OF THE ST. LAWRENCE AND PLANTS THE FRENCH FLAG SOMEWHERE ON DRY LAND. His discovery eventually prompted the establishment of French colonies and the formation of "New France."

1605   THE FIRST PERMANENT FRENCH SETTLEMENT IN NORTH AMERICA IS BUILT IN WESTERN NOVA SCOTIA, THEN CALLED ACADIA. Many decades later, French-speaking emigrants from Acadia made their way to Louisiana. The word used to describe a group of French-speaking people in that area today, "Cajuns," is a distortion of the term "Acadiens."

1608   SAMUEL DE CHAMPLAIN, COMMONLY REFERRED TO AS THE "FATHER OF CANADA," SETS UP A PERMANENT SETTLEMENT ON THE SITE OF THE PRESENT DAY CITY OF QUEBEC.

1610   HENRY HUDSON DISCOVERS HUDSON BAY. Hudson was left there to die by his crew, indicating that he was very adroit as an explorer but perhaps somewhat deficient when it came to employer-employee relations.

39

1627	THE COMPANY OF NEW FRANCE (SOMETIMES CALLED THE COMPANY OF THE HUNDRED ASSOCIATES) IS SANCTIONED BY THE CROWN TO PUSH AHEAD WITH THE DEVELOPMENT OF THE NORTH AMERICAN REGION. Unfortunately, the English and the French never seemed to get along very well back in the Old World and many of the able-bodied French had to remain in France in order to fight the wars, leading to a very slow development of the colonies in the Western world.
1642	FRENCH SETTLERS, LED BY MAISONNEUVE, SET UP SHOP IN WHAT IS NOW MONTREAL.
1663	LOUIS XIV, WITH THE ASSISTANCE OF JEAN COLBERT, TRANSFORMS NEW FRANCE INTO A ROYAL COLONY WITH THE FRENCH GOVERNMENT ASSUMING GREATER DIRECT CONTROL OVER THE AREA. The crown was represented in the colony by three major figures--the governor, the intendant, and the bishop. In addition, French civil law became the system of justice in New France. At this time, there were only 3,000 French-speaking people in the area and a good portion of these were coureurs de bois, the forerunners of the Jeremiah Johnson-type who probably did not have the looks of Robert Redford but were quite skilled when it came to hunting, exploring, fur-trapping, and mountain-climbing. Unfortunately, this type of person was not the optimal choice for establishing permanent settlements and bringing "civilization" to the New World.
1670	THE HUDSON'S BAY COMPANY IS GRANTED A ROYAL CHARTER BY ENGLISH AUTHORITIES TO DEVELOP TRADE IN THE AREA RUNNING FROM HUDSON BAY TO THE ROCKY MOUNTAINS. The company was able to keep this grant operative until 1870, when its domain was finally turned over to the Canadian government. In the decades following the granting of the charter, the French, the English, and the native peoples were all involved in a series of bloody confrontations, indicating that the two European powers were willing to extend their traditionally hostile relationship to the New World as well.

1713	THE BRITISH GAIN CONTROL OF NOVA SCOTIA (ACADIA) THROUGH THE TERMS AGREED TO IN THE PEACE TREATY OF UTRECHT.
1759	WOLFE'S FORCES DEFEAT THE FRENCH TROOPS UNDER MONTCALM IN THE FAMOUS BATTLE ON THE PLAINS OF ABRAHAM, A DECISIVE EVENT IN THE EVENTUAL BRITISH TAKEOVER OF NEW FRANCE. Both Wolfe and Montcalm were killed in the battle, perhaps persuading future military commanders to adopt a new strategy of coordinating battle plans at the rear of their troops instead of in front of them.
1763	AS A RESULT OF THE TREATY OF PARIS, GREAT BRITAIN FORMALLY TAKES OVER NEW FRANCE. At the time of the British takeover, there were 65,000 French Canadians.
1774	THE QUEBEC ACT GRANTS RELIGIOUS FREEDOM TO ROMAN CATHOLICS IN THE NEW WORLD AND PERMITS THE FRENCH CANADIANS TO RETAIN THEIR CIVIL LAW AND CULTURAL IDENTITY. The Act also extended the Quebec boundaries in order to include the Ohio territory, an action which helped fan revolutionary fires in the 13 colonies to the south.
1775	CANADA IS INVADED BY AMERICAN REVOLUTIONARIES AND MONTREAL IS SEIZED. However, all American troops were out of Canada by 1776 and in spite of the request by Lafayette and certain others to launch a new invasion, American leaders refused to do so.
1776	THE AMERICAN DECLARATION OF INDEPENDENCE IS PROCLAIMED BUT THE COLONISTS IN THE NORTH REFUSE TO JOIN THE REBELLION. During the course of the Revolutionary War and shortly thereafter, over 40,000 American colonists who refused to accept the revolt against Great Britain fled to Canada. This large grouping, known as United Empire Loyalists, became a major force in Canadian political development and formed the core of opposition to any unification of Canada and the United States.

1791	THE CONSTITUTIONAL ACT OF 1791 DIVIDES THE OLD PROVINCE OF CANADA INTO UPPER CANADA (NOW ONTARIO) AND LOWER CANADA (NOW QUEBEC). The rights of the Catholic Church were retained in Lower Canada whereas the prerogatives of the Church of England were strengthened in Upper Canada. Each colony was granted a separate government headed by a governor selected by the crown. Elected assemblies with very limited policymaking power were also established.
1812	THE WAR OF 1812 ERUPTS AND AN AMERICAN FORCE LAUNCHES AN UNSUCCESSFUL INVASION OF CANADA. The British and the Americans finally signed a peace treaty in 1814 with the Americans being extremely fortunate in avoiding forfeiture of some of their pre-1812 territories to Great Britain.
1837-38	DISILLUSIONED BY THE LACK OF RESPONSIBLE GOVERNMENT, REBELLIOUS CANADIANS STIR UP TROUBLE IN BOTH UPPER AND LOWER CANADA. William Lyon Mackenzie in Upper Canada and Louis Joseph Papineau in Lower Canada were the two pivotal leaders of these revolts. Papineau in particular favored the establishment of a republic which would be free of both European and church ties. This unrest eventually prompted British authorities to dispatch Lord Durham to the colonies to evaluate the situation.
1840	THE ACT OF UNION MERGES THE TWO CANADIAN COLONIES INTO ONE ENTITY. In his report issued in 1839, Lord Durham recommended the creation of one major province, the establishment of responsible government, and the institution of a program intended to assimilate French Canadians into the English system. Durham insisted that if these steps were not taken, the Canadians would eventually push for outright independence from Great Britain. With the Act of Union, the British parliament agreed to go along with Durham's first recommendation but not with the others.

1846   THE INTERNATIONAL BOUNDARY BETWEEN CANADA AND THE UNITED STATES IS EXTENDED ALONG THE 49TH PARALLEL FROM THE ROCKIES TO THE PACIFIC.

1855   FRANCE REESTABLISHES DIRECT DIPLOMATIC TIES WITH CANADA ALMOST A CENTURY AFTER THE FAMOUS BATTLE ON THE PLAINS OF ABRAHAM.

1864   THIRTY-THREE DELEGATES TO THE QUEBEC CONFERENCE DRAW UP 72 RESOLUTIONS WHICH WILL LEAD TO THE CREATION OF A CANADIAN CONFEDERATION. Most of these recommendations were later incorporated into the British North America Act which formally created the confederation. Keep in mind that the American Civil War was still being waged in the United States and that many Canadians were worried about the repercussions of this conflict. For example, the British had provided a great deal of support to the Confederacy, and many Canadians were concerned that the victorious North might attempt to seek revenge by seizing Canada from Great Britain. Thus these delegates, who later earned the title of the "Fathers of the Confederation," were intent on (1) instituting some form of self-government, (2) keeping Canada from being annexed by the United States, and (3) arriving at a formula to annex the Western prairie areas, then under the control of the Hudson's Bay Company, before the United States did. Consequently, the tragic events which transpired to the south of Canada had a definite impact on the creation of the Canadian confederation, including the recommendation of establishing a strong federal government because of the belief that the American states had been allowed to exercise too much authority and had thus plunged the American governmental system into utter turmoil.

1867   THE BRITISH NORTH AMERICA (BNA) ACT IS PASSED BY THE BRITISH PARLIAMENT AND THE CONFEDERATION IS FORMALLY CREATED. The Dominion of Canada at this time consisted of the United Province of Canada (Ontario and

Quebec), Nova Scotia, and New Brunswick. Powers were divided between the central dominion government and the provincial governments with the former seemingly receiving the greatest discretionary authority. Great Britain still retained control over Canadian external affairs and the court of last resort remained the Judicial Committee of the Privy Council in London. John A. MacDonald became the first Prime Minister of Canada.

1869   THE CANADIAN ACQUISITION OF THE RED RIVER AREA PRECIPITATES THE REVOLT OF THE MÉTIS LED BY LOUIS RIEL. This area, which had long been under the control of the Hudson's Bay Company, was ceded to Great Britain which then transferred control to the Canadian government. Unhappy with the turn of events, Louis Riel, a French Canadian, led his Métis and Indian followers in an unsuccessful revolt against Canadian authority. In 1870, the Red River area became part of the new province of Manitoba.

1871   BRITISH COLUMBIA BECOMES THE SIXTH PROVINCE IN THE CONFEDERATION. British Columbian officials opted for a place in the confederation mainly because they had been promised by Ottawa that a transcontinental railroad would be extended to the West Coast as soon as possible. This railroad, plagued by numerous economic and political woes, was finally completed in 1885.

1873   PRINCE EDWARD ISLAND OPTS FOR MEMBERSHIP IN THE CONFEDERATION.

1885   LOUIS RIEL LEADS A SECOND MÉTIS REBELLION IN SASKATCHEWAN. The revolt was soon put down and Riel was caught and hanged. Riel became a martyr for many French Canadians who perceived him as trying to protect French Canadian and native rights against English Canadian domination.

1896   SIR WILFRID LAURIER, LEADER OF THE LIBERAL PARTY, BECOMES CANADA'S FIRST FRENCH CANADIAN PRIME MINISTER.

44

1905   ALBERTA AND SASKATCHEWAN JOIN THE CONFEDERATION.

1914-18   CANADA PARTICIPATES IN WORLD WAR I. Because of its British ties, Canada declared war on the axis powers soon after the British declaration of war. In contrast, President Wilson was reelected in 1916 on a platform which pledged to keep America out of the European conflict. Wilson eventually changed his mind but America did not become involved in the war until 1917. The Canadians suffered more battlefield casualities (55,000 killed) in the war than the Americans (51,000 killed) and the Canadian nation was deeply divided in its opinions concerning Canadian participation. In particular, French Canadians felt that Canada was helping the British to attain their own imperialist goals, goals with which many French Canadians did not agree. The furor over the war effort reached its height in 1917 when mandatory conscription went into effect and many French Canadians refused to accept the draft.

1926   AN IMPERIAL CONFERENCE ASSERTS THE EQUALITY IN STATUS OF THE DOMINIONS AND GREAT BRITAIN. After being unable to work out a common foreign policy for the British empire, Great Britain and the dominions released a statement which stipulated that they were "equal in status, in no way subordinate one to another in any aspect of their domestic or external affairs, though united by a common allegiance to the Crown." Part of the impetus for this statement was provided by Canadian Prime Minister W. L. MacKenzie King who had faced a serious confrontation with the crown-appointed governor-general in 1921. The Liberals under King emerged victorious in the election of 1921 but the party was later involved in some serious scandals. As a result, King asked the governor-general to dissolve parliament and to schedule new elections. The crown appointee refused to go along with the prime minister's suggestion. Eventually, new elections were

45

held and King's party was returned to power. Nonetheless, King traveled to the Imperial Conference in 1926 to discuss the powers of the governor-general and to seek clarification concerning the "proper" relationship between Great Britain and the dominion nations.

1927   CANADA'S FIRST FOREIGN LEGATION IS ESTABLISHED IN WASHINGTON, D.C.

1931   THE STATUTE OF WESTMINSTER AFFIRMS THE INDEPENDENCE OF THE DOMINIONS IN MOST POLICY AREAS. In effect, the Statute proclaimed that the dominions such as Canada and Australia would be responsible for their own foreign policy, have the right to pass any legislation which they deemed necessary for the welfare of their respective countries, and have the privilege of ignoring any British legislation which might be considered as detrimental to their own particular interests. Canada was thus recognized as a sovereign nation with the exception that certain amendments to the BNA Act would still have to be passed by the British parliament and the final court of appeal on certain matters would still be the Judicial Committee of the Privy Council in Great Britain.

1933-36   NEW THIRD PARTIES SUCH AS THE COOPERATIVE COMMONWEALTH FEDERATION (CCF) AND SOCIAL CREDIT ARE CREATED. Much of the appeal of these new parties was regionalized and attributable to the discontent caused by Great Depression conditions.

1939-45   CANADA TAKES PART IN WORLD WAR II. Once again, because of its Commonwealth ties, Canada entered the war more than two years before the United States (which declared war after the attack on Pearl Harbor in December 1941).

1945   CANADA CONSTRUCTS THE FIRST NUCLEAR REACTOR OUTSIDE OF THE UNITED STATES. In addition, Canada, like the United States, emerged from the war in a state of full industralization,

46

a situation which contrasted markedly with the utter devastation on the European continent.

1949   NEWFOUNDLAND BECOMES THE LAST MEMBER OF THE CONFEDERATION AND THE CANADIAN SUPREME COURT BECOMES THE COURT OF LAST RESORT IN JUDICIAL MATTERS. CANADA ALSO JOINS THE NORTH ATLANTIC TREATY ORGANIZATION (NATO). Appeals to the Privy Council were finally abolished and the Canadian parliament received the right to amend the BNA Act in all matters except provincial and minority rights. These issues were still left in the hands of the British parliament.

1952   VINCENT MASSEY BECOMES CANADA'S FIRST CANADIAN-BORN GOVERNOR-GENERAL. Up until that time, governors-general were always selected from the Commonwealth countries, but the selection of Massey has been followed up by the appointment of other Canadian-born citizens to this largely ceremonial position.

1959   THE JOINT CANADIAN-AMERICAN ST. LAWRENCE SEAWAY PROJECT IS OPENED TO ALLOW SHIPS TO TRAVEL FROM THE GREAT LAKES TO THE ATLANTIC.

1960   THE CANADIAN BILL OF RIGHTS IS PASSED. The bill was passed as ordinary legislation by the Canadian parliament and among other things, prohibited discrimination on the basis of race, religion, sex, or national origin.

1961   THE CCF AND THE CANADIAN LABOUR CONGRESS MERGE TO FORM THE NEW DEMOCRATIC PARTY. This party would be ranked appreciably to the left of America's Democratic Party.

1963   A ROYAL COMMISSION ON BILINGUALISM AND BICULTURALISM IS ESTABLISHED. The commission studied relations between French-speaking and English-speaking Canadians and in its report issued in 1965 warned that Canada faced the danger of disintegration because of the widening opportunity gap favoring English Canadians and working against French Canadians.

1964   THE FULTON-FAVREAU CONSTITUTIONAL AMENDMENT FORMULA IS REJECTED. This formula would have transferred the ultimate power of constitutional amendment from Great Britain to Canada but did not receive the necessary unanimous support of the provincial governments.

1965   A NEW CANADIAN FLAG IS ADOPTED. Canada finally gave up its traditional British Union Jack in favor of the maple leaf design, an action which fomented a great deal of heated discussion in the country. During the same year, the Quebec provincial government signed a series of agreements with the French government.

1967   EXPO 67 IS HELD AND DE GAULLE MAKES HIS FAMOUS "QUEBEC LIBRE" STATEMENT. In commemoration of its centennial as a nation, Canada hosted the highly successful world's fair in Montreal. During his visit to Montreal to attend the fair, President de Gaulle addressed an audience in front of the Montreal city hall and voiced his support for a free Quebec. Canadian Prime Minister Lester Pearson called an emergency session of his cabinet and later declared that de Gaulle's remarks were inappropriate for a visiting head of state, prompting de Gaulle to cancel a scheduled visit to Ottawa and to return immediately to Paris.

1969   THE SUPREME COURT DRYBONES DECISION BECOMES THE FIRST MAJOR COURT APPLICATION OF THE CANADIAN BILL OF RIGHTS AND THE OFFICIAL LANGUAGES ACT IS PASSED PROVIDING FRENCH AND ENGLISH EQUAL STATUS FOR ALL PURPOSES OF THE FEDERAL GOVERNMENT.

1970   FLQ TERRORISM IN QUEBEC REACHES ITS PEAK WITH THE MURDER OF A QUEBEC OFFICIAL AND THE KIDNAPPING OF A BRITISH DIPLOMAT. THE WAR MEASURES ACT IS SUBSEQUENTLY INVOKED BY THE FEDERAL GOVERNMENT. One FLQ (Quebec Liberation Front) cell organization was responsible for the execution of Quebec Labor Minister Pierre Laporte while the British diplomat, James Cross, was eventually released unharmed by another FLQ group in return for safe passage to Cuba. The federal government eventually sent in troops to help quell the violence and the controversial War Measures Act, allowing the suspension of certain civil rights, was put into effect by federal authorities.

1971   THE VICTORIA CONFERENCE PROPOSES A NEW CANADIAN CONSTITUTION BUT FAILS TO RECEIVE THE SUPPORT OF THE QUEBEC GOVERNMENT. The far-reaching Victoria Charter included a basic statement on citizens' rights, support of the equal status of the French and English languages, and a method by which constitutional amendment would be a totally Canadian process. Although the other nine provinces accepted the new charter, the Quebec government refused to go along with it because it did not protect provincial control over certain social policies. As a result of the Quebec veto, Canada still lacked an acceptable formula for amending the constitution without having to ask the British parliament for its ultimate stamp of approval.

1976   THE PARTI QUÉBÉCOIS WINS THE QUEBEC PROVINCIAL ELECTIONS AND VOWS TO WORK FOR AN INDEPENDENT QUEBEC. Although directing his campaign toward a denunciation of the alleged corruption and inefficiencies in the previous Liberal government, PQ leader René Lévesque was always identified as a strong supporter of Quebec sovereignty, a goal which is still written in the PQ policy platform. On another front, the death penalty was abolished in Canada in 1976.

1977   THE QUEBEC NATIONAL ASSEMBLY PASSES BILL 101 (CHARTER OF THE FRENCH LANGUAGE). This new law declared that French is the only official language of Quebec and that with very few exceptions, French would be the mandated language to be used in the working place and in the schools.

49

1978   THE TRUDEAU GOVERNMENT PROPOSES A NEW
            CONSTITUTION FOR CANADA. The federal
            authorities explained that the chief purpose
            of the new document was to "renew" the
            Canadian confederation and to preserve
            national unity.

1980   THE QUEBEC VOTERS SOUNDLY REJECT A
            REFERENDUM ISSUE WHICH WOULD PROVIDE THE
            QUEBEC GOVERNMENT WITH A MANDATE TO
            NEGOTIATE SOVEREIGNTY-ASSOCIATION WITH THE
            REST OF CANADA.

1982   CANADA'S NEW CONSTITUTION AND CHARTER OF
            RIGHTS AND FREEDOMS GO INTO EFFECT. Nine
            provinces supported these new documents, but
            Quebec adamantly opposed both the new
            charter and the new constitutional amendment
            formula. Nevertheless, in spite of Quebec's
            opposition, the new constitution and charter
            were promulgated by Queen Elizabeth II in
            April 1982.

NOTES

[1]This poll was commissioned by the <u>Newsmagazine</u> television program and was made public on June 18, 1977. Eighty-three percent knew that Canada was a parliamentary democracy but only 29 percent identified Canada as a monarchy.

[2]Ibid. Fifty-one percent also stated that Queen Elizabeth II should continue to "reign" over Canada, 41 percent stated she should not, and eight percent had no opinion. Forty-two percent stated that having a monarch helped Canadian unity while 52 percent disagreed. The strongest support for the retention of the monarchy was found in the prairies and Atlantic provinces, while the weakest was naturally found in Quebec.

[3]See S. M. Lipset, "Revolution and Counter-revolution: The United States and Canada," in <u>The Canadian Political Process: A Reader</u>, 2nd ed., ed. Orest Kruhlak, Richard Schultz, and Sidney Pobihushchy (Toronto: Holt, Rinehart and Winston, 1973), pp. 3-29.

III

THE NEW CANADIAN CONSTITUTION: AN ACT OF
UNITY OR DISUNITY?

An Overview of Canadian Constitutionalism

In an historic ceremony held in Ottawa in April
1982, Queen Elizabeth II officially proclaimed Canada's
new constitutional act. Most Canadians were extremely
pleased to see the constitution finally "patriated,"
which means that future amendments to the constitution
will be made exclusively in Canada and will not require
ratification by the British parliament. Nevertheless,
the new constitution has sparked a great deal of
controversy and on the day that Queen Elizabeth
presided over the festivities in Ottawa,
counter-demonstrations were being held in neighboring
Quebec where Premier René Lévesque labeled the day as
one of the darkest in Quebec's history.

In many respects, the Canadian political system is
patterned after Great Britain's. The British have no
written constitution per se, but have traditionally
depended on certain key statutes, court decisions,
customs, and common law practices in order to safeguard
the rights of the people and to guarantee the orderly
functioning of government. Indisputably, the British
political system has generally stood out as a bastion
of democracy and a protector of citizens' freedoms,
even without a dominant constitutional document.

The Canadian system also has several statutes and
customs which are part of its constitutional heritage.
In the mid-1960s, a major Canadian forum was assembled
to study the state of constitutionalism in the country.
This forum identified the Canadian "constitution" at
that time as consisting of the (1) BNA Acts, 1867-1964,
(2) Manitoba Act of 1870, (3) Parliament of Canada Act
of 1875, (4) Canadian Speaker Act of 1895, (5) Alberta
Act of 1905, (6) Saskatchewan Act of 1905, and
(7) Statute of Westminster of 1931.[1]   Other
constitutional authorities have also included the Bill
of Rights and the War Measures Act (which allows, in
emergency situations, the arrest of citizens without
recourse to habeas corpus protections) as parts of the
"constitution."[2] Some of these documents, such as the

53

Bill of Rights of 1960, were passed by the Canadian parliament as simple legislation and could be annulled by a simple act of parliament. Nonetheless, acts such as these and other statutes and customs which protect certain civil liberties, provide an equitable system of law, and guarantee responsible governmental institutions, should be considered as a part of the overall constitutional structure with the Constitution Act of 1982 being the cornerstone of Canada's constitutional system.

The BNA Act

The BNA Act, which is referred to in the new constitution as the Constitution Act, 1867, has been described as "a document of monumental dullness which enshrines no eternal principles and is devoid of inspirational content."[3] The scholar who made these remarks went on to say that in spite of its "dullness," the BNA Act is a very pragmatic document and provides workable ground rules for the functioning of the Canadian system. The BNA Act is still the major portion of Canada's new constitution, with a Charter of Rights and Freedoms, a constitutional amendment formula, and a few other provisions being added to the older document in 1982.

The BNA Act is divided into eight major sections and has as its underlying premise the idea that the Canadian government should be patterned after the British model. Besides a short preamble, the BNA Act provides guidelines for (1) territorial unification, (2) federal executive powers, (3) federal legislative powers, (4) provincial constitutions, (5) the distribution of federal-provincial legislative authority, (6) judicial powers, (7) fiscal arrangements, and (8) various miscellaneous provisions.[4]

As is the case with the British system, the BNA Act stipulates that parliament will be the supreme governmental policymaking body, although there is a greater separation of powers among the executive, legislative, and judicial bodies in Canada than in present-day Great Britain. For example, Canada has a separate and distinct Supreme Court which has a limited power of judicial review (the right of the court to declare an act of the executive, legislature, or public

54

administration as unconstitutional). Great Britain does not have a separate high court and does not recognize the power of judicial review.

Canada also has a "responsible" government system, which means that the prime minister and his cabinet are responsible for their actions to a popularly elected parliament and are expected to resign if they lose the confidence of a majority of members in the House of Commons. In addition, the BNA Act created a federal system of government for Canada, whereas Great Britain has traditionally had a unitary system. In a unitary system, governmental authority is concentrated in the hands of a central government; in a federal system, governmental authority is divided between central and regional governments. The vast geographic size of the new confederation, combined with a strong sense of regional identity in certain areas, fairly well dictated that a federal system was the only feasible alternative available to the new nation back in 1867.

As Table III:1 indicates, the BNA Act mandates a fairly concise division of powers and responsibilities between the federal and the provincial governments. The Canadian founding fathers definitely favored the central government having the bulk of authority and made sure that the central government was granted reserved or residual powers (in other words, any powers not specifically granted to the provinces would be considered as within the domain of the central government). Within their own sphere of jurisdiction, however, the provincial legislatures are viewed as sovereign and not answerable to the parliamentary authority in Ottawa.

Some features of the BNA Act have become obsolete and some very important facets of contemporary Canadian government are not even mentioned in the Act. For example, the Act permits the federal government to disallow or withhold assent (through the lieutenant-governor, the crown's representative in each province) from provincial legislation. These powers, although still on the books, have fallen into disuse, In addition, the strong attachment to Great Britain which is alluded to in the Act has undoubtedly waned somewhat in recent years as Canada has asserted its independence.

55

TABLE III:1

CONSTITUTIONAL POWERS OF THE FEDERAL PARLIAMENT AND THE PROVINCIAL LEGISLATURES

Powers of the Federal Parliament
As Stipulated in Section 91
of the Constitution Act, 1867

1. the amendment of the constitution of Canada, subject to certain exceptions;
1a. the public debt and property;
2. the regulation of trade and commerce;
2a. unemployment insurance;
3. the raising of money by any mode or system of taxation;
4. the borrowing of money on the public credit;
5. postal service;
6. the census and statistics;
7. militia, military and naval service, and defence;
8. the fixing of and providing for the salaries and allowances of civil and other officers of the Government of Canada;
9. beacons, buoys, lighthouses, and Sable Island;
10. navigation and shipping;
11. quarantine and the establishment and maintenance of marine hospitals;
12. seacoast and inland fisheries;
13. ferries between a province and any country or between two provinces;
14. currency and coinage;
15. banking, incorporation of banks, and the issue of paper money;
16. savings banks;
17. weights and measures;
18. bills of exchange and promissory notes;
19. interest;
20. legal tender;
21. bankruptcy and insolvency;
22. patents of invention and discovery;
23. copyrights;
24. Indians, and lands reserved for the Indians;
25. naturalization and aliens;
26. marriage and divorce;
27. the criminal law, except the constitution of courts of criminal jurisdiction, but including the procedure in criminal matters;

28. the establishment, maintenance, and management of penitentiaries;
29. steamship lines, railways, ships, canals, telegraphs and other works and undertakings extending beyond the limits of a province, and other works declared by the Parliament of Canada to be for the general advantage of Canada.

In addition, under Section 95 of the BNA Act, 1867, the Parliament of Canada may make laws relating to agriculture and immigration concurrently with provincial legislatures, although, in the event of conflict, federal legislation is paramount.

Powers of the Provincial
Legislatures As Stipulated
In Section 92 of the
Constitution Act, 1867

1. the amendment of the constitution of the province except as regards the office of the Lieutenant-Governor;
2. direct taxation within the province in order to raise revenue for provincial purposes;
3. the borrowing of money on the credit of the province;
4. the establishment and tenure of provincial offices and the appointment and payment of provincial officers;
5. the management and sale of the public lands belonging to the province and of the timber and wood thereon (and pursuant to Section 109 of the Act, all lands, mines, minerals and royalties belong to the provinces as well);
6. the establishment, maintenance, and management of public and reformatory prisons in and for the province.
7. the establishment, maintenance, and management of hospitals, asylums, and charitable institutions in and for the province, other than marine hospitals;
8. municipal institutions in the province;
9. shop, tavern and other licences issued for the raising of provincial, local, or municipal revenue;
10. local works and undertakings, other than those expressly within federal jurisdiction;

11. the incorporation of companies with provincial objects;
12. the solemnization of marriage in the province;
13. property and civil rights in the province;
14. the administration of justice in the province, including the constitution, maintenance and organization of provincial courts, both of civil and of criminal jurisdiction, and including procedure in civil matters in those courts;
15. the imposition of punishment by fine, penalty, or imprisonment for enforcing any law of the province made in relation to any matter coming within any of the classes ot subject enumerated in this section; and
16. generally all matters of a merely local or private nature in the province and not enumerated in Section 91 as a matter coming under federal jurisdiction.

Furthermore, in and for each province the legislature may, under Section 93, make laws exclusively in relation to education, subject to certain restrictions relating to rights or privileges held by certain religious denominations with respect to schools.

The provinces also share powers of legislation respecting agriculture and immigration, and have an overriding legislative jurisdiction with respect to old-age pensions and supplementary benefits.

> Source: Department of External Affairs, Reference Papers, no. 70, August, 1975, pp. 8-9, 15-16.

The BNA Act also suggests that the powers of the governor-general, the crown's representative in Canada, are significant. This is greatly misleading, however, as the real decision-making power is concentrated in the hands of the prime minister and his cabinet, neither of which is even mentioned in the BNA Act.

Federal-provincial conferences have also emerged as a vital policymaking forum in recent years, but the BNA Act has nothing to say about them. Political parties are also ignored by the Act even though they have emerged as a pivotal force in the Canadian political system. In addition, the Canadian Supreme Court was not established in the BNA Act and had to be created later on.

The Evolution of Canada's New Constitution

On October 2, 1980, the federal cabinet under the tutelage of Prime Minister Pierre Trudeau unveiled an historic resolution which was designed to finally "patriate" Canada's major constitutional document, the BNA Act. In addition, the federal government announced plans to establish a constitutionally endowed bill of rights and to at long last enact a Canadian-originated formula for constitutional amendment. Trudeau's bold initiative was intended to rejuvenate Canada's troubled system of federalism and to enhance the sense of Canadian nationhood, but his unilateral approach, which for many months deliberately disregarded the desires of many provincial governments, undoubtedly exacerbated the severe cleavages which already existed within the federal-provincial framework.

Prior to the changes put into effect in 1982, the BNA Act had simply been a statute passed by the British parliament and had never been approved by the Canadian parliament nor by the Canadian people through a referendum. In addition, the amending of the BNA Act still had to be referred in certain cases to the British parliament for its approval. For example, approval was given by the British parliamentarians in 1964 for an amendment to the BNA Act which enabled the Canadian parliament to pass a law pertaining to a proposed pension plan. Over the past few decades, the British parliamentary approval had been automatic but many Canadians objected to having to appeal to London in the first place in order to pass legislation which was solely pertinent to Canada.

Yet in spite of the strong sentiment in favor of patriation, 13 constitutional conferences had been held over a period of more than a half century without achieving any notable success. The major stumbling block had not been the patriation of the BNA Act, but rather unanimous agreement on a constitutional amendment formula. If patriation were to occur without prior approval on an amendment procedure, each change in the constitution would have undoubtedly had to be ratified unanimously by the federal government and the

59

ten provincial governments, a situation which would openly invite stalemate and paralysis. In the mid-1960s with the Fulton-Favreau formula and again in 1971 with the Victoria amending procedures, the Canadian national and regional governments came very close to breaking the deadlock and agreeing on a process which would not require unanimity. In both cases, however, the Quebec government, fearing a possible diminution in its authority to protect the interests of the French-Canadian people, cast the sole dissenting vote. Ironically, the negotiations had been in a holding pattern over the past half century because of the ground rule which stipulated that the federal and provincial governments should first of all unanimously agree on an amendment formula to do away with unanimity in the passage of constitutional amendments. In contrast, in the case of the United States the approval of only 9 of the original 13 states was needed to implement the Constitution of 1787 and its accompanying amendment formula.

Given impetus by the Parti Québécois victory of November 1976, the Trudeau government launched a concerted campaign to finally patriate the constitution and develop an acceptable amendment formula. In the late spring of 1978, the government released a White Paper on constitutional reform which outlined a new Canadian constitution and amendment formula. Trudeau subsequently met with the provincial premiers in the autumn of 1978 and again in the winter of 1979. At those meetings, the government leaders agreed on the importance and urgency of constitutional change and the need for all governments to devote more time and effort to the task of constitutional renewal. The much-heralded report by the Task Force on Canadian Unity which was issued in January of 1979 echoed the same sense of urgency. However, in spite of the rhetoric, it was quite apparent that little of substance was being achieved and that several provincial governments were in no hurry to put a rapid end to the more than half-century on-again off-again struggle to ratify a new Canadian constitutional framework.

On May 20, 1980, the voters of the province of Quebec rejected by a 59.2 percent to 40.8 percent margin a referendum issue which would have provided the Lévesque government with a mandate to negotiate political sovereignty and economic association. During the referendum campaign, Pierre Trudeau had pledged to the Quebec electorate that if it voted against the Lévesque proposal, the federal government would immediately push forward with constitutional reform to improve Quebec's status within the framework of confederation. On the afternoon following the vitally important Quebec vote, Trudeau addressed the House of Commons and stated that he was honor-bound to launch constitutional renewal and "never stop working at it until Canada finally has a new constitution."[5]

Trudeau immediately dispatched Jean Chrétien, his Minister of Justice and chief architect of the federal referendum victory in Quebec, to the twelve provincial and territorial capitals to hold preliminary constitutional discussions with the subnational government leaders. In early June, Trudeau personally met with the provincial premiers in Ottawa, and ministers involved in federal-provincial relations held periodic meetings throughout the summer. In early September 1980, the first ministers of Canada met once again in a much-heralded conference which Trudeau hoped would culminate in a constitutional agreement. Instead, the meeting was characterized by a lack of consensus and among the dozen items linked to constitutional reform, tacit agreement was reached only on the issues of family law, fisheries, and a restructured Supreme Court system.[6] Trudeau personally stressed the need to patriate the constitution, prepare a charter which would constitutionally guarantee human, democratic, legal, and linguistic rights, and formulate a proposal protecting the right to education in their own language for French and English-speaking minorities. His priorities made little headway in the discussions, and most of the package of proposals formulated by the provincial premiers suffered a similar fate.[7]

Rebuffed by most of the provincial leaders, Trudeau subsequently made the decision to proceed unilaterally with the patriation of the BNA Act without the consent of the provinces. In outlining his plan of action, Trudeau maintained that his conduct was justified because the rule of federal-provincial unanimity had become "a tyrant" that had fomented constitutional paralysis for more than five decades.[8]

In the resolution presented before parliament in early October 1980, the Trudeau government asked Great

Britain to transfer both the text of the BNA Act and the power to amend the document to Canada. In addition, the British parliament was requested to include two significant amendments. The first would establish the Canadian Charter of Rights and Freedoms, a U.S.-style bill of rights which would be binding on both federal and provincial governments. This new constitutionally derived charter would guarantee fundamental democratic and legal freedoms (including mobility rights), outlaw racial and sexual discrimination, and insure bilingual education rights. The second amendment would constitutionally obligate the federal and provincial governments to continue the present system of equalization payments (which will be discussed in the next chapter) in order to maintain a roughly equal standard of public services across Canada.

Several provincial leaders objected to portions of the proposed Charter of Rights and Freedoms, and discussions continued to bog down on an acceptable constitutional amendment formula. For a time, René Lévesque of Quebec was joined by premiers from seven of the English-speaking provinces in expressing major opposition to Prime Minister Trudeau's constitutional proposals. However, the constitutional logjam was finally broken in November 1981 when the nine premiers of the English-speaking provinces voted to support Trudeau in exchange for certain concessions in the amendment formula and the Charter of Rights and Freedoms. In order to secure the support of these premiers, Trudeau agreed to delete a provision which would have permitted the Canadian public to vote in a referendum to resolve any future constitutional deadlock between the federal and provincial governments. Whereas the earlier Victoria Charter would have provided Ontario and Quebec with an absolute veto over constitutional amendments, Trudeau agreed that this would not be allowed in the new constitutional document. Moreover, the Canadian prime minister stated that he would support a very controversial measure permitting provincial governments to "opt out" of any constitutional amendment which directly impacted upon their provincial powers.

As for the Charter of Rights and Freedoms, Trudeau stated that he would reluctantly limit mobility rights and permit economically depressed provinces to extend preferential treatment to their own residents in seeking employment opportunities. Trudeau also conceded that in certain cases provinces could "opt out" from implementing new federal provisions dealing specifically with fundamental freedoms, legal rights, and equality rights. [9]

Once these concessions were made, Trudeau was able to rally support from all provincial leaders except René Lévesque. Thus, Quebec once again stood alone in the constitutional process but found this time that neither the federal government nor the nine provincial governments of English Canada would recognize Quebec's right to veto the entire constitutional process. Quebec eventually made an appeal to Canada's Supreme Court, claiming that the terms covering Quebec's entry into the confederation in 1867 and the custom of amending the constitution by a unanimous vote of the governments in Ottawa and the provinces made it necessary for all provinces to agree on the patriation of Canada's new constitutional document. In its decision, the Supreme Court conceded that a unanimous vote had been the customary practice used for amending the BNA Act in the past, but that unanimity was not grounded on legal principle and that Prime Minister Trudeau could therefore proceed with the patriation process without Quebec's approval.

On December 2, 1981, the Canadian House of Commons passed the final revised constitutional resolution by a vote of 246 to 24. Six days later, the Senate adopted the resolution and it was soon sent along to London for final approval by the British parliament. With only one-third of its membership present, the British House of Commons gave final approval to the constitutional package on March 9, 1982. The House of Lords approved the bill on March 25, paving the way for Queen Elizabeth to proclaim the new document in Ottawa on April 17 and to end once and for all Canada's dependence on Great Britain for the amendment of the Canadian constitution.

The Constitution Act of 1982

Table III:2 provides the text of the Constitution Act of 1982, including Canada's new Charter of Rights and Freedoms and new constitutional amendment formula. In addition, as pointed out in Part VI of the Constitution Act of 1982, some amendments were made to

63

TABLE III:2

THE CONSTITUTION ACT, 1982

PART I
Canadian Charter of Rights and Freedoms

Whereas Canada is founded upon principles that recognize the supremacy of God and the rule of law:

Guarantee of Rights and Freedoms

1. The Canadian Charter of Rights and Freedoms guarantees the rights and freedoms set out in it subject only to such reasonable limits prescribed by law as can be demonstrably justified in a free and democratic society.

Fundamental Freedoms

2. Everyone has the following fundamental freedoms:
   (a) freedom of conscience and religion;
   (b) freedom of thought, belief, opinion and expression, including freedom of the press and other media of communication;
   (c) freedom of peaceful assembly;
   (d) freedom of association.

Democratic Rights

3. Every Citizen of Canada has the right to vote in an election of members of the House of Commons or of a legislative assembly and to be qualified for membership therein.

4. (1) No House of Commons and no legislative assembly shall continue for longer than five years from the date fixed for the return of the writs at a general election of its members.

   (2) In time of real or apprehended war, invasion or insurrection, a House of Commons may be continued by Parliament and a legislative assembly may be continued by the Legislature beyond five years if such continuation is not opposed by the votes of more than one-third of the members of the House of Commons or the legislative assembly, as the case may be.

5. There shall be a sitting of Parliament and of each Legislature at least once every (12) months.

Mobility Rights

6. (1) Every citizen of Canada has the right to enter, remain in and leave Canada.

    (2) Every citizen of Canada and every person who has the status of a permanent resident of Canada has the right
        (a) to move to and take up residence in any province; and
        (b) to pursue the gaining of a livelihood in any province.

    (3) The rights specified in Subsection (2) are subject to
        (a) any laws or practices of general application in force in a province other than those that discriminate among persons primarily on the basis of province of present or previous residence; and
        (b) any laws providing for reasonable residency requirements as a qualification for the receipt of publicly provided social services.

    (4) Subsections (2) and (3) do not preclude any law, program or activity that has as its object the amelioration in a province of conditions of individuals in that province who are socially or economically disadvantaged if the rate of employment in that province is below the rate of employment in Canada.

Legal Rights

7. Everyone has the right of life, liberty and security of the person and the right not to be deprived thereof except in accordance with the principles of fundamental justice.

8. Everyone has the right to be secure against unreasonable search or seizure.

9. Everyone has the right not to be arbitrarily detained or imprisoned.

10. Everyone has the right on arrest or detention:
    (a) to be informed promptly of the reason therefor;
    (b) to retain and instruct counsel without delay and to be informed of that right; and
    (c) to have the validity of the detention determined by way of habeas corpus and to be released if the detention is not lawful.

11. Any person charged with an offence has the right:
    (a) to be informed without unreasonable delay of the specific offence;
    (b) to be tried within a reasonable time;
    (c) not to be compelled to be a witness in proceedings against that person in respect of the offence;
    (d) to be presumed innocent until proven guilty according to law in a fair and public hearing by an independent and impartial tribunal;
    (e) not to be denied reasonable bail without just cause;
    (f) except in the case of an offence under military law tried before a military tribunal, to the benefit of trial by jury where the maximum punishment for the offence is imprisonment for five years or a more severe punishment;
    (g) not to be found guilty on account of any act or omission unless, at the time of the act or omission, it constituted an offence under Canadian or international law or was criminal according to the general principles of law recognized by the community of nations;
    (h) if finally acquitted of the offence, not to be tried for it again and if finally found guilty and punished for the offence, not to be tried or punished for it again; and
    (i) if found guilty of the offence and if the punishment for the offence has been varied between the time of commission and the time of sentencing, to the benefit of the lesser punishment.

12. Everyone has the right not to be subjected to any cruel and unusual treatment or punishment.

13. A witness who testifies in any proceedings has the right not to have any incriminating evidence so given used to incriminate that witness in any other proceedings except in a prosecution for perjury or for the giving of contradictory evidence.

14. A party or witness in any proceedings who does not understand or speak the language in which the proceedings are conducted or who is deaf has the right to the assistance of an interpreter.

Equality Rights

15. (1) Every individual is equal before and under the law and has the right to the equal protection and equal benefit of the law without discrimination and, in particular, without discrimination based on race, national or ethnic origin, color, religion, sex, age or mental or physical disability.

    (2) Subsection (1) does not preclude any law, program or activity that has as its object the amelioration of conditions of disadvantaged individuals or groups including those that are disadvantaged because of race, national or ethnic origin, color, religion, sex, age or mental or physical disability.

Official Languages

16. (1) English and French are the official languages of Canada and have equality of status and equal rights and privileges as to their use in all institutions of the Parliament and Government of Canada.

    (2) English and French are the official languages of New Brunswick and have equality of status and equal rights and privileges as to their use in all institutions of the Legislature and Government of New Brunswick.

(3) Nothing in this charter limits the authority of Parliament or a Legislature to advance the equality of status or use of English and French.

17. (1) Everyone has the right to use English or French in any debates and other proceedings of Parliament.

(2) Everyone has the right to use English or French in any debates and other proceedings of the Legislature of New Brunswick.

18. (1) The statutes, records and journals of Parliament shall be printed and published in English and French and both language versions are equally authoritative.

(2) The statutes, records and journals of the Legislature of New Brunswick shall be printed and published in English and French and both language versions are equally authoritative.

19. (1) Either English or French may be used by any person in, or in any pleading in or process issuing from, any court established by Parliament.

(2) Either English or French may be used by any person in, or in any pleading in or process issuing from, any court of New Brunswick.

20. (1) Any member of the public in Canada has the right to communicate with, and to receive available services from, any head or central office of an institution of the Parliament or Government of Canada in English or French, and has the same right with respect to any other office of any such institution where
(a) there is a significant demand for communications with and services from that office in such language; or
(b) due to the nature of the office, it is reasonable that communications with and services from that office be available in both English and French.

(2)   Any member of the public in New Brunswick has the right to communicate with, and to receive available services from, any office of an institution of the Legislature or Government of New Brunswick in English or French.

21.   Nothing in Sections 16 to 20 abrogates or derogates from any right, privilege or obligation with respect to the English and French languages, or either of them, that exists or is continued by virtue of any other provision of the Constitution of Canada.

22.   Nothing in Sections 16 to 20 abrogates or derogates from any legal or customary right or privilege acquired or enjoyed either before or after the coming into force of this charter with respect to any language that is not English or French.

Minority Language Educational Rights

23.   (1)   Citizens of Canada
        (a)   whose first language learned and still understood is that of the English or French linguistic minority population of the province in which they reside, or
        (b)   who have received their primary school instruction in Canada in English or French and reside in a province where the language in which they received that instruction is the language of the English or French linguistic minority population of the province, have the right to have their children receive primary and secondary school instruction in that language in that province.

      (2)   Citizens of Canada of whom any child has received or is receiving primary or secondary school instruction in English or French in Canada, have the right to have all their children receive primary and secondary school instruction in the same language.

(3) The right of citizens ot Canada under Subsections (1) and (2) to have their children receive primary and secondary school instruction in the language of the English or French linguistic minority population of a province

    (a) applies wherever in the province the number of children of citizens who have such a right is sutticient to warrant the provision to them out of public funds of minority language instruction; and

    (b) includes, where the number of those children so warrants, the right to have them receive that instruction in minority language education facilities provided out of public funds.

Enforcement

24. (1) Anyone whose rights or freedoms, as guaranteed by this charter, have been infringed or denied may apply to a court of competent jurisdiction to obtain such remedy as the court considers appropriate and just in the circumstances.

    (2) Where, in proceedings under Subsection (1), a court concludes that evidence was obtained in a manner that infringed or denied any rights or freedoms guaranteed by this charter, the evidence shall be excluded if it is established that, having regard to all the circumstances, the admission of it in the proceedings would bring the administration of justice into disrepute.

General

25. The guarantee in this charter of certain rights and freedoms shall not be construed so as to abrogate or derogate from any aboriginal, treaty or other rights or freedoms that pertain to the aboriginal peoples of Canada including

    (a) any rights or freedoms that have been recognized by the Royal Proclamation of October 7, 1763; and

TABLE III:2 (continued)

(b) any rights or freedoms that may be acquired
by the aboriginal peoples of Canada by way of
land claims settlement.

26. The guarantee in this charter of certain rights
and freedoms shall not be construed as denying the
existence of any other rights or freedoms that
exist in Canada.

27. This charter shall be interpreted in a manner
consistent with the preservation and enhancement
of the multicultural heritage of Canadians.

28. Notwithstanding anything in this charter, the
rights and freedoms referred to in it are
guaranteed equally to male and female persons.

29. Nothing in this charter abrogates or derogates
from any rights or privileges guaranteed by or
under the Constitution of Canada in respect of
denominational, separate or dissentient schools.

30. A reference in this charter to a province or to
the legislative assembly or Legislature of a
province shall be deemed to include a reference to
the Yukon Territory and the Northwest Territories,
or to the appropriate legislative authority
thereof, as the case may be.

31. Nothing in this charter extends the legislative
powers of any body or authority.

Application of Charter

32. (1) This charter applies
(a) to the Parliament and Government of
Canada in respect of all matters within
the authority of Parliament including
all matters relating to the Yukon
Territory and Northwest Territories; and
(b) to the Legislature and Government of
each province in respect of all matters
within the authority of the Legislature
of each province.

71

(2)   Notwithstanding Subsection (1), Section 15 shall not have effect until three years after this section comes into force.

33.   (1)   Parliament or the Legislature of a province may expressly declare in an Act of Parliament or of the Legislature, as the case may be, that the act or a provision thereof shall operate notwithstanding a provision included in Section 2 or Sections 7 to 15 of this charter.

    (2)   An act or a provision of an act in respect of which a declaration made under this section is in effect shall have such operation as it would have but for the provision of this charter referred to in the declaration.

    (3)   A declaration made under Subsection (1) shall cease to have effect five years after it comes into force or on such earlier date as may be specified in the declaration.

    (4)   Parliament or a Legislature of a province may reenact a declaration made under Subsection (1).

    (5)   Subsection (3) applies in respect of a reenactment made under Subsection (4).

Citation

34.   This part may be cited as the Canadian Charter of Rights and Freedoms.

PART II

Rights of the Aboriginal Peoples

35.   (1)   The existing aboriginal and treaty rights of the aboriginal peoples of Canada are hereby recognized and affirmed.

    (2)   In this act, "aboriginal peoples of Canada" includes the Indian, Inuit and Métis peoples of Canada.

PART III

Equalization and Regional Disparities

36. (1) Without altering the legislative authority of
Parliament or of the provincial Legislatures,
or the rights of any of them with respect to
the exercise of their legislative authority,
Parliament and the Legislatures, together
with the Government of Canada and the
provincial governments, are committed to
  (a) promoting equal opportunities for the
  well-being of Canadians;
  (b) furthering economic development to
  reduce disparity in opportunities; and
  (c) providing essential public services of
  reasonable quality to all Canadians.

    (2) Parliament and the Government of Canada are
committed to the principle of making
equalization payments to ensure that
provincial governments have sufficient
revenues to provide reasonably comparable
levels of public services at reasonably
comparable levels of taxation.

PART IV

Constitutional Conference

37. (1) A constitutional conference composed of the
Prime Minister of Canada and the first
ministers of the provinces shall be convened
by the Prime Minister of Canada within one
year after this part comes into force.

    (2) The conference convened under Subsection (1)
shall have included in its agenda an item
respecting constitutional matters that
directly affect the aboriginal peoples of
Canada, including the identification and
definition of the rights of those peoples to
be included in the Constitution of Canada,
and the Prime Minister of Canada shall invite
representatives of those peoples to
participate in the discussions on that item.

(3) The Prime Minister of Canada shall invite elected representatives of the Governments of the Yukon Territory and the Northwest Territories to participate in the discussions on any item on the agenda of the conference convened under Subsection (1) that, in the opinion of the Prime Minister, directly affects the Yukon Territory and the Northwest Territories.

PART V

Procedure for Amending Constitution of Canada

38. (1) An amendment to the Constitution of Canada may be made by proclamation issued by the Governor-General under the Great Seal of Canada where so authorized by
    (a) resolutions of the Senate and House of Commons; and
    (b) resolutions of the legislative assemblies of at least two-thirds of the provinces that have, in the aggregate, according to the then latest general census, at least 50 percent of the population of all the provinces.

    (2) An amendment made under Subsection (1) that derogates from the legislative powers, the proprietary rights or any other rights or privileges of the Legislature or Government of a province shall require a resolution supported by a majority of the members of each of the Senate, the House of Commons and the legislative assemblies required under Subsection (1).

    (3) An amendment referred to in Subsection (2) shall not have effect in a province the legislative assembly of which has expressed its dissent thereto by resolution supported by a majority of its members prior to the issue of the proclamation to which the amendment relates unless that legislative assembly, subsequently, by resolution supported by a majority of its members, revokes its dissent and authorizes the amendment.

(4) A resolution of dissent made for the purpose of Subsection (3) may be revoked at any time before or after the issue of the proclamation to which it relates.

39. (1) A proclamation shall not be issued under Subsection 38(1) before the expiration of one year from the adoption of the resolution initiating the amendment procedure thereunder, unless the legislative assembly of each province has previously adopted a resolution of assent or dissent.

(2) A proclamation shall not be issued under Subsection 38(1) after the expiration of three years from the adoption of the resolution initiating the amendment procedure thereunder.

40. Where an amendment is made under Subsection 38(1) that transfers provincial legislative powers relating to education or other cultural matters from provincial Legislatures to Parliament, Canada shall provide reasonable compensation to any province to which the amendment does not apply.

41. An amendment to the Constitution of Canada in relation to the following matters may be made by proclamation issued by the Governor-General under the Great Seal of Canada only where authorized by resolutions of the Senate and House of Commons and of the legislative assembly of each province:
(a) the office of the Queen, the Governor-General and the Lieutenant-Governor of a province;
(b) the right of a province to a number of members in the House of Commons not less than the number of Senators by which the province is entitled to be represented at the time this part comes into force;
(c) subject to Section 43, the use of the English or the French language;
(d) the composition of the Supreme Court of Canada; and
(e) an amendment to this part.

42. (1) An amendment to the Constitution of Canada in relation to the following matters may be made only in accordance with Subsection 38(1):
    (a) the principle of proportionate representation of the provinces in the House of Commons prescribed by the Constitution of Canada;
    (b) the powers of the Senate and the method of selecting Senators;
    (c) the number of members by which a province is entitled to be represented in the Senate and the residence qualifications of Senators;
    (d) subject to paragraph 41(d), the Supreme Court of Canada;
    (e) the extension of existing provinces into the territories; and
    (f) notwithstanding any other law or practice, the establishment of new provinces.

    (2) Subsections 38(2) to (4) do not apply in respect of amendments in relation to matters referred to in Subsection (1).

43. An amendment to the Constitution of Canada in relation to any provision that applies to one or more, but not all, provinces, including
    (a) any alteration to boundaries between provinces, and
    (b) any amendment to any provision that relates to the use of the English or French language within a province, may be made by proclamation issued by the Governor-General under the Great Seal of Canada only where so authorized by resolutions of the Senate and House of Commons and of the legislative assembly of each province to which the amendment applies.

44. Subject to Sections 41 and 42, Parliament may exclusively make laws amending the Constitution of Canada in relation to the executive Government of Canada or the Senate and House of Commons.

45. Subject to Section 41, the Legislature of each province may exclusively make laws amending the constitution of the province.

46. (1) The procedures for amendment under Sections 38, 41, 42 and 43 may be initiated either by the Senate or the House of Commons or by the legislative assembly of a province.

    (2) A resolution of assent made for the purposes of this part may be revoked at any time before the issue of a proclamation authorized by it.

47. (1) An amendment to the Constitution of Canada made by proclamation under Section 38, 41, 42 or 43 may be made without a resolution of the Senate authorizing the issue of the proclamation if, within 180 days after the adoption by the House of Commons of a resolution authorizing its issue, the Senate has not adopted such a resolution and if, at any time after the expiration of that period, the House of Commons again adopts the resolution.

    (2) Any period when Parliament is prorogued or dissolved shall not be counted in computing the 180-day period referred to in Subsection (1).

48. The Queen's Privy Council for Canada shall advise the Governor-General to issue a proclamation under this part forthwith on the adoption of the resolutions required for an amendment made by proclamation under this part.

49. A constitutional conference composed of the Prime Minister of Canada and the first ministers of the provinces shall be convened by the Prime Minister of Canada within 15 years after this part comes into force to review the provisions of this part.

PART VI

Amendment to the Constitution Act, 1867

50. The Constitution Act, 1867 (formerly named the British North America Act, 1867) is amended by adding thereto, immediately after Section 92 thereof, the following heading and section:

Non-Renewable Natural Resources, Forestry Resources and Electrical Energy.

92A. (1) In each province, the Legislature may exclusively make laws in relation to
 (a) exploration for non-renewable natural resources in the province;
 (b) development, conservation and management of non-renewable natural resources and forestry resources in the province, including laws in relation to the rate of primary production therefrom; and
 (c) development, conservation and management of sites and facilities in the province for the generation and production of electrical energy.

(2) In each province, the Legislature may make laws in relation to the export from the province to another part of Canada of the primary production from non-renewable natural resources and forestry resources in the province and the production from facilities in the province for the generation of electrical energy, but such laws may not authorize or provide for discrimination in prices or in supplies exported to another part of Canada.

(3) Nothing in Subsection (2) derogates from the authority of Parliament to enact laws in relation to the matters referred to in that subsection and, where such a law of Parliament and a law of a province conflict, the law of Parliament prevails to the extent of the conflict.

(4) In each province, the Legislature may make laws in relation to the raising of money by any mode or system of taxation in respect of
 (a) non-renewable natural resources and forestry resources in the province and the primary production therefrom, and

TABLE III:2 (continued)

    (b)   sites and facilities in the province for the generation of electrical energy and the production therefrom, whether or not such production is exported in whole or in part from the province, but such laws may not authorize or provide for taxation that differentiates between production exported to another part of Canada and production not exported from the province.

  (5) The expression "primary production" has the meaning assigned by the Sixth Schedule.

  (6) Nothing in Subsections (1) to (5) derogates from any powers or rights that a Legislature or Government of a province had immediately before the coming into force of this section.

51. The said act is further amended by adding thereto the following schedule:

The Sixth Schedule

Primary Production from Non-Renewable Natural Resources and Forestry Resources.

  1. For the purposes of Section 92(a) of this Act,
    (a) production from a non-renewable natural resource is primary production therefrom if
      (i) it is in the form in which it exists upon its recovery or severance from its natural state, or
     (ii) it is a product resulting from processing or refining the resource, and is not a manufactured product or a product resulting from refining crude oil, refining upgraded heavy crude oil, refining gases or liquids derived from coal

79

or refining a synthetic equivalent of crude oil; and

(b) production from a forestry resource is primary production therefrom if it consists of sawlogs, poles, lumber, wood chips, sawdust or any other primary wood product, or wood pulp, and is not a product manufactured from wood.

PART VII

Generale

52. (1) The Constitution of Canada is the supreme law of Canada, and any law that is inconsistent with the provisions of the Constitution is, to the extent of the inconsistency, of no force or effect.

(2) The Constitution of Canada includes
(a) the Canada Act, including this Act;
(b) the Acts and orders referred to in Schedule 1; and
(c) any amendment to any Act or order referred to in paragraph (a) or (b).

(3) Amendments to the Constitution of Canada shall be made only in accordance with the authority contained in the Constitution of Canada.

53. (1) The enactments referred to in Column I of Schedule I are hereby repealed or amended to the extent indicated in Column II thereof and, unless repealed, shall continue as law in Canada under the names set out in Column III thereof.

(2) Every enactment, except the Canada Act, that refers to an enactment referred to in Schedule I by the name in Column I thereof is hereby amended by substituting for that name the corresponding name in Column III thereof, and any British North American Act not referred to in Schedule I may be cited as the Constitution Act followed by the year and number, if any, of its enactment.

54. Part IV is repealed on the day that is one year after this Part comes into force and this section may be repealed and this Act renumbered, consequential upon the repeal of Part IV and this section, by proclamation issued by the Governor-General under the Great Seal of Canada.

55. A French version of the portions of the Constitution of Canada referred to in Schedule I shall be prepared by the Minister of Justice of Canada as expeditiously as possible and, when any portion thereof sufficient to warrant action being taken has been so prepared, it shall be put forward for enactment by proclamation issued by the Governor-General under the Great Seal of Canada pursuant to the procedure then applicable to an amendment of the same provisions of the Constitution of Canada.

56. Where any portion of the Constitution of Canada has been or is enacted in English and French or where a French version of any portion of the Constitution is enacted pursuant to Section 55, the English and French versions of that portion of the Constitution are equally authoritative.

57. The English and French versions of this Act are equally authoritative.

58. Subject to Section 59, this Act shall come into force on a day to be fixed by proclamation issued by the Queen or the Governor-General under the Great Seal of Canada.

59. (1) Paragraph 23(1)(a) shall come into force in respect of Quebec on a day to be fixed by proclamation issued by the Queen or the Governor-General under the Great Seal of Canada.

    (2) A proclamation under Subsection (1) shall be issued only where authorized by the legislative assembly or government of Quebec.

    (3) This section may be repealed on the day paragraph 23(1)(a) comes into force in respect of Quebec and this Act amended and

renumbered, consequential upon the repeal of this section, by proclamation issued by the Queen or the Governor-General under the Great Seal of Canada.

60. This Act may be cited as the Constitution Act, 1982, and the Constitution Acts 1867 to 1975 (No. 2) and this Act may be cited together as the Constitution Acts, 1867 to 1982.

*The Constitution Act of 1982 and the Canadian Charter of Rights and Freedoms are reproduced by permission of the Minister of Supply and Services Canada.

the BNA Act (otherwise known as the Constitution Act, 1867), but for the most part the numerous sections of the BNA Act remain in force and are to be considered as an integral part of Canada's constitution.

The Charter of Rights and Freedoms

The Charter of Rights and Freedoms is enshrined in the new constitutional document because many Canadian leaders firmly believed that basic human rights and freedoms must be a part of the constitution and not simply a parliamentary act which could be changed any time in the future by a simple majority vote in the two chambers of parliament. The Bill of Rights of 1960 fell into this latter category and many people worried about how easy it would be to amend or even eliminate sections of this legislation which guaranteed essential human and civil rights.

The Charter is also designed to promote a sense of national community in a country suffering from major regional cleavages. The section of the Charter dealing with mobility rights guarantees the right of every citizen of Canada to pursue work opportunities in any province. In the past, several of the provincial governments have enacted legislation which clearly discriminates against workers, contractors, and suppliers from other provinces. Although Prime Minister Trudeau did concede in the constitutional negotiations that the poorer provinces could retain the right to favor their own workers under certain circumstances, the mobility rights should eliminate much of the protectionist legislation passed by several of the provinces and thereby strengthen Canada's national economy.

The Charter also reiterates that Canada is officially a bilingual country and that in their dealings with the federal government, Canadian citizens can demand services in either the English or French language, regardless of whether they are in Quebec City or Vancouver or any other city or town. Citizens are also guaranteed minority language education rights wherever numbers warrant, a provision which has stirred deep resentment in the ranks of the Quebec government. Quebec's Bill 101 mandates that French is the only official language of that province and only parents who have received their own education in the English

83

language in Quebec have the right to send their children to English language schools. The minority language education rights in the new constitution deny Quebec's government the authority to be so restrictive and Canadian courts have already annulled certain sections of Bill 101. The Parti Québécois leaders argue that Bill 101 is a survival measure designed to preserve the French language and French Canadian culture on a North American continent which is overwhelmingly English-speaking. They further insist that the minority language education rights found in the Charter are intended to restore English as a dominant language in the education and business spheres in Quebec, a situation which would erode progress made by French Canadians over the past two decades and hasten the assimilation of Canada's French-speaking minority by the English-speaking majority. On the other hand. approximately 20 percent of Quebec's population do not speak French. These non-francophones argue that they have the constitutional right to educate their children in English and that by doing so, these children will have a much better opportunity to find employment opportunities in Quebec and in Canada as a whole.

Groups representing the native peoples of Canada have bitterly complained that the Charter does not address the wrongs which have been perpetrated against the native people in the past nor does it provide any hope for restitution of rights and the settlement of native claims. Several associations representing the Indian, Inuit (commonly known as Eskimos in the United States), and Métis attempted in vain to convince the British parliament to hold up passage of the constitutional resolution until native grievances were addressed. The new Constitution Act does state that "existing aboriginal and treaty rights of the aboriginal peoples of Canada are hereby recognized and affirmed," but is totally mute when it comes to addressing the many land and resource claims which the native peoples have lodged against the provincial and federal governments. To be quite frank, the major governments in Canada are dominated by whites of European extraction and many admit that natives have been wronged in the past and resource-rich land has been abruptly taken away from the native peoples time and time again. However, these government leaders did not want a statement included in the constitution calling for the just settlement of native claims, a

84

settlement which would have likely involved billions of dollars and millions of acres of prime land. Moreover, there are only 500,000 native peoples in Canada, as compared to a population of almost 24 million non-natives. Consequently, the natives are generally not a major force at the ballot box (with the exception of the sparsely-populated Northwest Territories) nor in major governmental circles, and they have thus far made minimal progress in gaining support for their claims. To a significant extent, the same situation exists in the United States as in Canada.

With the inclusion of a formal civil rights section in the constitution, there is a fear that control over this important issue area will slip away from elected officials in parliament and into the hands of judges in the court system. Many Canadians frown upon the broad authority over social issues exercised by the American judicial system and insist that major decisions affecting civil liberties in Canada must be made directly by lawmakers voted into office by the electorate. As has been expressed by one source disgruntled with the recent turn of events, "the Charter of Rights will stand between the citizens and government as Gibralter stands between the Atlantic Ocean and the Mediterranean Sea."[10] There is no doubt that cases coming before the Canadian court system will increase substantially because of the Charter of Rights and Freedoms but it is too early to ascertain whether judicial authority will be greatly magnified at the expense of the legislative branch.

A related concern is linked to the power which the federal government may be able to exercise in areas of jurisdiction traditionally reserved for the provincial governments. For example, the provinces have been assigned control over the education system, but both the mobility and minority language education provisions in the Charter limit provincial authority in the educational sector. Other sections of the Charter of Rights and Freedoms may also pose major problems for provincial representatives and the Canadian court system will be kept busy working out solutions to these federal-provincial jurisdictional conflicts.

The Amendment Formula

As discussed previously, the lack of agreement on an acceptable amendment formula held up the patriation of Canada's constitution for more than 50 years. The new formula which went into effect in 1982 stipulates that a constitutional amendment must be passed by both chambers of parliament and by legislatures in at least seven provinces having 50 percent or more of the total population of all the provinces. Table III:3 compares this new constitutional amendment process with that found in the United States.

The big losers in the constitutional amendment process are Quebec and, to a lesser extent, Ontario. A few years ago, all of the provinces except Quebec agreed to support the Victoria Charter which stipulated that a constitutional amendment could be passed by a favorable vote in parliament and by legislatures in Ontario, Quebec, at least two of the four Atlantic provinces, and at least two of the four Western provinces having 50 percent or more of the total population of that region. Under the new arrangement, Ontario and Quebec are no longer granted an absolute veto over constitutional amendments and the Quebec government now fears that the English-speaking provinces will line up against Quebec and approve constitutional amendments which might jeopardize the rights of the francophone population.

There is still a possibility that the amendment formula may be altered and a conference is to be held among the federal and provincial leaders at some point in the future to discuss this issue. Prime Minister Trudeau has insisted that under certain conditions he would support Quebec being given a veto over constitutional amendments, but some of the provincial premiers would have a very difficult time supporting such a major concession.

The opting out clause in the amendment formula also raises the specter of checkerboard federalism and may be a major stumbling block to the achievement of greater national unity in Canada. Amendments must be passed by parliament and by legislatures in at least seven of the ten provinces having more than 50 percent of the total population of the provinces. Although most amendments will have to be implemented by all of the provinces, including the dissenting ones, there are

TABLE III:3

CONSTITUTIONAL AMENDMENT PROCEDURES IN CANADA
AND THE UNITED STATES

Canada

An amendment to the Constitution of Canada may be made by proclamation issued by the Governor-General under the Great Seal of Canada where so authorized by

(a) resolutions of the Senate and House of Commons; and

(b) resolutions of the legislative assemblies of at least two-thirds of the provinces that have, in the aggregate, according to the then latest general census, at least 50 percent of the population of all the provinces.

United States

Amendments to the Constitution must be proposed either by (1) a two-thirds majority in the House and the Senate, or (2) a convention summoned by Congress at the request of the legislatures of two-thirds of the states (never successfully utilized).

Amendments must be ratified either by (1) three-fourths of the state legislatures, or (2) ratifying conventions in three-fourths of the states (successfully utilized for the Twenty-First Amendment).

---

exceptions to the rule. For example, if a successful amendment impacts upon certain provincial powers, the one, two, or three provinces which did not originally ratify the amendment could simply disregard it. As a consequence, over a number of years and after the passage of several amendments, administrative and legal practices might differ rather substantially from province to province. Once again, the court system will face myriad headaches in trying to harmonize federal and provincial statutes and Canadian unity might suffer because of this patchwork quilt of legal and administrative practices.

A Comparison of the American
and Canadian Constitutions

The Articles of Confederation was America's first constitutional document but insufficient powers were granted to the central government and the new nation soon found itself on the verge of disintegration. As a result of this impending danger, delegates from each of the states gathered in Philadelphia and decided to formulate an entirely new constitution instead of merely amending the old Articles of Confederation. The framers of the new constitution provided the central government with much more authority and also stipulated a precise formula for the amendment of the constitution. An amendment to the constitution may be proposed by either a two-thirds vote of both chambers of Congress or by a national convention which is called by Congress on the application of two-thirds of the state legislatures. However, the proposing of an amendment is only half of the battle. Once the Congress or a national convention has ratified the formal proposal, three-fourths of the state legislatures, or special state conventions held specifically for the consideration of the amendment, must pass it before it officially becomes an amendment to the constitution. The overall process is extremely arduous and of the several hundred proposed amendments which have been brought before Congress over the past two centuries, only 26 have passed through the obstacle course and successfully emerged as full-fledged amendments.

In contrast, the BNA Act was not passed by Canadians and was not even intended to be a constitutional document. Moreover, the BNA Act contained no amending provisions. On the other hand, the provinces were provided with a much more uniform constitutional framework than the American states. For example, the length of state constitutions still varies dramatically, with the Vermont document consisting of 6,000 words and the Georgia constitution of 600,000. Furthermore, several state constitutional documents are archaic in certain areas and do not reflect modern governmental practices. Fortunately, the Canadian provinces have apparently avoided these constitutional pitfalls.

Both nations have also done fairly well in protecting the civil liberties of their citizens, with

88

certain notable exceptions. For example, during World War I, thousands of people of German and Austrian extraction were herded into Canadian internment camps. Both nations also interned thousands of people of Japanese ancestry and confiscated their property during World War II. To this day, compensation for this confiscated property has not been forthcoming either in Canada or the United States. Moreover, the protection of native and black rights in the United States has been slow to develop and natives have also lodged many complaints against the Canadian government. Indeed, Indians were not even permitted to vote in Canadian federal elections until 1960. In addition, French Canadians living outside of Quebec are still occasionally exposed to certain discriminatory practices and find it difficult at times to retain their language and cultural identity. However, even though isolated incidents of discrimination are still occurring today, both nations have done a comparatively good job in safeguarding the constitutional rights of their citizens.

Even though Canadian constitutionalism was less precise than its American counterpart, at least up to the 1982 constitutional changes, Canada has traditionally enjoyed an orderly system of government and has been able to avoid the bitter constitutional struggle between central and regional governments which helped provoke the tumultuous American Civil War. However, in terms of current constitutional problems, Canada undoubtedly finds itself in a somewhat more precarious situation than the United States. The Quebec challenge not only threatens the Canadian constitutional framework, but the entire future of the confederation as well. In comparison, the United States has not faced such a serious constitutional challenge since the Civil War.

There is no guarantee that any new constitutional arrangement would be completely satisfactory to Quebec, but its isolation from Ottawa and the other provinces in the discussions leading up to the ratification of the 1982 constitution does little to enhance Canadian unity. Many Quebec citizens consider that they have been treated as second-class citizens and that Pierre Trudeau and the premiers of the nine English-speaking provinces totally ignored Quebec's views in the constitutional deliberations. Quebec's failure to ratify the constitution and the very peculiar opting out clause in the amendment formula combine to take some of the luster off of this very significant constitutional achievement. Indeed, if the 1982 constitution is to be a source of greater national unity, much as the U.S. constitution proved to be in the post-1789 period, French-speaking citizens must be convinced that their language and cultural rights will be fully protected.

NOTES

[1]See Guy Favreau, The Amendment of the Constitution of Canada (Ottawa: Queen's Printer, 1965).

[2]See James G. Matkin, "The Canadian Constitution," in Constitutions of the Countries of the World, ed. Albert P. Blaustein and Gisbert H. Flanz (New York: Oceana, 1971-1976).

[3]Alan C. Cairns, "The Living Canadian Constitution," in Canadian Federalism: Myth or Reality, 2nd ed., ed. J. Peter Meekison (Toronto: Methuen, 1971), p. 143.

[4]W. L. White, Ronald H. Wagenberg, and Ralph C. Nelson, Introduction to Canadian Politics and Government (Toronto: Holt, 1972), p. 28.

[5]In his speech before parliament, Trudeau made the following observations:

Altogether, what Quebecers expressed . . . was a massive support for change within the federal framework. We cannot venture to ignore this will to change which reflects that of all other areas in the country and to fall short of the expectations of Canadians. This is why, on May 14, I solemnly undertook to launch the constitutional renewal and never stop working at it until Canada finally has a new constitution.

However, we would be deceiving ourselves, if we were to believe that it will be easy to keep this commitment. We shall need the constant support of the Canadian people and their representatives within this parliament. We are also counting on the support of all provincial governments, including that of Quebec. We shall all have to agree on the basic principles underlying our efforts. We have to be receptive to the needs and aspirations of all Canadians, to seek together for methods and mechanisms more effective than those used until now and to be willing to make every effort required to achieve success. For that purpose, I have asked the Minister of Justice to begin immediately a tour of the provincial capitals in order to obtain the views of the premiers on the best way to follow up

on their will to change. As for us, our only
pre-requisites for change are the two which I
outlined in Quebec as early as January 1977.
  First, that Canada continue to be a real
federation, a state whose constitution establishes
a federal parliament with real powers applying to
the country as a whole and provincial legislatures
with powers just as real applying to the territory
of each province. Second, that a charter of
fundamental rights and freedoms be entrenched in
the new constitution and that it extend to the
collective aspect of these rights, such as
language rights.
  . . . What we want is to give Canada a new,
modern and functional federal constitution which
will enable our governments to better meet the
needs and aspirations of all Canadians. This new
constitution could include, if the people so wish,
several provisions in our present organic laws,
but, it will also have to contain new elements
reflecting the most innovative proposals emerging
from our consultations or from the numerous
analyses and considered opinions that have flowed
in the last few years from the will to change of
Canadians.
Consult Canada Weekly, June 4, 1980, pp. 4-5, for
additional parts of Trudeau's text.

  [6]The items on the agenda for the constitutional
summit held from September 8 to 13, included:
  . . . a statement of principles; a charter of
rights, including language rights; the reduction
of regional disparities; the "patriation" of the
constitution; resource ownership and
interprovincial trade; offshore resources; powers
affecting the economy; communications; family law;
the Senate; the Supreme Court; and fisheries.

  [7]The package of provincial proposals included:
--giving the provinces some jurisdiction over
  interprovincial and international trade, on top of an
  existing federal offer;
--sharing jurisdiction over communications with more
  provincial paramountcy;
--creating a new Upper House totally appointed by the
  provinces that would ratify appointments to certain
  regulatory agencies and have power of suspension over
  federal bills affecting certain provincial areas;

--enlarging the Supreme Court to 11 from nine judges with a 6-5 split of common and civil judges;
--giving the provinces control of divorce laws;
--increasing the provincial role in management of fisheries through administrative arrangements;
--granting ownership of offshore resources to coastal provinces;
--entrenching equalization;
--entrenching the principle of economic union but allowing certain discriminatory practices;
--giving a commitment not to impose a tax on natural gas exports; and
--patriating the constitution on the basis of an amending formula acceptable to the provinces.

[8]New York Times, 4 October 1980, p. 3.

[9]Edward McWhinney, Canada and the Constitution, 1979-1982 (Toronto: University of Toronto Press, 1982), pp. 90-101.

[10]Bruce Welling and Richard McLaren, "The Charter of Rights and the 'Fundamental Wrong'," Business Quarterly, 46 (Spring 1981):6. The authors add that "the question for Canadians now becomes whether they prefer government by legal or political process: by lawyers or by politicians." The authors clearly prefer the political process.

IV

FEDERALISM, QUEBECISM, AND THE CANADIAN
CONFEDERATION: TO BE OR NOT TO BE, THAT
IS INDEED THE QUESTION

General Principles of Canadian Federalism

General Theories of Federalism

Canada has a federal political system, which places it in the same category as Switzerland, West Germany, India, Australia, Mexico, the Soviet Union, the United States, and several other countries. Federalism implies a division of governmental authority among central and regional units, but the sharing of such power may differ quite dramatically from one federal system to another. As an illustration, the Soviet Union claims to be a federal state but has more authority concentrated in the central party-governmental apparatus than is to be found in most unitary systems. The Swiss, on the other hand, have generally permitted the balance of governmental power to remain in favor of the cantons with the central government in Bern exercising quite limited authority. In the case of the contemporary Canadian and American systems, the former has undoubtedly provided the regional governments much more policymaking latitude than the latter.

Various theories of Canadian federalism exist, with at least five having received significant support at one time or another during the confederation's existence. The compact theory goes hand in hand with the argument proposed by states' rights advocates in the United States. Compact theorists insist that the Canadian union was conceived as a league of provinces which by compact delegated certain authority to a central government. Thus the central government must be considered as a creation of the provinces and ultimately answerable for its actions to the provincial governments.[1]

The centralist theory is the opposite of the compact theory. Centralists claim that the Canadian system should eventually evolve to the point where the provinces will be little more than administrative appendages of the central government. Some American political analysts have made a similar point about the states, claiming that states governments are antiquated and ill-equipped to cope with the problems of a modern urbanized society. These theorists claim that only Washington, D. C. and Ottawa have the resources and know-how to solve the major problems in the urban centers and that more governmental authority must by necessity be transferred to the federal government. Some critics of the centralist approach claim that if the centralists were to have their way, provincial and state lines of demarcation would be of little significance other than for Rand-McNally mapmakers.

The _coordinate_ concept endorses the idea of powerful governmental units at both the national and regional levels with each exercising sovereignty within its own area of jurisdiction. However, the federal government would retain the authority to overrule the provinces in cases of jurisdictional dispute and would have the power to guarantee the protection of minority rights in all of the provinces.

The _cooperative_ concept asserts that the two major levels of government must cooperate with each other and avoid petty rivalries. In particular, federal-provincial conferences should be the key institutional structure through which working agreements are reached by both sides. This concept also gained popularity in the United States after Franklin D. Roosevelt entered the White House in 1933. Cooperative theorists argue that up until that time in the U.S., the federal and state governments perceived each other as rival poker players in a game in which there would always be one winner and one loser and where mutual cooperation could not be tolerated. The cooperative proponents go on to say that Roosevelt was able to change the rules of the game and convince the states that both levels of government would have to work together in order to overcome the serious problems brought on by the Great Depression.

The final theory of federalism is particularly applicable to consociational federal structures. In the case of Canada, the _dualist_ concept strongly emphasizes the fact that there are two major cultures in the country and as the main representative of one of the cultures, Quebec should be granted special status within the confederation. In effect, the dualists

96

argue that Quebec is a province distinct from the other nine provinces because it is the home of most of the French Canadians. Thus in order to protect the rights and privileges of the French-Canadian minority, Quebec should be allocated special powers within the confederation which are perhaps greater than its population base would seem to warrant.

Although there are proponents of all five of these concepts of federalism in contemporary Canadian society, the cooperative theory probably has the largest support in English Canada and the dualist theory seems to have recently picked up momentum in French Canada. Even some well-known scholars in English Canada have suggested that the only way to keep the confederation together is to accept the dualist proposition concerning Quebec's special status.[2] Most English Canadians do not agree with this premise, however, even though some of them may now be willing to seek a middle ground between the cooperative and dualist arguments and provide Quebec with more authority than allocated in the 1982 constitution.

Federal-Provincial Interaction

The major areas of responsibility assigned by the Canadian constitution to the federal and provincial legislatures were listed in Table III:1 of the previous chapter. Each of the provinces has its own parliamentary system with the major governmental institutions being a premier-directed cabinet, a unicameral (one chamber) legislative body, a semi-distinctive court system, and a provincial civil service. Provincial legislative elections must be held at least once every five years and the party which garners a majority of the legislative seats is asked to form the new provincial government. If no party achieves a majority, then the party which captures the most seats will usually be asked to put together a new government. The leader of the victorious party will then become the premier of the province and will select members of his cabinet from the ranks of his party followers who were elected to the legislature. Oftentimes, a candidate who seeks a legislative post must be financially well off, because the legislator's pay is fairly low in many provinces. (See Table IV:1 which compares the pay of provincial and state officials). The cabinet which is chosen is responsible

97

TABLE IV:1

A COMPARISON OF ANNUAL SALARIES AND ALLOWANCES
AT THE PROVINCIAL AND SELECTED STATE LEVELS[1]

Province	Premier	MLA's Salary & Allow.	Members of Legislative Assembly (MLAs)[2] Exp. Allow.
Alberta	$41,265 +		$22,050 + 6,485 Exp. Allow.
British Columbia	35,800 +	"	26,200 + 13,100 "
Manitoba	26,600 +	"	28,450 + "
New Brunswick	32,970 +	"	21,980 + 8,792 "
Newfoundland	30,730 +	"	21,136 + 10,568 "
Nova Scotia	32,000 +	"	16,400 + 8,200 "
Ontario	33,200 +	"	30,000 + 10,000 "
Prince Edward Island	34,043 +	"	12,800 + 6,300 "
Quebec	43,043 +	"	33,110 + 7,500 "
Saskatchewan	32,136 +	"	10,908 + 15,625 "

State	Governor	Legislators[3]
Arkansas	$ 35,000	$ 7,500
California	49,100	28,110
Colorado	60,000	14,000
Illinois	58,000	28,000
Maine	35,000	3,500
Maryland	75,000	21,000
Massachusetts	60,000	20,335
Minnesota	66,500	18,500
Mississippi	53,000	8,100
New York	100,000	28,788
Rhode Island	49,500	300
South Carolina	60,000	10,000
South Dakota	55,000	3,000
Washington	63,000	11,200

1. Figures quoted are in Canadian dollars and American dollars respectively.
2. Some provinces also permit special cost-of-living, travel, and other types of allowances.
3. Some states also permit monthly allowances while the legislature is not in session, special session allowances, and allowances for travel and other related expenses.

for formulating and then approving major policy initiatives before submitting these proposals to the legislature. As long as the cabinet retains the confidence of the legislature and is not defeated on a bill of major importance, it will continue to govern for up to five years. There are no fixed dates for elections in Canada and the premier can call for new elections anytime within the five-year span.

The crown is represented in each province by a lieutenant-governor who is selected by the federal cabinet, paid with federal monies, and subject to removal by federal authorities. The lieutenant-governor serves a five-year term and is theoretically responsible for appointing the premier, dissolving the legislature and calling for new elections, and approving provincial legislation. When a bill which has been passed by the legislature is presented to him, he has the option of (1) signing the bill and thus making it law, (2) refusing to sign it and thus effectively vetoing it, or (3) placing the bill in reserve until the federal cabinet can make a decision concerning the bill. In the past, some holders of the lieutenant-governor's post have indeed withheld assent or placed a bill in abeyance. Some have also gone against the wishes of the provincial premier and have refused to dissolve the legislature and call for new elections. Nevertheless, today's lieutenant-governor largely performs ceremonial duties and follows the directives given to him by the premier. In addition, the power of vetoing or holding legislation in abeyance is still on the books but has not been used since 1961.

The provinces remain the master of their own constitutional development, although they cannot alter the power assigned to the lieutenant-governor. Unlike the trend in the United States, the powers of the provinces have actually expanded vis-à-vis the federal government. As an example, the authority assigned to the provinces in the Canadian constitution relating to "property and civil rights" has been broadly interpreted by the courts and the provincial legislatures and is now considered as including a dominant say over industrial affairs, provincial trade and marketing, labor union regulations, wages, welfare, health, and other related spheres. Under the 1982 constitutional provisions, some believe that the opting out clause may further increase provincial prerogatives, while many others believe that the

Charter of Rights and Freedoms and related sections will definitely solidify the authority of Ottawa.

The prime minister at the federal level always tries to insure that each of the provinces will have a spokesperson in his cabinet, but provincial representation in Ottawa is sporadic at best. For example, Prime Minister Trudeau has experienced a great deal of difficulty in finding Westerners to sit in his cabinet. It is customary for almost all cabinet members to be selected from the House of Commons, but Trudeau's Liberal Party has failed to elect even one candidate to the House of Commons from some of the Western provinces, particularly Alberta. As a result, some Western provinces have been represented in the cabinet by members of the Senate who are appointed by the prime minister and not voted into office by the provincial electorate.

The time-honored customs of cabinet solidarity (the cabinet members agreeing to accept and support a cabinet decision even if they are personally opposed to it) and party discipline (members of a party agreeing to accept the party's decision even if they personally dislike it) have made it very difficult for provincial interests to be adequately articulated in Ottawa, even though the provinces are undoubtedly the major interest group in the federal capital. In other words, unless it is an extreme case, a member of the cabinet or a member of parliament (an MP) is expected in Canada to go along with his cabinet's or party's stand on an issue, even if it might prove to be detrimental to his province's interests. In addition, the federal ministries are formed along functional lines (foreign affairs, transportation, etc.) with very little allowance being given for regional idiosyncrasies and concerns. Once upon a time it was considered that the Senate would provide the provinces with the voice they needed in Ottawa, but this legislative body currently plays a very minimal role in the policymaking process.

Partially as a result of the difficulties experienced by the provinces in having their demands listened to by federal officials, direct federal-provincial conferences have emerged in recent years as the major policy forum between Ottawa and the provincial capitals. The pivotal First Ministers' federal-provincial conference occurs once or twice a year and brings together the prime minister and provincial premiers in face-to-face meetings. Federal-provincial parleys between ministers with parallel responsibilities at the national and regional levels are also held on a regular basis.

A major issue of discussion at these conferences is money. As provincial powers and responsibilities have expanded, so has their need for additional funds, but taxing powers are highly centralized and definitely favor Ottawa. In Canada, taxes may be imposed by the three levels of government--federal, provincial, and municipal. However, the federal government is under no restriction in terms of levying taxes of any kind, whereas provincial governments are restricted to levying direct taxes. Direct taxes (such as the individual income tax) are those paid directly by the person on whom they are levied, whereas indirect taxes (such as a tax on manufactured items) are those passed on to other people. All provinces levy individual and corporate income taxes but in most cases it is the federal government which administers and collects these taxes on behalf of the provinces. Only Quebec collects its own individual and corporate taxes, and Ontario and Alberta have now started to collect their own corporate taxes. In order to attract new revenues, several of the provincial governments have also begun to impose heavy taxes on the sale of gasoline at the pump.

Although the provincial tax base has certainly expanded in recent years, the provincial governments desire additional taxing powers which would make them less dependent on transfer payments from the federal government for secured funding sources. For example, in 1980-1981, federal expenditures added up to 58 billion dollars, and 12.3 billion dollars of this were returned to the provinces through cash transfers (about 27 percent of total federal expenditures). Federal authorities, in turn, have been able to use their purse-string powers to gain additional leverage in negotiations with the provinces. As an illustration, the federal cabinet formulated a program in 1977 which would provide up to 350 dollars in grants for people who were willing to upgrade the insulation in their homes. However, the program would only be applicable to those provinces which agreed beforehand to (1) reduce their speed limits to 100 kilometers per hour, (2) stop taxing insulation materials, (3) tighten building codes and require better insulation standards, and (4) eliminate bulk meters in apartment houses. Thus in order for its citizens to take advantage of the federal insulation grants, each province was expected to fall in line with federal directives in these diverse policy areas.

It is clear that the federal government has certain distinct advantages in terms of securing revenue sources and the provinces often have to go hat in hand to the federal authorities in order to receive additional funding. Quebec has already decided to opt out of certain shared-cost programs and receives a higher abatement on personal and corporate income taxes and other duties in order to run separate programs at the provincial level. Some of the provinces would undoubtedly like to have their own independent taxing base and revenue sources, but whether the confederation could hold together under such a system is debatable.

The Canadian government has adopted a special system of equalization payments through which the richer provinces, such as Ontario, Alberta, and British Columbia, indirectly provide funds which will be redistributed to the poorer provinces. In recent years, federal subsidies to Ontario have represented less than two percent of its total annual income, whereas federal funding to Prince Edward Island has represented almost 50 percent of its annual income. The entire issue of equalization payments and federal fiscal support to the provinces has recently become quite controversial because of complaints lodged by officials in Quebec. The Quebec representatives claim that federal policies have cost its people several billion dollars in the period since 1961. Federal officials counter that Quebec residents gained more than two billion dollars since 1961 and are among the major beneficiaries of a confederated Canada.[3] The two sides obviously used different indicators to come up with their totals and the dispute over government financing continues to stir up problems between Ottawa and Quebec.

The Municipalities

In the Canadian system, the provinces are essentially sovereign in their specific spheres of jurisdiction and cannot be grossly interfered with by the federal government. Quite the opposite is true in the relationship between the provinces and the municipalities. The Canadian municipalities are considered as the creation of the provinces and are answerable at all times for their actions to the provincial authorities.

Municipal governments in Canada are fairly similar to their American counterparts with a separation of authority existing between the mayor's or city manager's office and the municipal council. Elections to municipal posts are usually nonpartisan (no party labels are allowed) in both nations, but Canadian officials are often elected annually or every two years, whereas American officials normally serve for a longer period.

The most common form of government to be found in the Canadian municipalities is the mayor-council type. Under this system, the municipal council has a chairperson who acts as the city's chief executive officer and is given special powers. This chief executive officer or mayor is elected by the voters and is expected to represent the community as a whole, whereas the other members of the council may represent specific wards or districts.

Another common type of municipal government in Canada is the council-manager plan. Under this system, a mayor and a small council are elected by the voters and a manager or executive director is hired by the city to act as the chief administrative officer. The municipal council is in charge of passing legislation for the city and the city manager makes sure that the council policy is carried out. In addition, the city manager may make policy recommendations for the council's consideration.

Moreover, many of the cities have elected school boards which are essentially independent of the municipal council and may in fact determine school policies for areas which extend beyond the boundaries of the city. The boards rely almost exclusively on property taxes for revenue to keep the school districts functioning. The local governments are also heavily dependent on property taxes for operating revenues, with four-fifths of all revenue coming from this source and the rest largely from provinical government grants-in-aid. Other funding may come from municipal sales taxes and the selling of licenses.

103

In 1980, Canada had only nine metropolitan areas with a population exceeding 500,000, as compared to 79 in the United States. However, the Toronto and Montreal metropolitan regions each have populations close to 3,000,000 and the Ontario capital has been particularly active in trying to adapt its government to the challenges faced by a megalopolis. In 1954, the Toronto Metropolitan Council was created with representatives from 13 municipalities in and around Toronto. Education in the greater metropolitan area was also placed under the direction of a 22-member board and transportation under the supervision of a 5-member commission. In 1966, the provincial government of Ontario reorganized the Toronto area further by consolidating 12 suburban communities into five large cities (called boroughs) and increasing the representation of the boroughs on the Metropolitan Council. Winnipeg, Ottawa, Quebec City, Montreal, and several other cities have taken steps in the same direction to better coordinate activities between the core city and the suburbs in order to prevent a needless duplication of services.

Canada has thus far been able to avoid the major urban disorders and fiscal problems which have plagued several American cities. If problems were to arise, they would probably occur in either Toronto or Montreal. The question then arises as to whether the provincial governments would be adequately prepared to cope with the problems of the large urban areas. This exact question has been posed many times in the United States as people wonder whether Albany can solve the fiscal and other assorted problems of New York City, or if Sacramento can handle the trials and tribulations experienced by either Los Angeles or San Francisco. Many mayors of the big cities in America have been bypassing the state governments and appealing directly to Washington for assistance, a phenomenon which critics claim is further eroding the power of the states and leading to the creation of a unitary system. The central government of Canada has generally steered clear of interfering with the provincial control of the municipalities, although tri-level conferences on intergovernmental relations involving federal, provincial, and municipal representatives are occasionally held. On the whole, the Canadian cities do in fact seem to be in much better shape than many of their American counterparts. On the other hand, the larger urban conglomerates are facing increasingly severe challenges and the route which the central and provincial governments take in reacting to these problems will have a major impact on the future evolution of Canada's federal system.

Regionalism

Quebec

The Traditional Grievances

Regionalism has always been prominent in Canadian political affairs and nowhere has it been more pronounced than in Quebec. Those French Canadians in Quebec who are now actively supporting separation from the confederation can readily check off a long laundry list of grievances to bolster their argument. They contend that French Canadians have long been slighted by the dominant English-speaking majority, calling to mind such incidents as the Acadian exodus, the two Riel revolts, and the 1890 Manitoba school controversy and the 1913 Ontario school crisis which were both linked to efforts to force all students to be educated in English. These French Canadians also resent Canada's traditionally close links with Great Britain, insisting that Canada was once actively involved in bolstering British imperial goals and wondering why it took so long to drop "God Save the Queen" as Canada's national anthem and the British Union Jack as Canada's national flag. In addition, they bitterly denounce the British parliament for agreeing to patriate Canada's constitution in 1982 without Quebec's approval and firmly believe that Ottawa has relegated Quebec to a second-class status because of the provisions in the new constitution.

Perhaps the most bitter grievance voiced by French Canadians today is the claim of economic discrimination. Many French Canadians believe that the French-speaking population has been short-changed in finding decent jobs in both the private sector and the federal civil service. Statistics apparently bear out at least part of the French Canadian claim, showing that the best jobs go to English-speaking people and that those French Canadians who do get ahead often do so because they have become very adept in the use of the English language. The Gendron Commission

105

investigation of employment in Quebec in the early 1970s indicated that English-speaking citizens held 75 percent of the jobs which paid over 15,000 dollars, even though anglophones represented less than 20 percent of the entire population of Quebec.[4]

Lingering in the back of many French Canadian minds is the fear that the six million French-speaking North Americans will eventually be swallowed up and assimilated by the 240 million English-speaking people who inhabit the continent. This apprehension is particularly strong among the one million French-speaking Canadians who live in the nine provinces outside of Quebec. Pressure upon them to accept the English Canadian way of life is especially strong, and even though some of them have organized La Fédération des Francophones Hors Québec (The Federation of French-Speaking People Outside of Quebec) to help preserve their cultural identity, they are undoubtedly fighting an uphill battle.

The Evolution of Quebec Society

The Duplessis Era

For almost a quarter of a century beginning in 1936, the Quebec political scene was completely dominated by Maurice Duplessis and his Union Nationale movement. The Duplessis regime was paternalistic and nepotistic, being sort of the French Canadian equivalent to the Tammany Hall machine of New York City. The Union Nationale movement helped to perpetuate the highly traditional values of Quebec society and did little to foster the modernization trend which was occurring in most of the other provinces. For example, women were granted the right to vote in the other provinces during the period 1916-1925. Female suffrage did not come to Quebec until 1940.

Some intellectual circles bitterly attacked the Duplessis regime and called for the modernization of Quebec society and the introduction of liberal democratic political values. These circles also attacked the strong secular role of the Catholic Church in Quebec, particularly in the area of education. A Montreal publication, the Cité Libre, became the major forum for attacks against the administration. This publication counted on the writing talents of Pierre Trudeau and several of his colleagues and advocated the rapid modernization of Quebec society and strong French Canadian attachments to the notion of federalism.

The 1949 Asbestos Strike pitting workers against the Johns-Mansville Company management helped to rally support for the modernization of Quebec. The strike lasted for five months with over 5,000 miners taking part. Many Quebec citizens came to the conclusion that the plight of the workers was indeed serious and were not particularly impressed when the Quebec government sided with the company and the Catholic Church officially refused to condone the actions of the strikers. Eventually the workers were forced back to their jobs, but it was abundantly clear to certain sectors of Quebec society that the traditional roots of French Canadian life would have to be torn asunder before the average Quebec resident could begin to prosper and to wield at least a modicum of political power.[5]

The Quiet Revolution

The death of Duplessis paved the way for the Liberal Party under the leadership of Jean Lesage to defeat the Union Nationale movement in the provincial elections of 1960. Although somewhat traditional in terms of his own personal preferences, Lesage nevertheless pushed for the modernization of Quebec society and for the recognition of Quebec's "special status" within the Canadian confederation. The rallying cry of the Lesage regime became "maître chez nous" and under the new administration's guidance, the "Quiet Revolution" to modernize Quebec society was launched. The long established Catholic Church domination over the Quebec public education system was drastically reduced and the government became more involved in the activities of the economic sector. For example, the Quebec government took control of the hydro-electric facilities in the province and assumed a greater role in supervising the mining industry which had grown so rapidly in the post-World War II era. The government thus began to expand its spheres of jurisdiction and definitely contributed to the "secularization" trend in Quebec society.

During the 1960s, relations between Quebec and France were also strengthened with several cultural and educational agreements being initialed by the two French-speaking governments. The renewed interest in direct Quebec-France ties was highlighted by the visit of French President Charles de Gaulle to the Montreal World's Fair in 1967. While giving a speech to an audience assembled in front of the Montreal City Hall, de Gaulle uttered the famous phrase, "Vive le Québec libre" (Long live free Quebec). Prime Minister Lester Pearson convened an emergency session of his cabinet and subsequently declared that de Gaulle's statement was unacceptable to Canadians. Upon learning of Pearson's pronouncement, de Gaulle immediately cancelled the remainder of his visit to Canada and returned to France.

The rationale for de Gaulle's statement is difficult to pinpoint. The French leader later suggested to an acquaintance that the enthusiasm of the Montreal crowd reminded him of the reception he had received on his triumphant return to a liberated Paris in 1944. Indeed, he may well have been overcome by the euphoria of the moment. Whatever the basis for his inflammatory statement, de Gaulle immediately convened the French Council of Ministers on his return to Paris and quickly rammed through a statement offering moral encouragement to the Quebec people. The rift in French-Canadian relations was eventually healed once de Gaulle vacated his Elysée post, but the French head of state had certainly succeeded in riveting world attention on the situation in Quebec.

The FLQ Movement

The Front de Libération du Québec (FLQ) was a radical left movement which contended that change was occurring much too slowly in Quebec and that anti-systemic tactics were necessary in order to awaken the average Quebec worker to his plight. One of the chief figures in the FLQ, Pierre Vallières, attracted a great deal of attention to the movement through his book, Les Nègres blancs. Written while he was in jail, Vallières' book asserted that the French Canadians were the "white niggers" of North America who had been ruthlessly exploited by the dominant Anglo-American community for over three centuries. He perceived the situation as a class struggle and insisted that Quebec

108

needed a revolution, just like any country enslaved by "capitalism and colonial imperialism."[6]

The FLQ was formally organized in 1962 and proclaimed its allegiance to national liberation and a socialist economic system. The felquistes (members of the FLQ) were responsible for scores of bombings during the 1960s and several deaths which resulted from the explosions. In October 1970, the FLQ kidnapped James Richard Cross, a senior British trade commissioner who was living in Montreal, and Pierre Laporte, the Quebec Labor Minister. The province was traumatized by these kidnappings and much attention was given by the world's press to the events which transpired in Quebec.

On October 16, Ottawa invoked the controversial War Measures Act which granted authorities the right to arrest suspects and to hold them without bail for up to 90 days. A massive manhunt was launched in Quebec for suspected FLQ members and parts of the province were transformed into virtual armed camps. This already tense atmosphere intensified further when the body of Pierre Laporte was discovered on October 18. Reaction against the FLQ in the province intensified and one well-known Quebec political figure, Réal Caouette, even suggested that the FLQ members then in custody should be placed before a firing squad and executed.[7]

Cross was eventually released in December and his kidnappers given safe passage to Cuba. Later in the month, the killers of Laporte were apprehended. The FLQ had succeeded in attracting a great deal of publicity for its cause, but also forfeited any goodwill which it might once have had among Quebec citizens. The unprecedented massive round-up of suspected FLQ members eventually succeeded in decimating the ranks of the movement, although many Quebec residents believed that the federal government could have taken swift action without invoking the War Measures Act, a law designed for wars and extreme national emergencies.

The Parti Québécois

The Parti Québécois (PQ) was formed in the mid-1960s and professed strong support for the eventual independence of Quebec. The PQ's rise to power was gradual as the party experienced serious difficulties in capturing seats in the provincial legislature, even though its percentage of the overall vote was fairly significant. Quebec has a single-member district, first past the wire electoral system, similar to what is found in the United States. This means that there is one candidate who will be elected in each electoral district and that the person receiving the most votes in that district, even if far short of a majority, will be elected. Laboring under this system, the PQ received 24 percent of the provincial vote in 1970 but only six percent of the seats in the legislature. In 1973, it increased its percentage of the overall vote in the province to 30 percent, but garnered only five percent of the Quebec National Assembly seats. Finally in 1976, running on a platform of "good government" with little mention of separatism, the PQ under the leadership of Réne Lévesque won 41 percent of the provincial vote and a majority of the legislative seats.

Even though Lévesque played down the separatist theme during the campaign, the PQ remained closely identified with Quebec independence and its victory sent shockwaves reverberating throughout English Canada (see Table IV:2 for the PQ platform concerning independence). During its first term in office, the PQ leaders steered Bill 101 through the Quebec National Assembly making French the only official language in Quebec and requiring children of newcomers to the province to attend French schools, even if the children were not from French-speaking families. The bill also requires the use of French in most major Quebec business enterprises. With the ratification of the new Canadian Charter of Rights and Freedoms, and rulings handed down in subsequent cases in the court system, portions of Bill 101 have now been nullified, especially the provisions linked to education.

The PQ also supports the concept of sovereignty-association, or in other words, a politically sovereign Quebec state which will have Common Market-type economic ties with the rest of Canada. Under such a system, Quebec would be completely sovereign over its own internal affairs and could thus insure the survival of the French Canadian culture. On the other hand, Quebec would continue to have a free trade area, a common currency, and certain common defense and foreign policy arrangements with the rest of Canada, including continued support of NATO and

TABLE IV:2

PLATFORM OF THE PARTI QUÉBÉCOIS
RELATING TO QUEBEC'S INDEPENDENCE

General Policy

Four centuries of common history have formed
French Quebecers into a nation, which has always
contained in its bosom a large minority of people from
a variety of backgrounds, whose basic rights it has
respected more than most other nations. This founding
people has always manifested the desire to develop its
own, distinctive culture. But it has become obvious,
with time, that this objective can only be achieved if
it has full control over the reins of its political
life.

Controlling its political life would entail
exercising control over Parliament--which makes laws,
spends the revenues from taxes, and determines the
direction of Quebec's cultural, economic, and social
development. At the present time, this political power
is divided in such a way that the majority of
Quebeckers, by force of circumstances, find themselves
relegated to the role of a minority in the Canadian
Confederation: in the federal Parliament, Quebec has
only 74 out of a total of 264 members; most of the time
at federal-provincial conferences it finds itself at
odds with the 10 other governments. In the past, these
combined pressures have obliged Quebec governments to
hand over more and more power to Ottawa, whereas only
the Quebec government is in a position to defend and
promote the culture of the majority of citizens it
represents.

Furthermore, the only government that this
majority controls is systematically hampered in key
areas because of a duplication of structures and
inadequate legal and financial resources to give its
policies a certain coherence and therefore ensure their
effectiveness. Economic development continues, to the
detriment of Quebec's interest, while Quebec
desperately needs a prosperous, dynamic economy to
ensure the long-term survival of its French culture.
Time and again federalism has proven to work against
the best interests of Quebec's majority. This is an

111

intolerable situation. No collectivity can indefinitely entrust its destiny to others without losing its dignity and severely compromising its survival.

Although Quebec has all of the material and human resources to attain political sovereignty, it cannot live in isolation--any more than any other people. Conscious of the ties of interdependence that bind the various nations together, it is ready to take its place among them as a responsible, dynamic partner, especially in view of the privileged links created by geography and history.

A Parti Québécois government therefore pledges to:

1. Obtain political sovereignty for Quebec through democratic means, and propose an economic association to Canada that would be mutually advantageous to both parties.
2. Provide Quebec with a constitution that would achieve a good balance between effective government and true democracy.
3. Decentralize the administration and place more importance on municipalities, at both the local and regional levels.
4. Guarantee the impartiality of the judicial system and make it more accessible to everyone.
5. Pursue a foreign policy of peaceful cooperation.

Achieving Independence

The right of all peoples to self-determination-- their right to choose their own political regime--is enshrined in the United Nations Charter, which Canada as a participating nation signed along with 130 other countries. Since Quebecers live in a democracy, it is up to them to determine their own destiny by whatever means they choose. The Quebec government intends to achieve political sovereignty through democratic means, while respecting the rights of its neighbours and any other countries with whom it maintains friendly relations based on mutual interest and the rules of international law.

A Parti Québécois government therefore pledges to:

1. Obtain by way of referendum during its first mandate, at the time it judges most opportune, the support of Quebecers for Quebec's political sovereignty.

2. Set in motion the machinery for achieving independence, by proposing that the National Assembly pass a law authorizing it to:

   a) Request from Ottawa the repatriation of all powers, excepting those which both governments will jointly agree to entrust to a joint commission for the purpose of economic association.

   b) With this objective in mind, enter into technical discussions with Ottawa on the orderly transfer of powers;

   c) Draw up agreements with Canada for the division of debits and credits as well as for ownership of the public domain, according to the rules of international law.

3. Systematically exercise all of the powers of a sovereign state in the event that it should have to act unilaterally.

4. During the remainder of the present political regime, promote Quebec's independence as much as possible.

5. Submit, to the Quebec people, a national constitution, drawn up by citizens at the county level, and adopted by their representatives at a constituent assembly.

6. Obtain recognition for Quebec by other states and request admission to the United Nations.

7. Respect those treaties, binding Quebec and Canada, which are favourable to Quebec, and revoke any others, in accordance with the rules of international law.

8. Reaffirm and defend Quebec's right to all of its territory, including Labrador and the islands off the New Quebec coast, the continental shelf, the 200-mile coastal limit, the so-called "federal" parks and the Quebec part of the area around the national capital; reclaim as Quebec territory the Arctic islands and territories that presently belong to Canada, by virtue of the same title as other Nordic countries; if no agreement can be reached on this question, occupy the

TABLE IV:2 (continued)

area through legal means (granting concessions, setting up institutions, etc.), and take the case to the International Court of Justice.

Source: Official Program of the Parti Québécois, 1978 Edition, pp. 7-8.

NORAD. In a speech presented at the Economic Club of New York in January 1977, Lévesque contended that "independence" was inevitable but that there would not be a large-scale nationalization of business and industry and that American investment would continue to be welcomed. PQ representatives have literally crisscrossed the globe since then explaining the government's policy priorities and hoping to prepare world opinion for an event which they consider to be inevitable--the creation of a politically sovereign, French-speaking Quebec nation.

However, the PQ was handed a major setback in its quest for political sovereignty in the May 1980 referendum. The referendum issue was actually watered down substantially, with the PQ government simply asking the electorate to give it a mandate to negotiate sovereignty-association with the federal government, promising to hold a second referendum once the negotiations were completed. Nevertheless, even this very mild wording was not sufficient to placate the concerns of the voters who worried about their economic security in a Quebec which might be cast off from the rest of Canada. Moreover, Prime Minister Trudeau, a native son of Quebec and a popular figure in the province, promised to work for the improvement of Quebec's status within Canada if the voters would reject the referendum. His wish was granted, although many Quebec residents still question whether he fulfilled his part of the bargain.

René Lévesque's PQ government rallied from the major referendum setback and decisively defeated the Liberal Party opposition in the 1981 provincial elections. In an effort to pare the province's huge budgetary deficit, Lévesque in late 1982 took the drastic action of asking the legislature to cut the salaries of Quebec civil servants who are among the

114

best paid public employees in the world. Lévesque was successful in this controversial move but he alienated many of the civil servants and labor unions which had provided the backbone of PQ electoral support in the past. The PQ fortunes in the next provincial election may therefore be in peril, but the party can still count on a fair degree of support as a result of the constitutional negotiations which left Quebec isolated from the rest of the country. A fair number of the French-speaking voters resent how Quebec's wishes were shunted aside during the constitutional deliberations and perceive that the 1982 constitution represents a potential threat to the survival of the French-Canadian language and culture. Lévesque and his compatriots will attempt to capitalize on this resentment and suggested in March 1983 that if the PQ were to receive a majority of the vote in the next provincial elections, this might be construed as a mandate to form a sovereign Quebec nation.

The Political Consequences of the PQ Policies

The PQ victory in the 1976 provincial elections certainly had a dramatic impact on the rest of Canada because the continuation of the Canadian confederation was placed in question. As an example of the PQ's impact, the federal government declined in 1976 to spend any money on the traditional July 1 festivities which commemorate the founding of the confederation in 1867. However, ever since the PQ victory, the Ottawa government has pumped millions of dollars into the July 1 celebration, and Canadian television audiences have been inundated with spot commercials and star-studded extravaganzas which extol the virtues and benefits of continued national unity. For its part, the PQ government has spent millions to upgrade Quebec's traditional St. Jean-Baptiste celebration which is now referred to as Quebec's "national holiday."

Many of the people in other parts of Canada concede that the French Canadians have at times been given a raw deal and therefore are willing to make significant concessions to Quebec, short of breaking up the confederation. However, if Quebec were to separate and keep its present boundaries, it would become the 17th largest country in the world in terms of geographical size (see Table IV:3). It would be

115

TABLE IV:3

QUEBEC AS A "SOVEREIGN" NATION

Population[1]	World Rank	Surface Area (Km²)	W.R.	Gross Domestic Product[2]	W.R.	Per Capita GDP[3]	W.R.
6,438,403	76th	1,540,687	17th	$76,000,000,000	25th	$11,875	12th

1. 1981 census figures.

2. 1981 figures in Canadian dollars.

3. 1981 figures in Canadian dollars.

Sources: Government of Quebec, 1982-83 Budget, and World Bank, World Development Report, 1982.

116

appreciably larger than the area which encompasses all of New England and the states of New York, New Jersey, Pennsylvania, Ohio, Indiana, Illinois, Michigan, Wisconsin, Minnesota, and Iowa. On the other hand, little more than ten percent of the province is settled and much of the region is virtually uninhabitable. Moreover, the new nation would still have to exist within an ocean of "Anglo-Saxons" in North America and would be largely dependent on trade and investment from these neighbors in order to prosper economically. Thus there are many "ifs" associated with Quebec independence, including a great deal of skepticism toward the practicality of any Common Market arrangement with the rest of Canada. Nonetheless, Quebec could probably go it alone if a majority of its people were willing in the short run to make major sacrifices and if an arrangement could be reached with the rest of Canada concerning workable economic and monetary linkages.[8]

From another perspective, some people question the continued survival of the rest of Canada if Quebec were to go its own way. As will be discussed in the next section, English Canada has never been as cohesive as Quebec and regional interests have often taken precedence over so-called "national" needs. A premier of British Columbia once suggested that if Quebec were to secede, the people of his province would undoubtedly be affected in a negative fashion. He went on to say that the natural geographic relationship of his province to Alaska on the north and Washington on the south might tempt British Columbians of the "next generation" to "fall for the siren song of being part of a large country".[9] At the other end of Canada, a premier from Nova Scotia stated that the Maritime provinces would probably have to join with the United States if Quebec were to abandon the confederation.[10]

Thus not only Quebec's status as a province is in question, but also the status of the rest of Canada if Quebec were to separate. With little doubt, many English Canadians are confident that the other provinces could get along quite well even without Quebec. Some even contend that English Canada would be better off without Quebec because a major source of devisiveness in the country would be removed. This attitude, however, certainly does not reflect the feelings of the majority of Canadians who want to see the confederation remain intact (see Table IV:4).

117

TABLE IV:4

CANADIAN ATTITUDES TOWARD QUEBEC FOLLOWING THE
1976 PQ VICTORY

	National			English-Speaking			French-Speaking		
	Yes	No	Don't Know	Yes	No	Don't Know	Yes	No	Don't Know
1. Should the government of Canada hold a national vote on Quebec independence?	46.7%	42.0%	11.0%	50.7%	38.5%	10.4%	34.5%	53.6%	11.6%
2. Should the government of Canada negotiate special political and economic agreements with Quebec to try to prevent separation?	47.4	43.6	8.7	38.3	54.2	7.1	66.9	23.2	9.6
3. Should the governments of Canada and the provinces promote and finance more extensive bilingualism throughout the country to try to prevent separation?	36.0	54.2	9.3	27.8	64.1	7.3	56.0	33.1	10.6
4. If a Quebec referendum favors independence, should Ottawa agree to negotiate separation?	45.7	40.6	13.1	41.5	46.6	11.1	57.7	28.0	14.3
5. Should Ottawa use force to prevent Quebec's separation?	18.7	72.4	8.8	19.2	73.4	7.3	16.7	73.4	9.9
6. If separation occurs, should Canada enter into an economic union with Quebec?	53.9	29.5	16.4	44.8	39.0	15.9	76.1	11.3	12.6

Source: Gallup Poll commissioned by The Canadian, 9 April 1977, p. 5.

Placating the demands of the French Canadians short of separation will be difficult to achieve. French Canadians do indeed stand lower on the socio-economic ladder than their English Canadian counterparts and the federal government would have to introduce some very strong and controversial legislation in order to rectify this situation. In addition, some Canadians now believe that separation is a dead issue as a result of the 1980 referendum and therefore are not willing to make significant economic concessions to the francophone population in Quebec.

Some observers believe that Quebec would remain in the confederation if it were given equal status with "English Canada" and if the French language were given an equal standing in not only federal governmental affairs, but in the provincial and private sectors as well. However, many English Canadians would balk at having an area with somewhat less than 27 percent of the overall Canadian population enjoy equal footing with the provinces which represent the other 73 percent. Moreover, French is the second language in Canada on the basis of overall figures, but is often not the second language in many provinces (see Table IV:5 for statistics on the use of English and French in Canadian homes). In addition, the 1981 Canadian census reveals the following statistics concerning population by "mother tongue," which refers to the first language learned in childhood and still understood by an individual: (1) in Alberta, German (91,480) and Ukrainian (68,130) outrank French (62,145); (2) in British Columbia, German (93,385) and Chinese (76,270) are ahead of French (45,620); (3) in Manitoba, French (52,555) trails both German (75,180) and Ukrainian (58,855); (4) in Saskatchewan, German (59,630) and Ukrainian (44,665) again lead French (25,540); and (5) in the Northwest Territories, more people list Inuktituk (13,200) and Athapaskan (4,090) than French (1,235) (see Table IV:6 for the overall ethnic composition of Canada). Thus the extension of special French privileges to all of the provinces might be actively resisted in regions where other ethnic groups might feel that their own interests had been slighted.[11]

TABLE IV:5

POPULATION BY MOTHER TONGUE
(1971)

Province	English Only	French Only	Both English and French	Neither English nor French
Alberta	1,525,575	3,310	81,000	17,990
British Columbia	2,054,690	1,775	101,435	26,725
Manitoba	881,715	5,020	80,935	20,585
New Brunswick	396,855	100,985	136,115	600
Newfoundland	511,620	510	9,350	625
Nova Scotia	730,700	4,185	53,035	1,035
Ontario	6,724,100	92,840	716,065	170,090
Prince Edward Island	101,820	680	9,110	30
Quebec	632,515	3,668,020	1,663,790	63,445
Saskatchewan	867,315	1,825	45,985	11,110
Northwest Territories	25,500	100	2,120	7,085
Yukon	17,130	5	1,210	35
Total	14,469,540	3,879,255	2,900,155	319,360
% of Total	67.5	17.1	12.7	2.7

POPULATION BY LANGUAGE MOST OFTEN SPOKEN AT HOME
(1971)

Province	English	French	Other
Alberta	1,477,960	22,700	127,210
British Columbia	2,027,120	11,505	145,995
Manitoba	816,560	39,600	132,085
New Brunswick	430,715	199,080	4,760
Newfoundland	517,210	2,295	2,595
Nova Scotia	753,725	27,220	8,015
Ontario	6,558,060	352,465	792,580
Prince Edward Island	106,795	4,405	440
Quebec	887,875	4,870,105	269,785
Saskatchewan	832,515	15,930	77,795
Northwest T.	20,225	590	13,995
Yukon	17,465	135	785

Source: 1971 Census of Canada.

TABLE IV:6

POPULATION BY ETHNIC GROUP
(1971)

Ethnic Group	Population	% of Population
British Isles	9,624,115	44.6
French	6,180,120	28.7
German	1,317,200	6.1
Other European	3,642,480	16.9
Asian	285,540	1.3
Indian and Inuit (Eskimo)		1.4
Black	34,445	0.2
Other	171,645	0.8
Total	21,568,310	100.0

Source: 1971 Census of Canada

121

Prime Minister Trudeau warned in a 1977 Washington speech that the separation of Quebec from Canada would have "much graver implications for the United States than the 1962 Soviet attempt to place nuclear missiles in Cuba".[12] Few Americans would currently accept the gravity of Trudeau's warning, although any Quebec separation would introduce an element of uncertainty which has been absent from 20th century Canadian-American relations. Consequently, Americans should indeed keep abreast of the events transpiring north of the border and hope than an amicable solution can be reached.

If the current confederation is to prosper, a formula must be devised which will quickly correct the injustices which the French-speaking population has suffered. In addition, official recognition of Quebec's "special status" in certain spheres and its concomitant right to act autonomously within certain cultural and educational areas must be given serious consideration by federal and provincial officials in the other regions of Canada.

Some people have also suggested that Canada must become a truly bilingual society, requiring all children to learn English and French and to protect the use of French in all spheres of activity. Indeed, most Canadians agree that if students were to learn both English and French, there would be a better understanding and rapport between the two cultural communities.[13] On the other hand, many English Canadians have no practical need to learn French. Moreover, the PQ strongly asserts that language usage is only one facet of the problem facing French Canadians in contemporary Canadian society. The PQ insists that the French Canadian culture can continue to survive on an anglophone-dominated continent only if the French Canadians are able to determine their own political destinies. Thus, according to the PQ, nothing short of political sovereignty is acceptable and the Canadian confederation, as now constituted, must be dismantled. Such a scenario, however, remains unpalatable to a large segment of English Canadian society and Quebec's future status in North America will continue in the foreseeable future to be a dominant issue in Canadian affairs.

Other Regions

Several of the Canadian provinces have deeply resented the "heartland-hinterland" dichotomy which has seemingly characterized Canada's development. Prime Minister Trudeau admitted the existence of this dichotomy at the 1973 Western Economic Opportunities Conference when he spoke of an historical Canadian national policy based on "a Central Canadian 'metropole' with an agricultural and resource 'hinterland' in the West."[14] The heartland is the area from Montreal in the east to Windsor in the west with the Toronto-Ottawa-Montreal triangle being the pivotal core area. The hinterland is all of the area to the east and to the west of Ontario, as well as most of Quebec with the exception of the English Canadian section of Montreal.

The province of Ontario has 35 percent of the total population of Canada, 38 percent of the total work force, and 40 percent of the country's gross national product. Ontario has almost one-half of all the manufacturing jobs in Canada and continues to outdistance the other provinces in attracting new industries. In addition, Ontario has long been the center for finance, commerce, education, and the mass media. The average income of Ontarians has recently fallen behind that of residents in Alberta and British Columbia, but is still a third higher than that in Price Edward Island and 40 percent higher than that in Newfoundland.

Not too surprisingly, the federal government is also headquartered in Ontario and Ontarians enjoy the largest representation of any province in parliament. Some of the provinces have been prompted to complain that the federal government has been complacent in its efforts to mitigate the overwhelming influence of Ontario. In particular, the Western provinces have insisted that they have been treated as resource colonies with raw materials being extracted from their land but turned into manufactured products in Central Canada where the industries and the jobs are concentrated.

This issue of provincial "colonialism" has become much more controversial in the 1970s and 1980s because of the added "worth" of oil and other commodities. For example, the province of Alberta, which has rarely in

123

its history had a government of the same political persuasion as the federal cabinet, has rapidly emerged as Canada's "Texas" and is now insisting that a significant percentage of non-renewable resources extracted from its territory be turned into finished products within the province. Although definitely hurt by the recession of the late 1970s and early 1980s, the province is still comparatively wealthy and for a time even floated loans to other provinces.[15] Alberta has no sales tax and has eliminated provincial taxes on oil and natural gas. A few stalwart Albertans have even asserted that the province, with its vast resource base and eleven billion dollar plus reserve in its Heritage Fund (a provincial savings account consisting of oil and gas royalties), would be better off as an independent country.[16] The Western Canada Concept (WCC) was formed in the early 1980s with the intent of taking Alberta and its neighboring Western provinces out of confederation. The movement succeeded in a byelection in electing one member to the Alberta legislature but later, hindered by internal bickering, failed to elect anyone in Alberta's 1982 provincial elections (although it did receive 11.9 percent of the total vote in the province). Nonetheless, resentment toward Ottawa and frustrations linked to the lack of Western representation in the nation's capital remain very strong. Pierre Trudeau and his Liberal Party are also greatly resented by many Westerners for what is perceived to be their pro-Central Canada sentiments. In 1983, only two Liberal Party members represented the Western provinces in parliament, and none west of Winnipeg, Manitoba. Moreover, the Liberal Party failed to hold one seat in the legislatures of British Columbia, Alberta, Saskatchewan, and Manitoba, and the two territorial assemblies in the Yukon and the Northwest Territories. Historically, the last Liberal Party government formed in Saskatchewan was 1971, in Manitoba 1958, in British Columbia 1942, and in Alberta way back in 1921. Westerners are deeply disturbed with various policies being pursued by the central government, and many are convinced that the West is discriminated against by Ottawa.

In contrast to the relative prosperity and abundant resource reserves of the Western provinces of Manitoba, Saskatchewan, Alberta, and British Columbia, the Atlantic provinces are the poorest in the confederation. Inhabitants of Newfoundland, Nova Scotia, Prince Edward Island, and New Brunswick have

124

average annual incomes well below those of residents in the other provinces and their governments are heavily dependent on subsidies from the federal government. Nonetheless, some hope is on the horizon, at least for Nova Scotia and Newfoundland. Nova Scotia will benefit from offshore natural gas discoveries, and Newfoundland is located near the Hibernia oil field, potentially one of the largest in the world. Leaders of Newfoundland have waged a bitter battle with Ottawa, claiming total control over the field whereas Ottawa insists that the federal government has jurisdiction. Regardless of the final settlement, the citizens of Newfoundland will benefit from the lion's share of royalties in the years ahead. However, economic prosperity is still an elusive dream for many citizens of the Atlantic provinces and quite a few question how beneficial confederation has been for their region.

With the major exception of Ontario, most provinces would like to see a decentralization trend in the Canadian economic and commercial spheres so that they could attract more industries and provide adequate employment for their young people.[17] In 1969, a Department of Regional Economic Expansion (DREE) was set up for this expressed purpose, but its accomplishments were very modest, and it was replaced in 1982 by a Department of Regional Industrial Expansion (DRIE). Ontario continues to attract the great bulk of new industries, to the consternation of the other provinces. Discontent in the "hinterlands" is in no way comparable to the disillusionment in Quebec, but the provinces of English Canada are far from unified. As a result, the federal government in Ottawa must not only cope with the serious challenge from Quebec, but must also begin to accommodate more fully the demands of the Eastern and the Western provinces.

The "Native" Dimension

Although the Europeans who settled in Canada generally treated the native population in a much less barbarous fashion than their counterparts south of the border, many Indians, Inuit (Eskimos), and Métis believe that the Canadian government has not done enough either to right the wrongs which were perpetrated against them or to protect their way of life from the white man's encroachment.

125

For example, in order to halt legal proceedings against the construction of a 12-billion-dollar hydro-electric project in the James Bay region of Quebec, the federal and Quebec governments agreed to award the 11,000 Indians and Inuits in the region 225 million dollars and control over 61,000 square miles of wilderness territory. Critics of the James Bay agreement claimed that the life-styles of the natives would suffer irreparable damage because of the expansion of the European civilization into the area. These critics were also quick to react to the much-publicized proposals to build a pipeline in the Northwest Territories through land which had traditionally been populated by natives. Representatives of certain native groups have claimed that the native peoples have never received just compensation for land already taken from them by the Europeans and that the construction of any such pipeline would not only deprive them of additional territory, but also adversely affect the native population's way of life. The declaration appearing in Table IV:7, which was formulated by a group claiming to represent the Dene tribe of the Northwest region, insists that the tribe should be recognized as a separate nation within the Canadian confederation. The declaration also vividly describes some of the problems faced by the natives and adequately portrays another of the challenges facing the Canadian government in trying to balance the demands of the natives against the seemingly insatiable thirst of the major population areas in Southern Canada for more natural resources from the Northern expanses.

Canada's Indian Act classifies approximately 310,000 of the nation's citizenry as "Status Indians." These Indians are placed under the direct jurisdiction of the federal government and about two-thirds of them continue to live on government reservations. Almost one year after the new constitution was promulgated, Canada's prime minister and the provincial premiers met to discuss expanding the constitutional rights of all native groups, particularly the Status Indians. The federal and provincial leaders agreed at this meeting to accord a constitutional status to any agreements resulting from the present or future negotiation of native land claims. The 1982 constitution protected only "existing" rights. In addition, the leaders decided to amend the constitution so that aboriginal rights would apply equally to men and women. Up until

TABLE IV:7

THE DENE DECLARATION

We the Dene of the Northwest Territories (NWT) insist on the right to be regarded by ourselves and the world as a nation.

Our struggle is for the recognition of the Dene Nation by the Government and people of Canada and the peoples and governments of the world.

As once Europe was the exclusive homeland of the European peoples, Africa the exclusive homeland of the African peoples, the New World, North and South America, was the exclusive homeland of Aboriginal peoples of the New World, the Amerindian and Inuit.

The New World like other parts of the world has suffered the experience of colonialism and imperialism. Other peoples have occupied the land--often with force--and foreign governments have imposed themselves on our people. Ancient civilizations and ways of life have been destroyed.

Colonialism and imperialism is now dead or dying. Recent years have witnessed the birth of new nations or rebirth of old nations out of the ashes of colonialism.

As Europe is the place where you will find European countries with European governments for European peoples, now also you will find in Africa and Asia the existence of African and Asian countries with African and Asian governments for the African and Asian peoples.

The African and Asian peoples--the peoples of the Third World--have fought for and won the right to self-determination, the right to recognition as distinct peoples and the recognition of themselves as nations.

But in the New World the native peoples have not fared so well. Even in countries in South America where the Native peoples are the vast majority of the population there is not one country which has an Amerindian government for the Amerindian peoples.

Nowhere in the New World have the Native peoples won the right to self-determination and the right to

127

recognition by the world as a distinct people and as Nations.

While the Native people of Canada are a minority in their homeland, the Native people of the NWT, the Dene and the Inuit, are a majority of the population of the NWT.

The Dene find themselves as part of a country. That country is Canada. But the government of Canada is not the government of the Dene. The Government of the NWT is not the government of the Dene. These governments were not the choice of the Dene, these were imposed upon the Dene.

What we the Dene are struggling for is the recognition of the Dene Nation by the governments and peoples of the world.

And while there are realities we are forced to submit to, such as the existence of a country called Canada, we insist on the right to a self-determination as a distinct people and the recognition of the Dene Nation.

We the Dene are part of the Fourth World. And as the peoples and Nations of the world have come to recognize the existence and rights of those peoples who make up the Third World the day must come and will come when the nations of the Fourth World will come to be recognized and respected. The challenge to the Dene and the world is to find the way for the recognition of the Dene Nation.

Our plea to the world is to help us in our struggle to find a place in the world community where we can exercise our right to self-determination as a distinct people and as a nation.

What we seek then is independence and self-determination within the country of Canada. This is what we mean when we call for a just land settlement for the Dene Nation.

---

this agreement, legislation openly discriminated against women because they lost their native rights if they married a non-native, whereas native men could marry non-natives and still retain their rights. The government leaders also decided to meet in constitutional conference with the representatives of the native groups at least three more times in the 1983-1987 period. Several months earlier, the federal government also agreed in principle to the eventual creation of a new federal territory called Nunavut (which means "our land" in the Inuit language). This new governmental unit, which would remain under Ottawa's jurisdiction, would be carved out of the eastern portion of the Northwest Territories and would primarily represent the interests of the Inuit. The residents of the Northwest Territories, in a referendum held in the spring of 1982, voted 56 percent in favor of this division and the electorate's verdict was later endorsed by the legislature of the Northwest Territories.

As can be seen by these negotiations, the federal and provincial governments have been willing to guarantee certain protections to native groups. Even Premier Lévesque, who refused to sign the 1983 agreements with the natives because it would imply acceptance by the Quebec government of the new constitution, stated that these provisions were needed and that he would ask the Quebec National Assembly to implement similar statutes. Nevertheless, many aboriginal groups consider that much more must be done by the governments in Canada and therefore continue to push for rights which will transfer more land to natives, protect traditional cultures and languages, and permit native peoples the opportunity to establish their own form of government. Progress on these key issues will most likely proceed at a snail's pace in the years ahead.

A Comparison of Federalism in Canada and the United States

The major difference between the Canadian and American federal systems is the much greater policymaking latitude enjoyed by the Canadian provinces. This great disparity in provincial-state powers is even more remarkable when one recalls that the founders of the Canadian confederation were clearly biased in favor of the central government and granted Ottawa the right to monopolize residual powers (which

129

were accorded to the states on the other side of the border). The provinces continue to battle Ottawa for additional governmental powers and during the 1970s and early 1980s the federal and provincial governments have been involved in bitter jurisdictional battles in areas as diverse as urban affairs, communications, language, culture, international trade, and natural resources. Provincial governments are also very much involved in economic activities and they control a large number of "crown corporations" which either monopolize activity in a certain economic sector or compete head-on with private companies.

In the United States, state interests are often articulated in Washington through Congress, the political parties, and the federal bureaucracy. In West Germany, the Länder (states) governments are directly represented in the legislature's second chamber, the Bundesrat. In Canada, however, the major negotiations take place within the framework of federal-provincial conferences, particularly the periodic meetings between the prime minister and the provincial premiers. The two chambers of parliament, the political parties, and the bureaucracy have poorly served the interests of the provinces in the nation's capital.

Although the American federal government does have a grants-in-aid formula which somewhat favors the poorer states, such as Mississippi, at the expense of the richer states, such as Connecticut, the Canadians have done a better job of compensating the poorer areas through their system of equalization payments. On the other hand, the Canadian government has had a poor track record in trying to encourage a broader distribution of businesses and industries among the provinces. Ontario undoubtedly dominates the Canadian economic, financial, commercial, media, and educational spheres to a much larger extent that even New York and California combined in the United States. The same may be said of Toronto's preponderant place in the Canadian system as compared to New York City and Los Angeles in the American system. Over time, Ontario's preponderance in the economic and political spheres will undoubtedly diminish somewhat as the Canadian population shifts westward, somewhat akin to Americans heading in greater numbers to the sunbelt region.

The Canadian governmental system is much more decentralized than its American counterpart but it also faces a much more serious danger of losing one of its integral units--Quebec. A Canadian expert on federalism once admitted that he had twice delayed the completion of a book on the Canadian federal system "because of the judgment that the federation would not last as long as it would take to finish the manuscript."[18] However, the manuscript was completed and the confederation still stands intact. On the other hand, the period of deep uncertainty continues to linger on, and regional and provincial loyalties will at times have a very detrimental impact on Canadian national unity.

[1]The five theories of federalism are thoroughly discussed in Edwin R. Black, Divided Loyalties: Canadian Concepts of Federalism (Montreal: McGill-Queen's University Press, 1975).

[2]See Professor Douglas Verney's comments along this line in Maclean's, May 16, 1977.

[3]Toronto Globe and Mail, 7 June 1977, p. 8, and Canadian News Facts, 1977, p. 1735. The Quebec officials claimed that the federal government had collected 4.3 billion dollars more in Quebec than it had spent in the province during the period 1961-1975.

[4]See the 1971 Gendron Commission Report, p. 132.

[5]For some insightful perceptions of the asbestos strike, consult Pierre Elliott Trudeau, ed., The Asbestos Strike, trans. James Boake (Toronto: James Lewis & Samuel, 1974).

[6]See Pierre Vallières, White Niggers of America, trans. Joan Pinkham (Toronto: McClelland and Stewart, 1971). FLQ theorists viewed Quebec's problems through a Marxist framework and contended that the French Canadians had been dominated through their history by three colonial masters--France, England, and the United States. These advocates of the FLQ cause thus concluded that revolution was the only alternative available to the French workers in order to throw off the colonial yoke. In a later book, Choose!, Vallières changed his philosophy somewhat and stated that the FLQ was no longer needed and that the necessary changes could be achieved within the current Quebec system.

[7]For a good account of the 1970 events, consult John Saywell, Quebec 70 (Toronto: University of Toronto Press, 1971). Caouette's remarks are found on page 106.

[8]Some Canadian scholars firmly believe that Quebec would be hurt by separation, claiming that the new nation would be more vulnerable to the American economic challenge, that a mass exodus of Quebec's most skilled individuals to the United States and English Canada would occur because of economic losses, and that

there would be a strong possibility of right-wing or left-wing authoritarianism in the new nation (see, for example, John Meisel's comments in his book, Working Papers on Canadian Politics, 2nd ed. (Montreal: McGill-Queen's University Press, 1975), pp. 209-210.

[9]Premier William Bennett was quoted in one of Gerald Clark's series of articles on English Canadian attitudes toward Quebec's possible separation. See the Vancouver Sun, 14 May 1977, p. 20.

[10]Ibid. This premier was Gerald Regan. Gerald Clark added that "the depth of goodwill toward Quebeckers is, regardless of the state of crises that the country now feels, astonishing and widespread. If Lévesque and others in the PQ have done nothing else, they have made English Canada aware that it is Quebec--with its distinctive flair and culture--that makes Canada different. And without the physical hinge that Quebec provides there could be no Canada; province by province, the rest would be forced to join the United States. The Maritimes, of no material use to Americans, would be pushed into tragic subsistence on its own and mass migration."

[11]The Gallup Report, May 19, 1976, indicated that 54 percent of Canadians interviewed felt that there was too much emphasis on bilingualism, whereas 22 percent felt that there was not enough, and 17 percent believed that it was just right. The figures among English Canadians were 73 percent too much, 10 percent not enough, and 12 percent about right. Among French Canadians, the figures were 16, 50, and 26 percent respectively, and among other ethnic groups 54, 12, and 19 percent.
In the Gallup Report published on September 11, 1976, Canadians were asked in which areas services should be available in both English and French. Thirty-seven percent said in all areas of Canada, 10 percent in areas where the language was used by at least 10 percent of the population, and 43 percent in areas where a majority used the language. The figures among (a) French-speaking, (b) English-speaking, and (c) other language groups were 67, 7, 21 percent; 26, 12, 52 percent; and 18, 10, and 52 percent respectively.

[12]Canadian News Facts, 1977, p. 1717.

[13]In the Gallup Report of June 16, 1976, people were asked if they thought "that if public school pupils learned both English and French, it would tend to a better understanding between French- and English-speaking Canada?" Sixty-four percent said yes and 28 percent no. The percentages among French-speaking Canadians were 79 percent yes and 15 percent no, and among English-speaking Canadians 58 percent yes and 34 percent no.

[14]Quoted in Donald V. Smiley, "Canada and the Quest for a National Policy," Canadian Journal of Political Science, 8 (March 1975):61.

[15]For example, the Alberta government granted a 50 million dollar loan to Newfoundland. The province has also purchased its own airline and its citizens are still not required to pay a provincial sales tax. Not too surprisingly, there has been a great influx of people into the province in the past few years.

Certain scholars, such as Ken Norrie and M. B. Percy, claim that this population growth and the inefficient use of resources have greatly mitigated the positive effects of the resource boom. See "Coping With A Resource Boom," Au Courant, no. 3, 1982, p. 5.

[16]As far back as the early 1970s, Eric Hanson suggested that Alberta could become another Switzerland and "would clearly be better off as a separate nation." See his article, "The Future of Western Canada: Economic, Social, and Political," Canadian Public Administration, 18 (Spring 1974):117.

The Alberta Heritage Savings Trust Fund was set up in 1975 as a "rainy day" savings account to be used when Alberta's revenues from non-renewable oil and natural gas sources begin to decline.

[17]A good synopsis of the viewpoints of the provincial governments concerning economic development is found in the Economic Recovery Program Communiqué issued at the 23rd Annual Premiers' Conference, Halifax, August 26, 1982.

[18]See the introduction in Donald V. Smiley's, Canada in Question: Federalism in the Seventies, 2nd ed. (Toronto: McGraw-Hill Ryerson, 1976).

V

PARTIES, ELECTIONS, AND POLITICAL
SOCIALIZATION: LIFE AMONG THE
CANADIAN POLITY AND OTHER SUCH CREATURES

The Canadian Society

Basic Characteristics of Contemporary
Canadian Society

The people living in Canada's advanced industrial
society are generally highly literate, civilized, and
affluent. Canadians not only have an average income
level many times higher than people in developing
nations, but they can also expect to live longer to
spend it. The average Canadian enjoys a life
expectancy of approximately 74 years, which contrasts
markedly with a Moroccan's 56 years, a Zambian's 49
years, an Ethiopian's 40 years, and an Afghanistani's
37 years. Canada as a whole also has a very low infant
mortality rate, although the rate of death among native
children does rival that of some of the developing
countries.

Canada's crime rate is fairly high in comparative
terms, but it ranks far below that of the United
States, with homicides in the entire country trailing
substantially behind the total in New York City (see
Table V:1 for comparative statistics). Canadian
society also compares quite favorably with other
advanced societies in terms of education levels, as
Table V:2 illustrates. Disruptions caused by work
stoppages have not overly burdened the Canadian
economy, but they do rank among the highest in the
advanced industrial world (see Table V:3).[1]

In comparative perspective, Canadians are
generally a very contented people. In a survey
conducted in the mid-1970s, people in several countries
were asked if they were very happy, fairly happy, or
not too happy. Eighty-five percent of Canadians stated
that they were very or fairly happy as compared to 90
percent in the United States and 80 percent in Western
Europe.[2] When asked if they wished to have more people
in their country, affirmative answers among Canadians
were appreciably higher than those in other advanced

industrial societies but lower than those in developing areas.[3] Very few Canadians stated that they had been in want of food or clothing during the past year and 59 percent were highly satisfied with their housing, as compared to 55 percent in the United States, 49 percent in Western Europe, 37 percent in Latin America, and 14 percent in both Africa and the Far East.[4] Canadians were also highly satisfied with their medical coverage and very few had gone without medical treatment because of lack of money.[5]

Canadians also rank comparatively high in their belief in God, belief in life after death, and the intensity of their religious beliefs (see Table V:4). On the other hand, Canada and several other advanced industrial societies are in the midst of a type of "social revolution" which is challenging many traditional values and beliefs. For example, marriage rates in Canada are up moderately whereas divorce rates are dramatically higher (see Table V:5).[6] A 1967 survey asked the question, "generally speaking, do you think family life today is more successful, or less successful than it was in your parent's day?" Forty-five percent of the respondents stated more successful, 33 percent less successful, 17 percent no different, and five percent undecided. When asked the exact same question in 1977, only 22 percent felt that family life was more successful, 60 percent less successful, 14 percent no different, and five percent no opinion.[7] Moreover, Canadians have become much more skeptical over the years concerning the influence of television on family life, with 41 percent in 1976 believing that television was a "good influence" and 41 percent "not a good influence."[8]

In effect, Canadians are materially prosperous and enjoy virtual "cradle to the grave" material security. Nevertheless, the traditional roles of the male, female, child, and "family unit" in Canadian society are being seriously questioned and this has precipitated a great deal of uncertainty and even malaise in various sectors of the population. These changing social attitudes, of course, have also had their effect on the political priorities of governments at both the regional and national levels.

TABLE V:1

COMPARATIVE HOMICIDE AND SUICIDE RATES, 1978
(per 100,000 people)

	Homicides	Suicides	
		Male	Female
Canada	2.6*	21.2	7.3
Australia	1.8	16.6	6.7
France	1.0*	23.3	9.9
Japan	1.1	22.6	13.6
United Kingdom[1]	1.2	10.7	6.5
United States	9.4	19.0	6.3
West Germany	1.2	30.1	15.1

[1]Includes only England and Wales
*1977 figures

Source: Statistical Abstract of the United States, 1981.

TABLE V:2

COMPARATIVE EDUCATIONAL STATISTICS, 1979

Country	Average Length of Schooling (years)*	Percent of 15-19 Year-Olds Enrolled in School	Percent of GNP Spent on Public Education	Percent of GNP Spent on Public Higher Education
Canada	14.1	64.9	7.7	18.3
France	14.7	55.9	3.5	17.8
Japan	13.2	71.4	5.8	20.1
United Kingdom	12.2	46.2	5.7***	13.8**
United States	15.2	75.0	6.4	17.7***
West Germany	12.3	45.4	4.7	13.6

*1970 figures
**1977 figures
***1978 figures

Sources: UNESCO, Statistical Yearbook, 1982, and OECD Observer, March 1982.

TABLE V:3

WORKING DAYS LOST FROM INDUSTRIAL DISPUTES

Country	1965		1970		1978	
	No. Days Lost	Days Lost/ 1000 Wrkers	No. Days Lost	Days Lost/ 1000 Wrkers	No. Days Lost	Days Lost/ 1000 Wrkers
Canada	2,349,870	361	6,539,560	1,004	7,393,000	840
Australia	815,869	193	2,393,700	493	2,131,000	451
France	979,861	50	1,742,175	84	2,187,000	129
Japan	5,669,362	129	3,914,807	74	1,357,000	36
United Kingdom	2,925,000	119	10,980,000	431	9,405,000	421
United States	23,300,000	333	66,413,800	950	36,923,000	438
West Germany	48,520	2	93,203	4	4,281,000	206

Source: Year Book of Labor Statistics.

139

TABLE V:4

ATTITUDES TOWARD RELIGION

Percentage Stating That They Believe in God
(Believe in Life After Death)

	1948	1968	1975
Canada	95 (78)	* (*)	89 (54)
Australia	95 (63)	* (*)	80 (48)
France	66 (58)	73 (35)	72 (39)
Japan	* (*)	* (*)	38 (18)
United Kingdom	* (49)	77 (38)	76 (43)
United States	94 (68)	98 (73)	94 (69)
West Germany	* (*)	81 (41)	76 (33)

Importance of Religious Beliefs, 1976

	Very Important	Fairly Important	Not too Important	Not at all Important	Don't Know
Canada	36	36	19	9	*
Australia	25	33	29	13	*
France	22	33	23	20	2
Japan	12	34	44	10	*
United Kingdom	23	26	26	20	5
United States	56	30	8	5	1
West Germany	17	30	37	14	2

Source: Gallup Opinion Index, Religion in America, 1976.

TABLE V:5

MARRIAGE AND DIVORCE RATES IN CANADA
(per 100,000 people)

	Marriages	Divorces
1922	720	6.1
1930	700	8.6
1940	1080	21.2
1950	910	39.3
1960	730	39.1
1970	880	136.5
1980	1,085	259.0
1981	1,129	278.0

Source: Statistics Canada, Vital Statistics, 1981.

Political Socialization

Canadian children are generally taught in the schools and at home to be supportive of their political system and to work within that system to bring about any changes that they believe are necessary. Comparatively, Canadians show a high level of obedience to civil authority and seemingly show more deference for political leadership than do Americans. On the whole, Canadians also seem to be less politicized than Americans, but certainly have been much more willing to vote than their counterparts to the South.

The WASP (white, Anglo-Saxon, Protestant) male from a highly privileged background dominates the political elites of both the United States and Canada. Females have continued to face severe problems in achieving membership in the elite club, and Canadian ethnic groups are also under-represented in the top political circles.[9]

The average Canadian's sense of political efficacy and political trust tends to vary from one region to another. For example, using 1965 and 1968 post-election data, Simeon and Elkins determined that approximately 60 percent of the residents of the Atlantic and French-speaking regions ranked relatively low in terms of a sense of political efficacy (the sense that one can personally influence political decisions and have one's opinion heard by political leaders). This figure compared to approximately 40 percent in the prairie region, 33 percent in Ontario, and 25 percent in British Columbia.[10] In terms of political trust (the feeling that the government leaders and politicians are generally competent, worthy of respect, and concerned with the individual citizen's welfare), residents of the Atlantic region continued to rank fairly low while people in the other regions of Canada ranked fairly high.[11]

People in most parts of Canada feel closer to their provincial governments than to their federal government. Ontario is somewhat the exception, but one should remember that this province serves as the headquarters for the federal government.[12] A national election study conducted in 1974 indicated that about six out of every ten Canadians think of their country in regional terms, with the strongest regional identification in English Canada being centered in the Western provinces.[13]

Although regional and cultural identification are generally stronger in Canada than in the United States, the best indicator of political party support in Canada still remains religious identification, even though Canada's two major parties are very similar in their stances on religious issues (see Table V:6 for statistics on Canadian religious denominations).[14]

Canada's Liberal Party perennially attracts above average support from Catholics. In addition, the party usually garners an above average following from people with high-ranking occupations, higher class self-images, and more years of schooling. It also does quite well among French-speaking and recent immigrant groups, younger people more than older people, and the urbanized more than the ruralized.

The Conservative Party, on the other hand, does better among Protestants, farmers, and lower ranking occupational groups. Anglophones, Canadian-born, and pre-World War II immigrant groups have also been more prone to vote Conservative. In addition, this party attracts more older voters than younger voters, more women than men, and more rural dwellers than urbanites. The Conservatives have also suffered historically from the image in Quebec that they are anti-French, a tendency somewhat equivalent to the Republicans' anti-Dixie reputation in the South.

The New Democratic Party (NDP), which is more socialist than any other major party in Canada or the United States, draws greater support from non-Catholics and non-French-speaking people. Men support this party more than women and urbanites more than rural dwellers, with non-French, non-English ethnic groups providing greater support than those from the two founding cultural groups. Much of the urban male support is attributable to union ties with over 60 percent of NDP voting support coming from working class people.

The Electoral System

With a few minor exceptions, all Canadians 18 years and over are allowed to vote in federal elections.[15] Federal and provincial electoral requirements

TABLE V:6

POPULATION BY RELIGIOUS DENOMINATION, 1971

Denomination	Membership	% of Denomination Membership
Anglican	2,543,180	11.8
Baptist	667,245	3.1
Greek Orthodox	316,605	1.5
Jewish	276,025	1.3
Lutheran	715,740	3.3
Mennonite	168,150	0.8
Pentecostal	220,390	1.0
Presbyterian	872,335	4.0
Roman Catholic	9,974,895	46.2
Salvation Army	119,665	0.6
Ukrainian Catholic	227,730	1.1
United Church	3,768,800	17.5
Other	767,980	3.6
No Religion	929,575	4.4
Total	21,568,310	100.0

Source: 1971 Census of Canada.

are fairly much the same, except that the provinces normally require six to twelve months of residency before a person can vote in the provincial elections. Lists of qualified voters are compiled by specially appointed registrars who do house-to-house canvassing prior to an election. Thus it is easier for a person to be registered to vote in Canada than it is in almost all of the states south of the border. In addition, the percentage of Canadians who exercise their right to vote is invariably higher than the percentage of Americans (see Table V:7).

In terms of methods used to determine the winners of elections, many parliamentary systems in Western Europe use the proportional representation (PR) voting formula. Canada also has a parliamentary system, but has steered clear of the PR format, instead relying on a single-member district, first past the wire system which is also used in the United States and Great Britain.[16] In a PR system, the electorate generally votes for a party of its choice and the number of seats at stake in parliament is divided among the parties according to their overall share of the vote. Although rarely this simple, under a PR system a party which secures 20 percent of the overall vote would be entitled to approximately 20 percent of the parliamentary seats.

In the next general elections which must be held no later than 1985, membership in the Canadian House of Commons will be increased from 282 to 310 seats. Thus, the nation will be divided into 310 constituency districts with roughly an equal number of voters in each.[17] The candidate who receives the most votes in each electoral district, even if less than a majority, will then be elected to the House of Commons. This single-member district, first past the wire system has historically worked disproportionately in favor of the parties which receive the highest percentage of the votes and those parties which have strong regional followings. Table V:8 clearly illustrates the bias of the electoral system in translating votes into seats in Canadian and American national legislative contests.[18] Because Canada depends strictly on general parliamentary elections to determine the formation of its government, whereas the United States has a separate election to select its chief executive, the bias of the electoral system in Canada may well be more significant. Canada could probably avoid much of this

145

TABLE V:7

VOTER TURNOUT FOR AMERICAN PRESIDENTIAL AND CANADIAN FEDERAL ELECTIONS

United States	Canada
1960 - 63%	1957 - 74%
1964 - 62%	1958 - 79%
1968 - 61%	1962 - 79%
1972 - 56%	1963 - 79%
1976 - 54%	1965 - 75%
1980 - 53%	1968 - 76%
	1972 - 77%
	1974 - 71%
	1979 - 76%
	1980 - 70%

Sources: Report of the Chief Electoral Officer on the General Elections, and Statistical Abstract of the United States.

TABLE V:8

BIAS OF ELECTORAL SYSTEM IN TRANSLATING VOTES
INTO SEATS IN U.S. HOUSE OF REPRESENTATIVES AND
CANADIAN HOUSE OF COMMONS ELECTIONS

HOUSE OF REPRESENTATIVES
Rank Order of Parties in Terms of % of Vote

Year	1	2	3
1940	Dem 1.20	Rep 0.82	Other 0.39
1946	Rep 1.06	Dem 0.98	Other 0.09
1952	Dem 0.98	Rep 1.03	Other 0.22
1958	Dem 1.15	Rep 0.81	Other 0.00
1964	Dem 1.18	Rep 0.76	Other 0.00
1970	Dem 1.10	Rep 0.92	Other 0.00
1974	Dem 1.16	Rep 0.80	Other 0.00
1980	Dem 1.19	Rep 0.78	Other 0.00

HOUSE OF COMMONS
Rank Order of Parties in Terms of % of Vote

Year	1	2	3	4
1940	Libs. 1.43	Cons. 0.53	CCF 0.39	Socred 1.52
1945	Libs. 1.24	Cons. 1.00	CCF 0.73	Socred 1.29
1949	Libs. 1.49	Cons. 0.53	CCF 0.37	Socred 1.03
1953	Libs. 1.32	Cons. 0.62	CCF 0.77	Socred 1.06
1957	Libs. 0.97	Cons. 1.09	CCF 0.88	Socred 1.09
1958	Cons. 1.46	Libs. 0.55	CCF 0.32	Socred 0.00
1962	Cons. 1.17	Libs. 1.01	NDP 0.53	Socred 0.97
1963	Libs. 1.17	Cons. 1.09	NDP 0.49	Socred 0.76
1965	Libs. 1.23	Cons. 1.13	NDP 0.44	Cred. 0.72
1968	Libs. 1.30	Cons. 0.88	NDP 0.47	Cred. 0.88
1972	Libs. 1.09	Cons. 1.16	NDP 0.65	Cred. 0.76
1974	Libs. 1.24	Cons. 1.03	NDP 0.38	Cred. 0.69
1979	Libs. 0.99	Cons. 1.34	NDP 0.50	Cred. 0.43
1980	Libs. 1.17	Cons. 1.12	NDP 0.57	Cred. 0.00

[1]The measurement of "discrimination" is determined by dividing the percentage of seats won in the legislature by the percentage of votes won by the party (% seats/% votes). Any figure above 1.00 indicates discrimination in favor of the party, any figure below 1.00 illustrates discrimination against the party.

Sources: Alan C. Cairns, "The Electoral System and the Party System in Canada, 1921-1965," Canadian Journal of Political Science, 1 (March 1968); Statistics of the United States, 1976; and Statistical Abstract of the United States, 1981.

electoral bias by switching over to the proportional representation system. Better yet, in view of Canada's federal structure, a system similar to West Germany's "half and half" formula might be appropriate. In West Germany, the voter chooses both a party and an individual candidate. Although certain variations do occur, approximately 50 percent of the seats in the German Bundestag are filled through proportional representation, and the other 50 percent by the election of individual candidates in each constituency area. In the eyes of most Canadians, however, the degree of bias built into the electoral system is relatively insignificant and it is highly unlikely that the system will be altered in the foreseeable future.

Candidates for seats in the House of Commons are usually selected by party conventions at the local constituency or "riding" level. In clear contrast to the American system, there are no primaries in Canada. The prospective candidate for office will usually appear with his spouse before the local party gathering, give a short speech, and then answer questions. The local party faithful will then vote until one candidate receives a majority. This person will then become the party's nominee in the general election because the national party organization rarely overrides the local group's choice. Occasionally, a candidate will be "parachuted" into a riding. This means that the national party leadership has a special interest in making sure a certain person is elected and thus searches for a safe riding where the chances are very good that the person will emerge as the winner. The person has little, if any, roots in the local riding and it is expected that the party label will suffice to bring him victory. However, the electors clearly prefer candidates who live in their constituency area and parachuting is a fairly rare phenomenon.

The party's nominee for a seat in the House of Commons must fulfill the same qualifications as a voter and if elected, must not at the same time be a member of the Senate, the provincial legislature, nor the civil service, and must not be employed as a government contractor. Once selected by the party organization, the nominee will then file a petition with local election officials bearing the names of at least 25 qualified voters. In order to dissuade frivolous candidates from running, a deposit of 200 dollars must

148

be posted, returnable if the candidate receives at least one-half of the total votes garnered by the winner. As a result of the Canada Elections Act of 1970, the candidate can now have his political affiliation placed on the ballot beside his name.

As is typical in the United States, Canadian candidates for office are prone to make rather strong promises to the voters, promises which are oftentimes difficult to keep once elected. As an illustration, two seats were at stake in provincial by-elections held a few years ago on Prince Edward Island. These elections were crucial because the two major parties were evenly split in the provincial legislature and if either party could sweep the two seats, it would be able to form the provincial government. The government then in power quickly rushed in road equipment to pave the streets in the region where the by-elections would be held, and promised to name that region's candidate, who had never been in the legislature before, as the new Minister of Highways and Public Works. Each party also promised a generous increase in pensions to older residents if it emerged victorious in the by-elections. Surprisingly enough, the government party did not win as the voters were evidently more enticed by the opposition party's pledges. Nevertheless, the strategy of both parties was appropriately summed up in this phrase: "If it moves pension it; if it doesn't pave it."[19] Such is part of the substance of modern political campaigns.

Electoral officers selected by federal and provincial authorities make sure that the election is conducted fairly and efficiently. In Ontario, for example, a returning officer is selected by the provincial cabinet for each riding. This officer selects the places where the people in the riding will vote and supervises the general activities associated with any election. The returning officer is also assisted by an election clerk of his own choosing, and each major party selects hundreds of enumerators who are responsible for collecting the names of eligible voters.

If any disputes arise during the course of the campaign or on election day, appeals may be made to the district court judges within the province. This court will then render a decision, subject to ultimate appeal to Canada's Supreme Court.

149

Electoral campaigns are very expensive in both Canada and the United States and have often been beyond the means of the average citizen who would like to run for office but simply cannot afford it. In the United States and in Canada in 1974, new campaign finance laws were passed which limit contributions by interest groups, place ceilings on campaign spending, and transfer some of the campaign costs to the government. Both of these major pieces of legislation were heavily influenced by the gross irregularities which occurred in Richard Nixon's 1972 reelection bid. The American law, which is mainly applicable to presidential elections, was first tested in 1976 and has had very mixed results. Because of loopholes and subsequent court decisions, Political Action Committees (PACs) representing big business and labor groups are able to spend whatever they want. In the 1980 presidential and congressional elections, these special committees and individual contributors provided Republican candidates with far more money than was available to Democratic candidates, meaning that Republicans could generally spend appreciably more than their Democratic competitors on staff support and advertising. According to the U.S. Federal Election Commission, PAC spending has increased steadily, totalling 75.6 million dollars in 1977-1978, 124.6 million dollars in 1979-1980, and 187.7 million dollars in 1981-1982.

The influence of PACs is offset somewhat in presidential elections by public funding of some of the candidate's activities. A candidate seeking his party's nomination for president during the primary and caucus phase of the campaign is entitled to matching funds from the federal government if he is capable of raising 5,000 dollars in each of twenty states with no individual contribution counting for more than 250 dollars. Thus, once the candidate has raised at least 100,000 dollars under the specified conditions, he is entitled to matching funds from then on, although only the first 250 dollars of each individual contribution will qualify for federal funding. If the candidate is then successful in winning the Democratic or Republican Party's nomination for the presidency, he will be entitled to an extra 20 million dollars in federal funding to wage the general election campaign. Taxpayers in the United States are able to designate on their individual tax forms that one dollar each year be added to this election fund, and this provision has proven to be adequate in providing federal financing

150

for both the primary and general election phases of the presidential campaign. In 1980, the Federal Election Commission doled out 188 million dollars from this fund to presidential contenders and it is expected that at least as much money if not more will be available for future presidential contests. However, this fund is only used for presidential elections and very little has thus far been done to offset the powerful influence of PACs and wealthy individuals in the congressional and gubernatorial races.

The Canadian law has worked much better than its American counterpart in limiting, although certainly not negating, the influence of big money groups. Canada's Election Expenses Act of 1974 provides public money to defray approximately one-third of the expenses of parliamentary candidates who acquire at least 15 percent of the total vote cast in a riding. These candidates receive the postage cost of mailing one item to every voter in the riding and receive an additional eight cents for each voter up to 25,000 and six cents for every voter above 25,000. Federal funding also pays for part of the cost of television time for parties and stipulates that a total of six-and-a-half hours of prime-time television must be provided to registered parties during the campaign, allocated on the basis of a party's percentage of the overall vote in the past election and the number of seats it holds in the House of Commons.

The Election Expenses Act also limits what individual candidates and parties can spend during the electoral campaign. Candidates can spend no more than one dollar for each of the first 15,000 voters in the constituency area, 50 cents for those between 15,000 and 25,000, and 25 cents for each voter above the 25,000 figure. National parties may also spend no more than 30 cents per voter for the total number of voters registered in constituencies where the party runs candidates. In the 1980 election, parties with candidates in each and every riding were permitted to spend 4.5 million dollars based on a total of 15 million registered voters throughout Canada. The use of campaign advertising is also prohibited by law until 29 days before an election. Moreover, candidates must report the names of donors who contribute in excess of 100 dollars to the campaign.

Canada's election laws are clearly designed to subsidize some of the expenses of serious candidates, limit overall campaign spending, and provide public disclosure of all large funding sources. Problems still remain concerning full disclosure of financial contributions and the Liberal Party and Conservative Party continue to be heavily dependent on corporate donations, whereas the New Democratic Party relies on contributions from the large labor unions. Nevertheless, Canadians have a much better handle on campaign spending practices than do the Americans and many of the Canadian regulations could be effectively implemented in the United States, where elections at the local, state, and federal levels cost 1.2 billion dollars in 1980.

As a consequence of the stronger following of third parties in Canada than in the United States, several of the Canadian national governments in recent years have been "minority" regimes. For example, the majority of House of Commons seats garnered by the Liberals in the 1980 election was only the fourth majority in the last ten Canadian elections. A "minority" government means that the party selected to lead the nation does not command majority support in the House of Commons and could theoretically be ousted at any time by a disgruntled and unified opposition. Minority governments are also very common in Western European parliamentary systems. In Western Europe, however, the party which has been asked to form the government will normally establish a coalition with one or more other parties in order to have majority support in the legislature. These coalition parties will be provided representation in the new cabinet and will play a role in the formulation of the government's policies. In contrast, Canada does not have a tradition of coalition governments. Yet in spite of its precarious status, the minority party which has formed the government in Canada has generally been able to govern fairly effectively and with a few notable exceptions (such as the Conservative Party's very short tenure in 1979), has usually been able to serve its full allowable term in office.

The Party System

A Two Party Dominant System

Throughout its 200-year history, the United States has had a two-party system. George Washington frowned upon political factions, considering that they would be a devisive force in an infant nation which needed all the unity it could muster for survival. But within Washington's own cabinet, two opposing political tendencies were already clearly in evidence. Secretary of the Treasury Alexander Hamilton eventually became a major spokesman for the Federalists and Secretary of State Thomas Jefferson the prime mover behind the Democrats. The Federalists eventually gave way to the Whigs and the Whigs in turn eventually succumbed to the challenge of the Republicans just a short time before Abraham Lincoln assumed the presidency. Third parties have never survived for long in the American system and the two major political movements have evolved into "catch-all" parties which attempt to muster support from liberals, conservatives, and middle-of-the-roaders alike.

Since the confederation was formed in 1867, Canada has also typified a two party dominant system with either the Liberals or the Conservatives prevailing in every national general election. The Conservatives monopolized governmental leadership during the formative years of the confederation, holding power for 24 of the 33 years between 1867 and 1900. Conversely, the Liberals have been in power during most of the 20th century (see Table V:9). Yet in spite of this two-party domination, Canada has differed from the United States because third parties have shown much more resiliency and have been much more influential in the political affairs of the Canadian system.

The Major Parties

The Liberal Party

The National Liberal Federation of Canada successfully ended the hegemonic position of the Conservatives at the end of the 19th century. The Liberals have traditionally received strong support among the French Canadians and all three French Canadian Prime Ministers, Laurier, St. Laurent, and Trudeau, have come

153

TABLE V:9

CANADIAN GENERAL ELECTION RESULTS
1900-1980

Year	Total Seats	Liberals		Conservatives		CCF-NDP		Social Credit		Other		Party Forming Govt.
		Seats	% Votes	Seats	% Votes	Seats	% Votes	Seats	% Votes	Seats	% Votes	
1900	213	132	52%	81	47%					0	1%	Lib.
1904	214	139	52	75	47					0	1	Lib.
1908	221	135	51	85	47					1	2	Lib.
1911	221	87	48	134	51					0	1	Con.
1917	235	82	40	153	57					0	3	Con.
1921	235	116	41	50	30					69	29	Lib.
1925	245	99	40	116	46					30	14	Lib.
1926	245	128	46	91	45					26	9	Lib.
1930	245	91	45	137	49					17	6	Con.
1935	245	173	45	40	30	7	9%	17	4%	8	12	Lib.
1940	245	181	51	40	31	8	8	10	3	6	7	Lib.
1945	245	125	41	67	27	28	16	13	4	12	12	Lib.
1949	262	193	49	41	30	13	13	10	4	5	4	Lib.
1953	265	171	49	51	31	23	11	15	5	5	4	Lib.
1957	265	105	41	112	39	25	11	19	7	4	2	Con.
1958	265	49	34	208	54	8	9	0	2	0	1	Con.
1962	265	100	37	116	37	19	14	30	12	0	0	Con.
1963	265	129	42	95	33	17	13	24	12	0	0	Lib.
1965	265	131	40	97	32	21	18	5	4	11	6	Lib.
1968	264	155	45	72	31	21	17	0	1	14	6	Lib.
1972	264	109	38	107	35	31	18	0	0	17	9	Lib.
1974	264	141	43	95	35	16	16	0	0	12	6	Lib.
1979	282	114	40	136	48	27	9	5	2	0	0	Con.
1980	282	147	52	103	36	32	11	0	0	0	0	Lib.

Sources: Howard A. Scarrow, Canada Votes, 1962, and Report of the Chief Electoral Officer on the General Elections.

from the Liberal fold. The Liberals have traditionally favored an English-French accommodation and greater centralization of authority. Although very weak in the Western provinces since the mid-1950s, the Liberal Party has nonetheless managed to dominate Canadian national elections over the past several decades, relying on almost total electoral domination in Quebec and strong support in Ontario.

The Conservative Party

The Progressive Conservative Party of Canada has roots which extend back to the pre-confederation era. The first leader of the party, John A. MacDonald, was instrumental in pushing for Canadian independence and played the major role in keeping the fragile union together after the confederation was formed. The party has not done well at the national level in recent years, having been in power in this century only from 1911 until the early 1920s, 1930 until 1935, 1953 until 1963, and for a few months in 1979. The party has been traditionally identified with private enterprise and with a limited centralization of government authority. The Conservatives have also been stereotyped as being pro-British and generally insensitive to the aspirations of the French Canadians. The party's perennial dismal showing in Quebec is one major reason why the Conservatives have formed very few national governments in recent decades.

The New Democratic Party

The New Democratic Party (NDP), which has never held power at the national level but which has formed several provincial governments, has no counterpart in the United States. Without a doubt, the NDP is appreciably to the left of any major political movement in Canada or the United States and is very vocal about its socialist leanings. On the other hand, it is undoubtedly more conservative than many of its sister movements in Western Europe.

The NDP had its roots in the Cooperative Commonwealth Federation (CCF), a moderate socialist party which was formed during the Great Depression period of the 1930s. In 1961, the CCF joined with the Canadian Labour Congress to form the NDP. The CCF ruled Saskatchewan for two decades beginning in World

155

War II and the NDP has since formed provincial
governments in Saskatchewan, Manitoba, and British
Columbia. The party also succeeded in electing a
record 32 representatives to the House of Commons in
1980, but has never been a major threat to the hegemony
enjoyed by the two leading parties. Nonetheless, the
NDP remains competitive in many ridings and retains a
substantial provincial base of support in the West,
with the major exception of Alberta. The NDP's
willingness to join with the Liberals in voting down
the Conservative budget in 1979 was the primary reason
that the Conservative government was forced to resign
after just a few months in office.

The dominant philosophy of the NDP is Fabian
socialism with origins tracing back to British
political philosophers and not to Marx. The party
generally favors greater governmental control over the
private economic sector, an expanded social welfare
system, and much more stringent controls on American
investment in Canada. The NDP has also strongly
advocated a non-nuclear world role for Canada.

The NDP has generally been a pragmatic movement
and has been willing to tone down some of its
ideological stances in order to win legislative seats.
On the other hand, some factions within the movement
have generated a great deal of publicity because of
their radical policy positions. For example, the
"Waffle" or "Watkins" faction issued a much-publicized
manifesto at the 1969 NDP national party convention
which called for the creation of an independent
socialist Canada. The Waffle Manifesto also asserted
that the "essential fact of Canadian history in the
past century is the reduction of Canada to a colony of
the United States" (see Table V:10). This resolution
submitted by the Waffle faction was not passed by the
NDP convention and a much less emotional platform was
eventually adopted.

The Minor Parties

The Communist Party has been a totally
insignificant force in Canadian political affairs at
both the national and provincial levels. On the other
hand, some regionally based parties have done fairly
well at times. The Social Credit Party and its
independent counterpart in Quebec, the Créditiste

156

TABLE V:10

EXCERPTS FROM THE NDP "WAFFLE"
RESOLUTION OF 1969

Our aim as democratic socialists is to build an independent socialist Canada. Our aim as supporters of the New Democratic Party is to make it a truly socialist party . . . .

The most urgent issue for Canadians is the very survival of Canada. Anxiety is pervasive and the goal of greater economic independence receives widespread support. But economic independence without socialism is a sham, and neither are meaningful without true participatory democracy.

The major threat to Canadian survival today is American control of the Canadian economy. The major issue of our times is not national unity but national survival, and the fundamental threat is external, not internal.

American corporate capitalism is the dominant factor shaping Canadian society. In Canada, American economic control operates through the formidable medium of the multi-national corporation. The Canadian corporate elite has opted for a junior partnership with these American enterprises. Canada has been reduced to a resource base and consumer market within the American empire.

The American empire is the central reality for Canadians. It is an empire characterized by militarism abroad and racism at home. Canadian resources and diplomacy have been enlisted in the support of that empire. In the barbarous war in Vietnam, Canada has supported the United States through its membership on the International Control Commission and through sales of arms and strategic resources to the American military-industrial complex.

The American empire is held together through world-wide military alliances and by giant corporations. Canada's membership in the American alliance system and the ownership of the Canadian economy by American corporations precluded Canada's playing an independent role in the world. These bonds must be cut if corporate capitalism and the social priorities it creates is to be effectively challenged.

Canadian development is distorted by a corporate capitalist economy. Corporate investment creates and fosters superfluous individual consumption at the expense of social needs. Corporate decision-making concentrates investment in a few major urban areas which become increasingly uninhabitable while the rest of the country sinks into underdevelopment . . . .

The struggle to build a democratic socialist Canada must proceed at all levels of Canadian society. The New Democratic Party is the organization suited to bringing these activities into a common focus. The New Democratic Party has grown out of a movement for democratic socialism that has deep roots in Canadian history. It is the core around which should be mobilized the social and political movement necessary for building an independent socialist Canada. The New Democratic Party must rise to that challenge or become irrelevant. Victory lies in joining the struggle.

Party, are conservative movements which have occasionally been powerful at the provincial level. Formed during the Depression period of the 1930s, the Social Credit movement dominated Alberta provincial politics for almost 30 years but has now fallen on hard times in that province. The movement has recently formed a provincial government in British Columbia but its sister movement in Quebec has declined precipitously. At the federal level, the Social Credit movement is no longer a force to be reckoned with in Canadian politics.

Quebec has actually given birth to more minority parties than most of the other provinces combined. Some of Quebec's third-party movements, such as the Union Nationale and the Parti Québecois , have been successful in attracting enough seats in the legislature to form provincial governments. And even though the PQ is powerful only at the provincial level and has no national base, that party's independence stance may well give it more influence over Canada's destiny than any other third-party movement in the nation.

The Party Leader Selection Process

Each of the major parties holds national nominating conventions for the purpose of selecting the party's leader and of formulating a national platform. These conventions are now held on a fairly regular basis. A party leader is very pivotal in Canada because if his party comes out on top in the parliamentary elections, he will become the nation's prime minister. In contrast, the American president is usually considered as the leader of his party, but the leadership of the opposition party is often in doubt. And even though Gerald Ford was president when he attended the Republican National Convention in 1976, he was only considered as the "leader" of the moderate faction, with Ronald Reagan being ascendant over the conservative grouping and supporters of Nelson Rockefeller being dominant over the liberal forces. In spite of the fact that some factions might be disgruntled with his leadership, a Canadian prime minister will usually be respected as the sole leader of his party (although John Diefenbaker did face in 1967 some very vociferous opposition from elements within the Conservative Party).

All of the prospective candidates for the national leadership post are expected to address the convention and voting is by secret ballot, two features which are quite different from American convention practices. Delegates to the Canadian conventions also have more flexibility in terms of whom they may vote for, whereas delegates to American conventions are generally bound to support a specific candidate through the first round or two of voting. Otherwise, American and Canadian conventions have much in common with a great deal of hoopla and ubiquitous media coverage.

Although a debatable assumption, the Canadian conventions may well have sparked more excitement in recent years than their American counterparts. For example, at the 1976 Conservative convention, Joe Clark did not nail down the victory for party leader until the fourth round, edging Claude Wagner by 65 votes. In contrast, Republican conventions in the United States have not gone beyond the first ballot since 1948 and the Democratic conventions since 1952.

The party leaders are also very important in the Canadian political process because governments are

159

traditionally formed by a single party and that party's members in parliament are expected to vote in accordance with the party leadership's recommendations. Parliamentarians who either belong to the party of the government or of the opposition and who grossly deviate from the party leaders' recommendations open themselves to severe discipline or even expulsion from the party.

On the other hand, the national party leadership has little influence over the provincial party organizations. Not infrequently, a party forming a government at the national level will be bitterly criticized by the national party's counterparts at the provincial levels. The Canadian party system is definitely decentralized and party organizations outside of the national and provincial legislative structures are inordinately weak and poorly organized. As a result of these weak hierarchical structures, the Canadian parties have played a minimal role in mediating federal-provincial disputes.

A Comparison of the Canadian and American Party Systems

The wider range of choices available in the Canadian political spectrum would probably be welcomed by critics of the American party system who consider choices offered by the Democrats and the Republicans as synonymous with the differences between Tweedledum and Tweedledee. On the other hand, no third party in Canada has as yet successfully challenged the traditional domination of the two major parties and none has really molded a national constituency following (see Tables V:11 through V:13 for federal and provincial election results).

Moreover, the limited success experienced by the socialist-oriented NDP appears to be a remarkable achievement when compared to the fate of the socialists in the United States. The best performance by a socialist movement in the United States was six percent of the national vote in the 1912 presidential election. The party came alive briefly during the Depression but has since performed dismally and has never even controlled a state government. Admittedly, some of the issues traditionally espoused by the socialists have been co-opted by the two major parties as state influence has increased over the private sector and

160

TABLE V:11

MEMBERS ELECTED TO PARLIAMENT BY PARTY AFFILIATION IN 1980 GENERAL ELECTIONS

Province	Liberal	P-C	N.D.P.	Social Credit	Other	Totals
Alberta	0	21	0	0	0	21
British Columbia	0	16	12	0	0	28
Manitoba	2	5	7	0	0	14
New Brunswick	7	3	0	0	0	10
Newfoundland	5	2	0	0	0	7
Nova Scotia	5	6	0	0	0	11
Ontario	52	38	5	0	0	95
Quebec	74	1	0	0	0	75
Prince Edward Island	2	2	0	0	0	4
Saskatchewan	0	7	7	0	0	14
Yukon	0	1	0	0	0	1
Northwest Territories	0	1	1	0	0	2
Totals	147	103	32	0	0	282

TABLE V:12

PARTY SEATS IN PROVINCIAL PARLIAMENTS

	Alb (1982)	BC (1983)	Man (1981)	NB (1982)	Newf (1982)	NS (1981)	Ont (1981)	PEI (1982)	Que (1981)	Sas (1982)
Liberal	0	0	0	18	8	13	34	10	42	0
Progressive-Conservative	75	0	23	39	44	37	70	22	0	57
New Democratic	2	22	34	0	0	1	21	0	0	7
Social Credit/Créditistes	0	35	0	0	0	0	0	0	0	0
Parti Québécois	0	0	0	0	0	0	0	0	80	0
Other	2	0	0	0	0	1	0	0	0	0

TABLE V:13

CANADIAN PROVINCIAL ELECTIONS

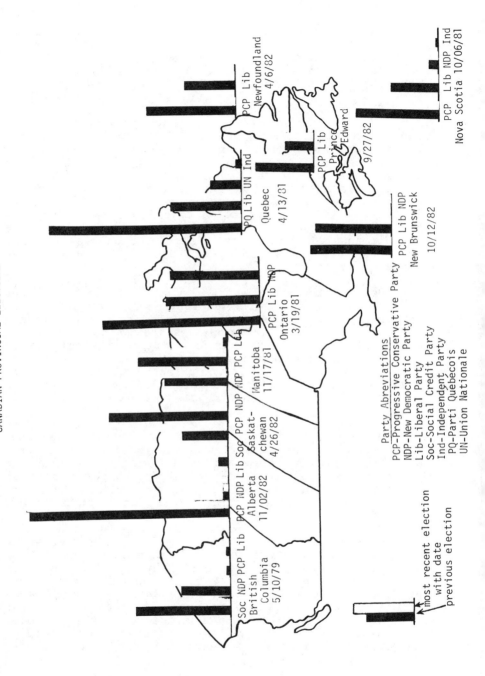

PCP Lib
Newfoundland
4/6/82

PCP Lib NDP Ind
Nova Scotia 10/06/81

PCP Lib
Prince
Edward
9/27/82

PQ Lib UN Ind
Quebec
4/13/31

PCP Lib NDP
New Brunswick
10/12/82

PCP Lib NDP
Ontario
3/19/81

PCP Lib NDP NDP PCP Lib
Manitoba
11/17/81

PCP NDP Soc PCP NDP
Saskat-
chewan
4/26/82

PCP NDP Lib Soc
Alberta
11/02/82

Soc NDP PCP Lib
British
Columbia
5/10/79

Party Abreviations
PCP-Progressive Conservative Party
NDP-New Democratic Party
Lib-Liberal Party
Soc-Social Credit Party
Ind-Independent Party
PQ-Parti Quebecois
UN-Union Nationale

most recent election
with date
previous election

163

governmental power has been increasingly centralized. On the other hand, the United States remains a bastion of capitalism and the word "socialist" has a pejorative connotation for a larger sector of the American public than the Canadian public.

Party discipline is also much more important in the Canadian political system than its counterpart to the south. With few exceptions, Canadian parliamentarians are bound to support the policy preferences of their party hierarchy. As one former parliamentarian stated, "the price of survival was constant loyalty to party and leader," and this loyalty often came before conscience and constituency interests.[20] In contrast, party discipline in Congress is moderate and it is not unusual for moderate Republicans to side with liberal Democrats and for Southern Democrats to line up with conservative Republicans.[21]

Both political systems also lack hierarchical party structures and the national party organizations have minimal control over the actions of the provincial and state parties. Many state and provincial organizations also experience similar difficulties in coordinating the activities of their local constituency groups. Some local units, in fact, such as the late Mayor Richard Daly's Cook County machine, actually ran the state party apparatus, somewhat akin to the tail wagging the dog.

Both party systems have fairly similar convention structures for the selection of national party leaders and for the formulation of party platforms, although the party's parliamentary delegation often dominates Canadian conventions to a greater extent than do congressional delegations. On the other hand, primaries have been used widely for American presidential, congressional, and state gubernatorial and legislative races. Some argue that primaries are a much more democratic electoral technique than local selection conventions because many more people are involved in the primary voting. Conversely, others assert that the political activists are much more astute and knowledgeable than the rank-and-file voter in choosing competitive candidates and that the public will have the last say anyway at the general election. Whatever the rationale, Canada has never experimented with the primary system.

In recent years, the Canadians have also been somewhat more tolerant in permitting relatively inexperienced political figures to assume top leadership posts. In the United States, candidates for the presidency normally spend long political apprenticeships in a vice-presidential suite, an office on Capitol Hill, or in a governor's mansion. In contrast, Pierre Trudeau was first elected to parliament in 1965 and became prime minister in 1968.

Many of the differences existing between the two-party systems must be attributed to the contrasting governmental structures. Canada has a parliamentary system with members of the government chosen predominantly from the ranks of the House of Commons. If the parliament ever loses confidence in the governing cabinet, the prime minister and his associates are expected to resign and new elections are usually held. This helps to explain why party discipline is so important in Canada. If party members were nonchalant about voting for their government's policies, the government would probably suffer a premature demise. Conversely, the President of the United States is totally independent of Congress and cannot be removed by the legislative branch except for impeachable offenses. If the president loses a major policy battle in Congress, his pride might be hurt but he will certainly not be expected to resign. Moreover, if a member of the president's party in Congress votes against an administration bill because of constituency interests, he will rarely face any disciplinary action. In fact, the members of Congress are unified in their desire to be reelected and do not expect a fellow party member to buck the constituency's interests, even if the president might be disappointed. Thus within the American political system, there is rarely the urgency for party discipline which exists in the Canadian parliamentary structure.

NOTES

¹Canada also had a total of 274 industrial disputes in 1960, 542 in 1970, and 1,058 in 1978.

²Gallup Report, April 14, 1976.

³Ibid., November 27, 1976. Thirty-eight percent in Canada stated that they wished that there were more people in their country as compared to three percent in Japan, eight percent in the United States, 17 percent in Western Europe, 38 percent in the Far East, 49 percent in Latin America, and 82 percent in Africa. However, in a Gallup Report released on May 20, 1978, only 28 percent of Canadians stated that they wanted an appreciably larger population, as compared to 62 percent who were opposed to such an increase in population.

⁴Ibid., December 24, 1976. When asked if during the past year there had been times when they did not have money enough to buy food, six percent in Canada said yes, as compared to eight percent in Western Europe, 14 percent in the United States, 40 percent in Latin America, 58 percent in the Far East, and 71 percent in Africa. When asked the same question about clothing, 12 percent answered affirmatively in Canada, 19 percent in both the United States and Western Europe, 53 percent in Latin America, 60 percent in the Far East, and 81 percent in Africa.

⁵Eighty-four percent of Canadians stated that they had received "good value" from the Canadian medical program with only 12 percent answering in the negative (Ibid., October 23, 1976). Only four percent of Canadians stated that they had not had enough money for medical or health care, as compared to five percent in Western Europe, 15 percent in the United States, 40 percent in Latin America, 48 percent in the Far East, and 57 percent in Africa (Ibid., December 24, 1976).

⁶When asked if they felt a couple should live together for a time before deciding to get married, 22 percent of Canadians surveyed said yes in 1971 and 38 percent in 1976. Among the 18 to 29 year old age cohort, 40 percent said yes in 1971 and 62 percent in 1976.

⁷Ibid., April 27, 1977. People over the age of 50 were more negative in their feelings toward family life than any other age cohort, with only 16 percent of this group stating that family life was more successful, 69 percent less successful, 11 percent no different, and four percent no opinion.

⁸Ibid., July 28, 1976. In 1956, 66 percent believed television was a good influence and 19 percent a negative influence. In 1966, the figures were 48 percent good and 27 percent negative.

⁹The Royal Commission on the Status of Women stressed that in Canada more attention must be given to the advancement of women within the political and economic realms.

¹⁰Richard Simeon and David J. Elkins, "Regional Political Cultures in Canada," Canadian Journal of Political Science, 7 (September 1974): 404.

¹¹Ibid.

¹²See Allan Gregg and Michael Whittington, "Regional Variation in Children's Political Attitudes," in David J. Bellamy, John H. Pammett, and Donald C. Rowat, eds., The Provincial Political Systems (Toronto: Methuen, 1976), p. 83.

¹³Jon H. Pammett, "Public Orientation to Regions and Provinces," in Ibid., p. 87.

¹⁴See Meisel, Working Papers, p. 13.

¹⁵Federally appointed judges, officers in charge of elections, prisoners, the mentally deficient, and a few other very limited categories are prohibited from voting.

¹⁶Manitoba and Alberta once experimented with modified PR systems at the provincial level, but all of Canada now uses a system fairly similar to that used in the United States.

¹⁷Independent commissions now determine the boundaries of each electoral district and the population from one district to another cannot differ more than ± 25 percent.

[18]For a good discussion of the bias of the Canadian electoral system, consult Alan C. Cairns, "The Electoral System and the Party System in Canada, 1921-1965," Canadian Journal of Political Science, 1 (March 1968): 55-80.

[19]Frank MacKinnon, "Prince Edward Island," in Canadian Annual Review of Politics and Public Affairs, 1966, ed. John Saywell (Toronto: University of Toronto Press, 1967), p. 151.

[20]Gordon Aiken, The Backbencher (Toronto: McClelland and Stewart, 1974), p. 118.

[21]The tight party discipline found in Canada should not be interpreted as meaning that there is an absence of factionalism within the parties. For example, at the 1976 Conservative Party convention, 49 percent of the delegates described themselves as right-wingers, 34 percent as centrists, and 17 percent as leftists (see Maclean's, March 8, 1976, pp. 18-23).

VI

PUBLIC POLICYMAKING IN CANADA:
THE HIGHLY DEVELOPED ART OF MUDDLING THROUGH

The Executive

The Executive Structure

The nominal head of state in Canada is the British monarch and he or she is represented in the North American nation by a governor-general. The powers of the governor-general, however, are largely ceremonial and some may say that the post itself is anachronistic and out of phase with modern democratic practices.[1] Nonetheless, the governor-general does free the prime minister from some of the more onerous ceremonial functions by representing the government at the opening of the national flower show or other such momentous events. Of course, the same trend is noticeable in the United States. As chief of state, the president was once expected to attend many such ceremonial functions. Now the president increasingly dispatches his wife, or the vice president, or a cabinet officer to represent him, thus allowing him to spend more time on important policy matters.

The governor-general is appointed by the monarch on the recommendation of the federal cabinet, serves a five year term, and is paid by the federal government. In return for his salary, he is expected to (1) select a prime minister when that office is vacant, (2) act on the advice of the prime minister in dissolving parliament, (3) periodically "advise" the prime minister, and (4) perform the aforementioned ceremonial duties.

Other elaborately named institutions, which are really facades for cabinet decision-making, are the governor-general-in-council and the Privy Council of Canada. The former institution simply issues directives which have been formulated by the federal cabinet. The latter group is open to all active and former cabinet members and certain other dignitaries who serve as privy councillors for life. In 1982, there were approximately 175 members of this group. However, the Privy Council, which was created in 1867

169

to advise the crown on governmental affairs in Canada, is actually dominated by the cabinet in power in Ottawa and reflects that cabinet's desires. Thus, when one is finally able to sift through the various ornamental institutions which have their origins in British political lore, one discovers that the true repository of executive authority is the prime minister and his cabinet (see Table VI:1 for a chart of the basic structure of the Canadian government).

The duties and responsibilities of the prime minister and his cabinet have never formally been written down. For example, the Canadian constitution is silent on the entire subject of what a cabinet is or what it is supposed to do. Nevertheless, custom has dictated that the prime minister, who is the leader of the party capable of forming a government and maintaining sufficient support in parliament, will choose his cabinet ministers from the ranks of parliament or make sure that they are elected to parliament at the subsequent round of by-elections.[2] The cabinet will then be expected to formulate the policies of the government, supervise the civil service, endorse and then defend programs submitted to parliament, and assume collective responsibility for the overall activities of the government.[3]

Most of the members of the cabinet will be assigned specific "portfolios," which means that they will direct a certain department or agency. A few, however, will not be assigned specific tasks but rather will act as troubleshooters for the prime minister. These people are often referred to as "ministers without portfolio."

The real power in the cabinet is centralized in the hands of the prime minister who is definitely more than just _primus inter pares_ (first among equals) in the cabinet. The prime minister is in fact the Canadian chief executive and is ultimately responsible for the conduct of the government, although the monarch remains Canada's nominal head of state. The prime minister personally selects the members of the cabinet and may change cabinet assignments whenever he deems it necessary. Although he must certainly pay attention to the desires of the regions, factions within his own political party, and certain key interest groups when forming his cabinet, the prime minister has a great deal of personal latitude in making his selections. In

170

TABLE VI:1

THE STRUCTURE OF THE CANADIAN GOVERNMENT

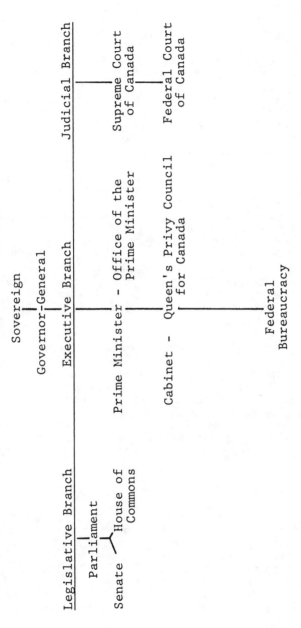

many countries with cabinet systems fairly similar to Canada's, coalition governments are the norm. The prime ministers in these countries must therefore heed the advice of not only their own party activists in choosing the members of the cabinet, but the coalition party partners as well. In spite of the propensity toward minority governments in recent years, coalitions have been strictly avoided in Ottawa and the prime minister has remained relatively free to work within his own party framework in order to form the cabinet. Just the same, the Canadian prime minister must remain cognizant of the importance of interpersonal relations within the cabinet and cannot ride roughshod over his ministers. Such imprudent actions will normally lead to widespread discontentment in the cabinet and may well precipitate the downfall of the government, as occurred with the Diefenbaker government in 1963.

The importance of the prime minister's position is illustrated by the persistent growth in two offices which work very closely with him. The Prime Minister's Office (PMO) and the Privy Council Office (PCO) have grown steadily in recent years and now employ approximately 300 people. Both the PMO and the PCO brief the prime minister daily on issues and keep him abreast of activities within the ministries. There are fewer policy specialists to be found in these organizations than in the White House's Executive Office, thus the scrutinizing of policy issues is more constrained in these Canadian institutions. Nonetheless, the PCO performs the important function of coordinating cabinet activities for the prime minister by setting agenda, taking minutes of cabinet sessions, and conveying cabinet decisions to the bureaucracy. The PMO helps to coordinate the prime minister's personal schedule and attempts to keep him abreast of possible trouble spots in federal-provincial relations.

Executive Policymaking

With only a few rare exceptions, important Canadian policies are formulated in the cabinet and not in the parliament. Even though cabinet sessions are held in secret, the policy priorities of the cabinet are generally determined in the following manner. Approximately a year before a new legislative session is to commence, the clerk of the Privy Council Office asks the heads of the executive departments and agencies to submit a priority list of proposals for legislative action and to explain in writing why these proposals demand urgent enactment. Once these lists are received by the PCO, they are rank ordered to coincide with the overall priorities of the prime minister and his cabinet. A group within the cabinet known as the committee on priorities and planning will then scrutinize the restructured list of priorities for legislative action. Next, the entire cabinet will examine the recommendations of this committee and determine the final list of governmental policy objectives. The departments will then be asked to prepare legislation and the overall goals of the government will be presented in the Speech from the Throne which opens every new parliamentary session. This speech is delivered by the governor-general (just as the monarch gives the opening speech in the British parliament), but the text is prepared by the prime minister and the cabinet and is equivalent to the U.S. president's annual State of the Union address.

As long as the government commands a majority in the House of Commons and can depend on disciplined party support, the cabinet's proposals, which have already been carefully scrutinized and discussed within the executive framework, will normally be passed by parliament with very few, if any, revisions. In addition, the cabinet's power is further strengthened by the tradition that only the government, and not individual members of parliament, will present bills involving the expenditure of funds or the raising of revenues (although all members are entitled to propose reductions in spending). Thus this control over both initiation and amendment provides the cabinet with awesome authority in terms of financial matters.

The cabinet also directs the activities of the executive bureaucracy and is responsible for enacting what is called orders-in-council. These orders include appointments to the courts and the fulfillment of various executive functions. For example, during the turbulent 1970 period in Quebec, the cabinet ordered federal troops into the province and invoked the War Measures Act. The prime minister and his associates thus resorted to strong executive powers which were available to them in order to combat what they perceived to be an FLQ reign of terror.

The cabinet also spearheads the activities of the federal government in the very important federal-provincial conferences. For example, approximately 500 different federal-provincial committees are currently functioning and the overall coordination for the federal programs presented at these conferences remains under the direction of the cabinet. In an overall perspective, there should be little doubt that the Canadian federal cabinet dominates the formulation of public policy in the Canadian political system.

A Comparison of the Canadian and American Executives

Even though there are significant structural differences between the two political systems, the Canadian and American executive branches clearly dominate in the formulation and the implementation of national public policy.

The president and his cabinet are not members of Congress, whereas the prime minister and his cabinet continue to be members of parliament and are integrally involved in parliamentary activities. If the Canadian cabinet loses the confidence of the House of Commons, it is expected to step down. In the United States, the president might represent one party and a majority in Congress the other, leading to many executive initiatives being poorly treated on Capitol Hill. Yet, the president is never expected to resign. Gerald Ford, a Republican president, faced just such a difficult situation because the House of Representatives and the Senate were dominated by huge Democratic Party majorities.

The separation of powers is much more extensive in the United States with the executive, legislative, and judicial branches exercising a great deal of autonomy in their own respective spheres. The situation is quite different in Canada where federal activities clearly revolve around parliament and the parliamentary party which has formed the cabinet.

The Canadian cabinet is also much more important in the executive process than its American counterpart. The cabinet must approve all policies in Canada and takes a very active part in the overall policymaking process. In sharp contrast, recent American presidents such as Kennedy, Johnson, and Nixon have rarely used their cabinets and meetings of the cabinet were few and far between. Instead, these presidents relied much more extensively on their White House advisers in the formulation of policy and even occasionally circumvented the cabinet and the executive departments altogether. For example, Richard Nixon had little confidence in the State Department apparatus and thus relied on his National Security Adviser, Henry Kissinger, and a few other Executive Office advisers to iron out America's foreign policy priorities. Rarely did Nixon ever consult with his Secretary of State, who was a member of the cabinet, or use the policymaking services available in the State Department's bureaucratic network.

Because of the separation of powers and only limited party discipline, the American governmental system centered in Washington often has less unity of purpose than its Canadian counterpart. For example, once the Canadian cabinet formulates a comprehensive energy package, it will usually be passed quickly by parliament and put into effect immediately thereafter. On the other hand, Gerald Ford and his advisers proposed a comprehensive energy policy which was intended to combat some of the problems linked to the sudden rise in oil prices. For over a year, Congress not only did not pass Ford's recommendations, but it failed to come up with a comprehensive substitute package of its own. In addition, some of the more ardent critics of the Ford plan were members of his own Republican Party. Likewise, Jimmy Carter faced similar difficulties in convincing Congress to accept many of his own energy proposals, even though both chambers of Congress were dominated by members of Carter's own party. Ronald Reagan has encountered the same type of problems with several of his defense and foreign policy initiatives.

In clear contrast to the American system, Canada retains some of the relics of its by-gone days in the British empire. In particular, the post of governor-general stands out. Even though this post is largely ceremonial and powers assigned to it in the Canadian constitution are largely forgotten, Canadians must still worry about a repetition of a situation which occurred not too long ago in Australia. Australia is a former member of the British empire and

now a fellow member with Canada in the Commonwealth of
Nations. In 1975, the Australian governor-general
unexpectedly used some of the assigned constitutional
powers which many Australians had considered would
never be utilized again. The leader of the opposition
party in Australia had announced that his followers
were going to block the government's proposed budget in
the Senate, the weaker of the two chambers in the
Australian parliament. The prime minister insisted
that the opposition had no right to use this tactic in
order to topple the government. A bitter controversy
ensued and the governor-general suddenly dismissed the
prime minister and asked the opposition leader to form
a new government. The prime minister's party, which
dominated the main chamber of parliament, quickly
passed a no-confidence vote against the new government
and asked for the reinstatement of the former
administration. The governor-general refused and
instead dissolved both chambers of parliament and
called for new elections. Canada has not suffered such
a crisis in many years but the Australian experience
should clearly illustrate the need to carefully
delineate the powers of the governor-general within the
contemporary governmental framework.

The Public Bureaucracy

In 1983, the Canadian public bureaucracy employed
approximately one million people at the federal,
provincial, and local levels of government. The
federal bureaucracy is essentially divided into four
main component parts. Each of the government
departments falls directly under the supervision of a
cabinet minister and of a deputy minister who is the
top civil servant in the organization. The main duties
of these departments are to assist the minister in the
formulation of policy and to carry out the laws passed
by parliament. The department corporations, on the
other hand, are responsible for the administration,
supervision, and regulation of certain special services
provided by the government. Such corporations include
the Unemployment Insurance Commission and the National
Research Council. The third major group consists of
the agency corporations. These corporations are
responsible for the management of quasi-commercial
operations, as well as the procurement, construction,
and disposal of certain products. The Crown Assets
Disposal Corporation and National Harbours Board are

examples of such agency corporations. The last group is comprised of the proprietary or crown corporations which normally provide services in competition with private companies. The Canadian Broadcasting Corporation and Air Canada fall within this last category. In December 1982, the Canadian government controlled 306 crown corporations and subsidiaries which employed 263,000 people, more than the number of civilian employees in the federal government itself. The assets of these crown corporations have a total value in excess of 32 billion dollars (Canadian).

Another Canadian government creation, the Royal Commission, is somewhat equivalent to special presidential or governor's commissions in the United States. These commissions may be appointed by either the federal or provincial governments and are assigned the task of gathering information on very specific topics. For example, recent allegations have been made concerning improprieties committed by the Royal Canadian Mounted Police, Canada's national police force. In light of the publicity generated by these allegations, the Trudeau government was prompted to appoint a Royal Commission to investigate the past activities of the Mounties. These commissions, which usually have from one to six members plus staff assistance, summon witnesses and collect briefs from various interested parties. After these briefs have all been examined and the legal summation concluded, a report is prepared by the commission members and submitted to the cabinet. The cabinet, in turn, then has the option of doing whatever it desires with the Royal Commission's recommendations.

Largely as a result of decisions rendered early in the century, the Canadian federal bureaucracy is now governed by a merit system. French Canadians, however, have long contended that the federal bureaucratic system has traditionally favored the English-speaking populace. In 1962, an official study concluded that French Canadians were not adequately represented in the federal bureaucracy and that the country's bilingual and bicultural character was not adequately reflected in the federal civil service. The 1969 Official Languages Act finally provided the French language equality of use in all federal institutions. However, many civil servants are still not conversant in French and the improvement in federal employment opportunities for the French-speaking populace has been fairly modest up to this point.

In an overall perspective, the public bureaucracy undoubtedly enjoys a great deal of independence from detailed ministerial control and is often granted significant decision-making latitude within its specific spheres of competence. Nonetheless, the elected officials in Ottawa are ultimately responsible for determining the policies of the government and must make sure that the bureaucracy conforms with the broad policy guidelines which the government leadership has formulated. Parliament does exercise some control over the bureaucracy through the Public Service Commission and the office of the auditor-general. The Public Service Commission supervises the staffing of the bureaucracy and makes sure that the entry into and advancement within the system are based on merit criteria. This commission is also in charge of promoting bilingualism in the public bureaucracy. The auditor-general, on the other hand, makes sure that there are no irregularities in expenditures made by the various parts of the bureaucracy. In addition, some of the provinces have now hired ombudsmen who are in charge of investigating complaints lodged against the bureaucracy by private citizens. Apparently, the ombudsmen have performed their tasks fairly efficiently and the residents of these provinces are satisfied that they have an advocate on their side when interacting with what is often perceived as a faceless bureaucratic structure. The federal parliament, however, has thus far refused to appoint an ombudsman at the national level, perhaps fearing that he or she might interfere with the traditional relationship between the individual member of parliament (MP) and his constituency. In other words, the MP might fear that instead of coming to him with his complaints or suggestions, a member of his constituency might go directly to the ombudsmen, thus interfering with the parliamentarian's right to "represent" his voting public.

The Parliament

The Parliamentary Structure

The House of Commons

Canada's chief legislative body is the House of Commons. The chamber currently has 282 members, but this number will grow over the next several years under a new formula passed by parliament. The Representation Act of 1974, which established this formula, stipulates that no province will lose seats and that the small provinces will still have "adequate" representation in the House of Commons. Nevertheless, the act asserts that parliamentary representation must be more in line with "one person-one vote" guidelines, and that Quebec will always remain the pivotal element in the process of redistributing seats. The representation formula is quite complicated, but the big winners in the next few years will be Ontario and the Western provinces. A redistribution of seats will occur periodically based on Canada's official census results which are taken every ten years. It is expected that the House of Commons will have approximately 352 members by the year 2001.

The Canadian House of Commons is essentially patterned after the British model with the prime minister and his cabinet occupying the front benches on one side of the House, and the opposition leaders the front benches on the other side. The MPs who are not in the cabinet nor opposition leadership posts are strewn out on the back benches (which thus explains why they are called "backbenchers"). A Speaker and Deputy Speaker (who are invariably from different language groups) preside over the House and make sure that order is maintained. On the whole, there is a great deal of decorum which accompanies the House proceedings and party leaders on both sides do a good job at keeping their forces in line.[4] The government's House Leader represents the interests of the entire cabinet in the House and supervises the activities of the party whips who in turn make sure that party discipline remains intact. The House Leader arranges periodic meetings with his party forces in the Commons to discuss the government's plan of action and the voting priorities for the future. The opposition forces also meet periodically to chart their course of action in making

179

life as difficult as possible for the governing hierarchy.

Salaries in 1983 ranged from 124,600 dollars (Canadian) in salary and expense allowances for the prime minister to 105,000 dollars for cabinet ministers to 50,300 dollars in salary and 16,800 dollars in expense allowances for an ordinary member of parliament.

The Senate

Of all the second chambers in Western advanced industrial societies, the Canadian Senate is without a doubt the most obsolete and anachronistic, clearly nosing out even the British House of Lords for this dubious honor.

At its creation, the Senate was viewed as protecting provincial rights as well as safeguarding the values of the propertied classes. The senators, who must be at least 30 years old and own real property (land or a house) valued at least 4,000 dollars, and have a total net worth of at least 4,000 dollars, are appointed by the governor-general-in-council (in other words, the prime minister and the cabinet) and may serve until the age of 75. The appointees to the Senate must also maintain a residence in the province which they represent. The Maritime provinces are allocated 24 seats in the Senate, Quebec 24, Ontario 24, the West 24, and Newfoundland 6, with certain provisions for extra seats under very special conditions. In reality, no matter what were the original intentions of the founders of the confederation for the Senate, Senate seats are now allocated by the cabinet as political plums for those who have rendered special service to the party, the province, or the nation, in no particular order. Oftentimes, the seats are given to people who are near the end of their careers and rarely does a Senate appointment serve as a stepping-stone to political advancement. In 1983, a senator made a tidy 50,300 dollars (Canadian) a year plus 8,200 dollars for annual expenses. When one party is in power for a long period of time, as the Liberal Party has been for much of this century, the Senate is bound to be top heavy with members of that particular political movement. Moreover, since two major parties have always directed

the affairs of the Canadian government, it is only
through their token generosity that any third party
members ever receive an invitation to sit in the
Senate. In September 1982, there were 15 vacancies in
the ranks of the Senate and most Canadians could care
less whether they are ever filled. At that time, the
Senate consisted of 61 Liberals, 23 Conservatives, one
Social Credit devotee, 4 independents, and 15 empty
seats.

In an effort to avoid being too condescending
toward this august legislative body, one should remark
that some of the senators are very dedicated to serving
the people and definitely earn their salary. The
Senate has completed some very illuminating
investigations on science policy, the mass media,
poverty, foreign affairs, etc. The cabinet at times
shows an interest in these studies, but very little
else associated with the Senate. The cabinet is not
responsible to the Senate for its actions and cannot be
removed from office by a Senate vote of no confidence.
At least one senator is always included in the Prime
Minister's cabinet, but links between the cabinet and
the Senate are at times quite tenuous. Nor has the
Senate done a satisfactory job in articulating and
protecting the interests of the provinces. Instead,
this important function has been fairly much taken over
by the federal-provincial conferences.

Members of the Senate are permitted to introduce
legislation, with the exception of money bills which
must begin in the House of Commons. The Senate must
also ratify all legislation before it can become law,
but only one in ten bills is ever modified by the
Senate and these revisions are generally very minor.
Moreover, the Senate has not rejected a bill sent to it
by the House of Commons in more than forty years.

The citizens of the provinces would undoubtedly be
better off if a major facelifting were performed on
this chamber. If Canadians really desire that the
Senate articulate the interests of the provinces, then
they should probably pattern the institution after the
German Bundesrat. The Bundesrat is composed of civil
servants from each of the Länder (state) governments.
These civil servants are appointed by each Länder
administration and must vote as a unit. The larger
Länder are assigned five seats in the Bundesrat, the
middle-sized four, and the smaller ones three, making a

181

grand total of 41 voting members. The Bundesrät takes
an active part in the passage of German legislation and
retains an absolute veto power over federal legislation
which is concerned with matters within the exclusive
jurisdiction of the Länder. Länder civil servants who
are attached to Bonn keep track of the daily
legislative matters and the Bundesrät only needs to
meet in formal session about twice a month in order to
handle its business.

The Canadian federal government might well be
reluctant to give up control over all of the patronage
seats in the Senate, so a modified reform of the Senate
might be more feasible. Perhaps a system could be
adopted which would allow the federal government to
choose one-half of the seats and the provincial
governments the other half. Indeed, Prime Minister
Trudeau suggested in June 1978 that a new House of the
Federation be formed to replace the Senate. According
to the Trudeau government, this new chamber would
better represent the interests of the provinces and of
the linguistic communities. Half of the membership
from each province would be chosen by the House of
Commons and the other half by the provincial
legislature. However, the powers of this new House
would be more restricted than those of the current
Senate and some provincial leaders have greeted
Trudeau's proposal with skepticism. Table VI:2
provides an alternate plan for Senate reform which was
formulated by the provincial government in Alberta.
Alberta officials assert that the Senate membership
should be appointed by provincial governments and that
the Senate should exercise an absolute veto over
federal legislation which might impact on provincial
authority. In addition, the allocation of seats to
each province would be done in such a way as to insure
that the Western and Eastern provinces could not be
outvoted by Ontario and Quebec.

No matter what solution is finally agreed on, most
anything would be better than the Senate system as now
constituted, even its abolition. Certainly the Senate
does fulfill some useful investigatory functions, but
this work could be turned over to selected Royal
Commissions with the same results at much less expense.
The Senate plays a minimal role in the governmental
process and Canada has been plagued for too long with
this albatross which should have been humanely disposed
of years ago.

TABLE VI:2

THE ALBERTA GOVERNMENT'S
RECOMMENDATIONS FOR
SENATE REFORM

1. The Senate be appointed.

2. Senators be appointed exclusively by the
    provincial governments.

3. Provincial representation in the Senate be based
    on a weighted system of representation.

4. The Senate should exercise an absolute veto over
    certain matters:

    a) "Exceptional" federal powers including the
        emergency power, the declaratory power, and
        the powers of reservation and disallowance;

    b) The federal spending power in areas of
        provincial jurisdiction; and

    c) The exercise of other federal legislative
        powers which significantly affect provincial
        jurisdiction.

5. The Senate have a role in approving the following
    matters:

    a) Appointments to federal boards and agencies;
    b) Ratification of international treaties;
    c) Appointments to the Supreme Court of Canada
        and certain Provincial Courts.

6. A mechanism to resolve potential deadlocks between
    the House of Commons and a reformed Senate be
    established.

Source: Government of Alberta, A Provincially-
         Appointed Senate: A New Federalism for
         Canada, August 1982.

The Parliamentary Policymaking Process

The Government and Opposition Forces

As is the case in the United States, the Canadian legislative body is almost totally dependent on the executive for policy initiatives. The Canadian parliament essentially "refines" and "ratifies" the government's policies and most of this work is performed in the popularly-elected House of Commons. For its part, the Senate amends very few bills and usually goes along with whatever the government and the House of Commons have recommended.

The government's task in making sure that its programs become law is greatly simplified by the strict party discipline. In most cases, the cabinet can fairly much dictate to the party members in the House how they are supposed to vote on a particular issue. Some government backbenchers have complained that this emphasis on party discipline sometimes turns them into "trained seals" and stands between them and their constituents.[5] Nevertheless, if the government is to survive it must insure that it has enough support to win key legislative votes. As a consequence, party discipline remains an indispensable part of the parliamentary system.

When the party which forms the government commands a strong majority in the House of Commons, the opposition parties have little chance of blocking important legislation. In fact, the opposition is heavily dependent on media coverage in order to rally public support for its point of view. Major avenues available to the opposition to make sure that its viewpoint is heard include the following. First, for eight days after the Speech from the Throne is delivered, general debate takes place in the House relating to the pros and cons of the government's policy priorities. Second, near the beginning of almost every meeting, ministers or their representatives are expected to answer questions from the floor of the House and publicly defend the government's programs. Obviously, some of the questions from the opposition MPs can be very pointed. Third, three times a week at the end of a session, members can introduce topics for general debate. And fourth, 25 days are allotted in each session for the opposition to introduce motions related to the government's policies. Six of these motions can lead to no-confidence votes against the government, and if successful, can precipitate the premature downfall of the prime minister and his cabinet. Thus even though a governmental majority can fairly well dominate the parliamentary policymaking process, the opposition parties can at least make their opinions and alternate policy choices known to the general public.

In March 1982, the Progressive Conservative Party opposition took the drastic step of refusing to answer the division bells during a session of the House of Commons and continued to do so for more than two weeks, thereby bringing the parliamentary process to a grinding halt. The Progressive Conservatives objected to the Liberal government's attempts to ram a comprehensive energy bill through the House without sufficient debate on the various sections of the energy package. Failing to answer the division bells basically means not returning to the floor of the House of Commons to take part in a vote. Parliamentary rules stipulate that the MPs cannot proceed with any other legislative business until a vote is held, so the Conservative Party was successful in preventing the consideration of other legislation until the Liberal government was willing to make a compromise on the energy proposal. Eventually, the Liberals agreed to set aside some additional time for debate and the Conservative Party opposition returned to the House.

Table VI:3 indicates the usual scheduling of activities in the House of Commons. Many parliamentarians consider that the process of making laws must be streamlined and in 1982 a group of backbenchers from all parties released a report urging major reforms. This report recommends that a fixed parliamentary calendar be established with regular autumn, winter, and spring sittings from mid-September until the end of June. This calendar would provide 175 days of parliamentary sessions, ten more than have occurred over the past few years. Monday, Tuesday, and Thursday sessions would begin at 11:00 a.m. (the time already set aside for Friday meetings) and no evening sessions would be held except for emergency debates. The maximum length of most speeches would be reduced from 40 minutes to 20 minutes with an additional 10 minutes set aside for questions to the speaker or for rebuttals to the speech. Fifteen minutes would also be

TABLE VI:3

CUSTOMARY SCHEDULE OF ACTIVITIES
IN THE HOUSE OF COMMONS

(1) Opening ceremonies at 2:00 p.m. (except on Fridays when the House convenes at 11:00 a.m.).

(2) Formal motions are made by the government and private members relating to the business of the government and of the House of Commons.

(3) Ministerial answers to written questions submitted by MPs are read.

(4) A 40 minute oral question period follows the reading of the answers.

(5) Government business or opposition resolutions are considered until 5:00 p.m.

(6) Just before the dinner break, private member bills and resolutions are allowed to surface.

(7) Government business or opposition resolutions are considered from 8:00 until 10:00 p.m.

(8) Three days a week at 10:00 p.m., a short period of time is set aside for debates which are monopolized by the backbenchers.

(9) Some time prior to the late, late show on television, the House adjourns and the MPs stagger home.

Source: Robert J. Jackson and Michael M. Atkinson, The Canadian Legislative System (Toronto: Macmillan, 1974).

allocated at the beginning of the daily question period to permit MPs 1½ minutes each to speak on issues of particular concern to them. The power of the Speaker of the House to adjourn sessions in which fewer than 20 MPs are on the floor would be substantially curtailed by permitting 15 minutes to assemble the necessary membership before adjournment could be ordered. In addition, the report recommends that the membership of the House of Commons standing committees be reduced and that the powers of these committees to initiate inquiries into the activities of government departments, agencies, and crown corporations be significantly increased.

No major reform of parliament has occurred since 1969, but it is likely that the House of Commons will enact some of these recommendations on an experimental basis. In particular, there is an excellent chance that the time allocated for speeches will be reduced in order to cut down on debates, and many MPs will also support the curtailment of evening sessions.

The Making of a Law

The parliament in Canada formally consists of the monarch (represented by the governor-general), the Senate, and the House of Commons. A bill can become law only after it has successfully passed through both legislative chambers and has received the assent of the governor-general. The bill can originate in either chamber, except for financial legislation which must first be considered by the House. The first reading is the formal introduction of the bill into the chamber and no debate or amendment of the bill is permitted at that time. The second reading is much more crucial and general debate is allowed. A bill which passes the second reading is then assigned to one of the 18 permanent committees or to a special committee in the House. Although certainly not enjoying the power or the resources of its American counterparts, the committees in the House make a thorough examination of the bill, may call witnesses and seek additional information from the government and other sources, and may amend the bill. Once the bill is sent back to the floor by the committee, the third reading takes place and the parliamentarians must either accept or reject the bill without further amendment. The bill must be passed in exact form by both chambers and is then sent along to the governor-general for his assent, which is automatically given.

In an overall sense, the government remains the formulator of legislation and the parliament only refines and then approves it. Very few private bills proposed by individual MPs are ever passed and parliament as a whole initiates very few pieces of legislation. Thus as long as the cabinet can depend on disciplined party support in parliament, its policy recommendations will usually be passed with only minor revisions made by the legislative chambers.

A Comparison of the Canadian and the American Legislatures

The ranks of Canadian and American lawmakers are both dominated by white, middle-aged males with professional backgrounds (see Table VI:4 for the characteristics of Canadian lawmakers). Members of the U.S. Congress do tend to have longer tenures and thus more legislative experience than their Canadian counterparts, largely attributable to fewer "safe" constituency districts in Canada and the desire of a relatively large number of Canadian legislators to leave the House of Commons after one or two terms in office.

Congress undoubtedly has more influence over the policymaking process than the Canadian parliament, although both legislative systems are overwhelmed by the numerical superiority, expertise, and resource advantages of the executive branch. As a consequence, both legislatures remain almost totally dependent on policy initiatives supplied by the executive branches in their respective countries. The lack of rigid party discipline and the definite existence of regional and ideological factions within both major party movements make it very difficult at times for the U.S. president to be assured that his proposals will become law. In addition, congressional committees are much better staffed and have more resources at their disposal than their Canadian counterparts. Those who chair congressional committees have lost some power in recent years because of reforms introduced on Capitol Hill, yet some still exercise inordinate power and at times can single-handedly determine the fate of a piece of legislation.

TABLE VI:4

CHARACTERISTICS OF MEMBERS OF
THE 30TH HOUSE OF COMMONS, 1976

	House of Commons		Canadian Populace[4]	
	No.	%	No. (000)	%
Total	264	100.0		
Male	255	96.6	10,795	50.1
Female	9	3.4	10,773	49.9
Under 40	54	20.5	14,538	67.4
40-49	96	36.4	2,502	11.6
50-59	74	28.0	2,008	9.3
60-69	28	10.6	1,397	6.5
70+	5	1.9	1,124	5.2
N.K.[1]	7	2.7		
0-2 yrs. in Parliament[2]	54	20.5		
2-9	152	57.6		
10-19	49	18.6		
20+	8	3.0		
N.K.	1	0.4		
Lawyers	64	24.2		
Professional or Managerial	149	56.4	1,466	17.0
Blue Collar, Sales, Clerical, Service, etc.[3]	27	10.2	6,649	77.1
Farmer, Rancher or related	16	6.1	512	5.9
N.K.	8	3.0		
Some College or University	207	78.4	1,644	8.6
High School or less	52	19.7	17,462[5]	91.4
N.K.	5	1.9		

1. Not known
2. Based on start of 30th Parliament, 30 September 1974
3. Includes insurance agents and other related occupations
4. Based on 1971 census
5. Population 5 years and over

The individual member of Congress also has much greater staff assistance than his Canadian compatriot, being allowed personnel to work in his office as well as additional staff for each of his committee assignments. In fact, the American Congress is far and away the "country club" of all of the world's legislative bodies, prompting some critics to insist that the members of Congress have become too engrossed with the trappings of the office and have lost track of what is occurring in the real world. The member of Congress pockets over 60,000 dollars (U.S.) a year in salary, as compared to 67,000 dollars (Canadian) in salary and allowances for his Canadian colleague. The member of Congress also receives more than a dozen trips home a year at the taxpayer's expense, liberal telephone and postage allowances, low cost usage of television and recording studios, subsidized meals in the various restaurants and cafeterias on Capitol Hill, the use of a gymnasium and other recreational facilities built on the Hill for his patronage, low cost use of medical facilities at Walter Reed Hospital, and so on. The Canadian parliamentarian receives assistance for trips back to his constituency district and a modest sum for staff assistance, but falls far short of receiving the amenities available to his colleagues south of the border.

In the policy arena, even when Congress does pass a major piece of legislation submitted by the executive branch, it is much more likely than its Canadian counterpart to have amended that legislation substantially. In addition, Congress has much more influence over the government's purse strings, even though the major budgetary guidelines are formulated by the executive branch. For example, Congress eventually cut off assistance for American involvement in Indochina in the early 1970s and has occasionally refused to grant presidents funds for certain overseas activities. The president certainly has various options open to him in diverting funds from one executive program to another after Congress has rejected one of his proposals, but these options must be used sparingly and judiciously in order to avoid the wrath of Capitol Hill.

The U.S. Senate is also much more powerful than its Canadian counterpart and is perhaps the most powerful upper chamber in the world. Ironically, the Senate was also intended by the founding fathers to protect the interests of the propertied classes and, originally, the senators were not elected by the people. That was soon changed, however, and the Senate now plays a very important role in the revision of legislation submitted by the executive branch and several of its members are among the most prominent political figures in the United States. Not infrequently, a seat in the Senate has served as a stepping-stone to a cushioned chair in the White House Oval Office.

Although assuredly more powerful than the Canadian parliament in the overall policymaking process, the American Congress has had a tendency of disposing of executive initiatives without proposing its own constructive alternatives. In this respect, even though the Canadian cabinet can often steamroll its policy preferences through parliament, there is nonetheless more unity of purpose in Canada on what policies are needed and how they should be enacted. And if the cabinet begins to drift too far away from the desires of the Canadian electorate, the next general election usually remedies that situation.

The Judiciary

The Structure and Decision-Making Process

Although parliamentary supremacy is an avowed principle of the Canadian political system, the Canadian judicial branch has played a substantial role in the nation's political development through decisions related to civil rights, federal-provincial division of powers, economic regulations, taxation, and other related spheres. Moreover, even though the justices have been influential in the public policymaking arena, they are fairly much insulated from political pressure which might emanate from the executive and legislative sectors. Once selected, the justices receive a guaranteed salary and permanent tenure until the age of 70 or 75, depending on the level of the court. A justice can only be removed from his post by a joint Senate-House decision based solely on gross misbehavior.

Minor provincial courts are at the grassroots level of the Canadian judicial system and hear most of the cases which come before the judiciary (see Table

191

VI:5 for a chart of the judicial system). These minor courts include surrogate (probate), division, magistrate, juvenile, family, arbitration, and a few other sectors. In addition, these courts fall completely under the control and the maintenance of the provincial governments in terms of judicial appointments, remuneration, tenure, etc.

The county and district courts are the next higher echelon in the provinces and exercise original jurisdiction in fairly minor disputes. The highest court in the province is the provincial Supreme Court and it varies in size from one province to another. Normally, the Supreme Court is divided into appeals and trials divisions, with the former hearing appeals from the lower courts and the latter having original jurisdiction over specified cases. Although provincial legislatures are empowered to create and maintain courts within their areas of jurisdiction, judges at the county, district, and provincial Supreme Court levels are all paid by the federal government and appointments to the highest provincial courts are made by the federal cabinet and not by provincial authorities.

The two major judicial bodies in the federal system are the Federal Court and the Supreme Court of Canada. The Federal Court was created in 1970 and has both appeals and trials divisions. It includes a chief justice, associate justice, and up to ten other justices. It is basically concerned with cases in which the government is a party and is particularly interested in disputes involving air and maritime law. This court is unique in that its justices travel around the country hearing cases. Its appeals division will hear appeals of lower court decisions based on technicalities of the law. Its trial division is the court of original jurisdiction for matters involving customs, income taxes, patents, national defense, immigration, and a few other related areas.

The Canadian Supreme Court, which was established in 1875 by an act of parliament and which was not even mentioned in the BNA Act, is composed of one chief justice and eight associate justices. By statute, three of the justices must come from the Quebec bar and thus are trained in French civil law rather than the common law tradition of English Canada. The Supreme Court meets three times a year and remains in session

192

TABLE VI:5

THE CANADIAN JUDICIAL SYSTEM

Supreme Court of Canada

(1)   appellate jurisdiction
(2)   reference cases from federal cabinet

The Federal Court

(1)   appellate   division
      for   administrative
      tribunals
(2)   trial   division   for
      specialized cases

Provincial Supreme Courts

(1)   appellate division
(2)   original jurisdiction division

District or County Courts

(1)   appellate division
(2)   original criminal jurisdiction
(3)   original civil jurisdiction

Local Courts

(1)   small claims division
(2)   surrogate division
(3)   family division
(4)   criminal division
(5)   other divisions

normal appeal route

until all of the cases on the docket are settled. Only five justices are needed to form a quorum and conduct cases, and this number can be reduced to four if both litigants agree. In the case of certain appeals petitions, only three justices are needed to form a quorum. All nine justices are usually present only when constitutional and capital offense cases are heard.

Up until 1949, the court of final resort for selected cases in Canada was not the Canadian Supreme Court but the Privy Council of Great Britain. Since that time, however, the Supreme Court of Canada has exercised the final word on judicial issues. In addition, if federal or provincial authorities issue a formal request, the Canadian Supreme Court or lower courts may issue an opinion pertaining to the legality of certain provisions contained in forthcoming legislation.

Prime Minister Trudeau proposed in the late 1970s that the membership of the Supreme Court of Canada be expanded and that the provincial governments be given a voice in the nomination and the appointment of new justices. The rationale for this recommendation appears in Table VI:6.

A Comparison of the Canadian and
American Judicial Systems

The Canadian judicial system is in many respects unitary, whereas the American system is federal. Two distinct federal and state court systems exist in the United States with each system exercising jurisdiction over criminal and civil disputes. For example, the principle of double amenability exists in the United States and not in Canada. Although a person cannot be tried for the same crime twice (referred to as double jeopardy), a person may be tried in both the federal and state systems on closely related charges. To illustrate double amenability in action, a suspected murderer may be tried in a federal court for violating the civil rights of the victims, and then tried in a state court for the more serious charge of murder. In Canada, the federal government has the sole jurisdiction over criminal matters and an alleged lawbreaker would be subject to trial in only one court.

194

TABLE VI:6

THE FEDERAL GOVERNMENT'S PROPOSAL TO
EXPAND THE MEMBERSHIP OF THE
CANADIAN SUPREME COURT

The Supreme Court of Canada is the highest court in the land. Its jurisdiction covers all matters of constitutional, federal and provincial law.

Although one of Canada's basic institutions, it exists only by virtue of a federal law (The Supreme Court Act) that any majority in Parliament could repeal or change.

In order to provide a more appropriate status for the Court, the Government intends to make its composition, organization and role part of the Constitution of Canada, beyond the capacity of any single government to change unilaterally.

This change in the status of the Court is particularly important in view of the Government's intention to enshrine a Charter of Rights and Freedoms in the new Constitution. It would be the Court's new and heavy responsibility to apply and interpret that Charter in keeping with the spirit of the new Constitution.

The Government also intends to ensure that the Court adequately reflects Canada's regional diversity by (i) increasing the number of judges to 11 to permit a more balanced regional distribution of judges and (ii) providing provincial governments with a voice in nominations and appointments.

In this connection, it is proposed that there be four Supreme Court judges from the Quebec Bar, one more than now. The remaining seven positions would be filled so that there would always be at least one judge from each of four areas: the Atlantic Provinces, Ontario, the Prairie Provinces, and British Columbia.

Appointment to the Supreme Court would be made subsequent to agreement between the federal government and the relevant province. If no agreement is reached, then an impartial nominating council would be responsible for selection. The person finally selected

195

would have to be approved by the proposed House of the Federation where provincial interests would be represented.

The Court would continue to be the general Court of Appeal of Canada. However, the judges of the Court appointed from the Quebec Bar would be the sole judges of questions relating to Quebec civil law.

These changes are intended to enhance the unique role of the Supreme Court of Canada as an integral part of Canada's federal system. Strengthening the position of the Court in this manner will help to ensure that it remains a court of law based on the soundest traditions of the judicial process rendering justice freely and equitably, whether between citizen and citizen, citizen and government or government and government.

Source: Government of Canada, The Constitutional Amendment Bill, 1978: Explanatory Document, 1978.

The Canadian tradition of allowing the courts to give "opinions" to governmental authorities is not practiced south of the border. On the other hand, the U.S. Supreme Court exercises a much stronger judicial review power than its Canadian counterpart. Judicial review was never mentioned in the American constitution, but evolved as a result of the Marbury v. Madison decision rendered by Chief Justice John Marshall and the other members of the Supreme Court in 1803. Although lacking a constitutional base, judicial review is now taken for granted and permits the judicial branch to declare acts of the Congress, executive branch, or other public agencies as unconstitutional and thus null and void. Unlike the British Court system, the Canadian Supreme Court does exercise a limited judicial review power and both the Canadian and American courts have used this power effectively at times to enhance their own political clout.

The federal cabinet makes appointments for all federal and many provincial court openings, whereas the American president nominates candidates for federal judgeships who must then receive the approval of the Senate. For inclusion on the Canadian Supreme Court, a justice must have at least ten years of judicial experience. Aside from this qualification, religion, race, and party are also important criteria for selection, as they are in the United States. Normally, candidates to both Supreme Courts have solid reputations and long judicial experience. At the lower court levels, however, there are occasionally some questions about a nominee's qualifications. For example, in choosing people to sit on the federal district courts, the president invariably allows the senator from his own party from the state where the judge will preside to make the nomination. If there is no senator from his party in that state, then other state party officials will be consulted. Oftentimes, the nomination submitted is based on past service to the party rather than on the experience and expertise of the nominee. The Canadian selection process may be somewhat less blatant, but partisan considerations are undoubtedly important. The higher courts have also been dominated by males and it was not until the 1980s that government leaders in both Canada and the United States selected a woman to sit on the Supreme Court. Bertha Wilson became the first woman on the Canadian Supreme Court in 1982 and Sandra Day O'Connor was the first selected for America's highest court in 1981. Once seated, justices in the United States serve for life whereas members of Canada's Supreme Court must step down at age 75 and members of the Federal Court must resign at age 70.

The Canadian Supreme Court hears appreciably fewer cases than its American counterpart. Moreover, the fact that Canada's highest court must have three justices from Quebec who are steeped in the French civil code is another distinguishing feature of the Canadian court system. Moreover, all justices on the American Supreme Court must hear the cases which come before it, unless they are ill or have disqualified themselves because of possible conflicts of interest. In Canada, only a quorum of five, and even at times three for appeals petitions, is necessary to conduct the court's business.

Both systems depend fairly extensively on precedence (referred to as stare decisis) as a basis for making their rulings. In other words, earlier court decisions often serve as a guide for the

197

rendering of future decisions. In addition, both lower court systems look upon their respective Supreme Courts as providing guidance for decisions which the lower courts might be asked to make. Furthermore, both high courts serve as the courts of last resort for all judicial matters.

In addition, the Canadian jurists seem to be more in tune with a "strict constructionist" philosophy, whereas American jurists have at times been noted for their judicial activism. Strict constructionism means that constitutional or quasi-constitutional documents are interpreted in a very strict, legalistic fashion. In contrast, judicial activists may attempt to give documents written centuries ago a contemporary relevance. In essence, judicial activists are more likely to become embroiled in sensitive societal issues, such as busing, the death penalty, or abortion. On the other hand, the strict constructionists, who seem to be quite prominent in the Canadian system and who are certainly not absent in the American system, are less prone to delve into these policy issues, perceiving these issues as being in the domain of the lawmakers in the legislature. In effect, strict constructionists contend that their job is to determine what law is, not what law ought to be.

With the major revisions in Canada's constitution enacted in 1982 and the inclusion of a Charter of Rights and Freedoms, it is to be expected that the courts will play a much more influential role in determining future Canadian policy. Judicial review powers will be exercised much more frequently by the higher courts and the Supreme Court will be asked repeatedly to settle disputes between federal and provincial governments. For example, the courts have already struck down certain provisions in Quebec's controversial Bill 101, claiming they violate guarantees put forth in the Charter of Rights and Freedoms. Some Canadians lament the expanded role of the court system, insisting that important decisions should be left in the hands of public officials directly elected by and answerable to the Canadian voters. For these critics, major decisions should emanate from the federal parliament and provincial legislatures, or in major federal-provincial conferences attended by the elected representatives of the people. Provincial rights advocates also fear that the expanded power base of the federal court system will bring about greater centralization of authority in Canada. In spite of these fears and reservations, it is clear that the judicial system will now play a much more prominent role in the overall policy process in Canada and may eventually attain a power base comparable to that of the judicial branch in the United States.

NOTES

[1]Alan Cairns has asserted that federal-provincial interactions represent the real "essence" of Canadian governmental activities. He contends that "with rare exceptions, the anticipated reaction of the prime minister of Quebec is a more important factor in the decisions of the federal Cabinet than that of the Governor-General, and yet tradition induces the institutionally oriented political scientists to pay more attention to possible, but unlikely, conflicts between the Prime Minister and the Governor-General than to chronic conflicts with the provinces which at times threaten to tear the system apart." Quoted in Cairns, "Alternative Styles in the Study of Canadian Politics," Canadian Journal of Political Science, 7 (March 1974): 106.

[2]By-elections occur between general elections to fill vacancies in the House of Commons which have arisen because of the death or the resignation of certain MPs.

[3]Collective responsibility means that each minister will defend and take responsibility for decisions issued by the cabinet, even if he or she opposed the decision during cabinet deliberations. The notion of collective responsibility has its origins in the British governmental system.

[4]For the purpose of maintaining order, direct name-calling on the floor of the House is considered as taboo. However, the following incident illustrates how the members can introduce some excitement into an otherwise dull session: "On one occasion, Drummond Clancy was being raked over by another Member. After taking it for awhile, he finally got to his feet. 'Mr. Speaker,' he asked, properly addressing the Chair, 'would it be out of order if I called the honorable Member a S-O-B?' The Speaker nodded his head. 'I thought so,' said Clancy, resuming his seat." (Aiken, Backbencher, p. 66). In the heat of debate, Prime Minister Trudeau occasionally invited members of the opposition parties to step out in the parking lot to engage in a few rounds of fisticuffs. As far as can be determined, this verbal sparring never actually turned into an actual boxing match.

[5]Ibid., p. 8.

VII

CANADA IN THE WORLD, OR HOW TO SURVIVE
ON THE EDGE OF THE ELEPHANT PIT

The Foreign Policymaking Process

Foreign Policy at the Federal Level

Similar to a trend which has occurred in many
Western advanced industrial societies, foreign policy
in Canada has increasingly come under the direction and
the control of the chief executive and a few key
advisers. Prime Minister Trudeau has particularly
taken an active role in formulating the major foreign
policy guidelines for Canada and has had an abiding
interest in several ongoing projects related to the
foreign policy arena. In addition, Trudeau has
achieved a reputation as a world's statesman and has
been a major figure at many international conferences.

Much of the day-to-day logistical support given to
the prime minister in the area of foreign affairs is
provided by the Department of External Affairs.
Starting off with a handful of employees situated in a
modest office over a barber shop, this department now
employs close to 6,000 personnel in Canada and abroad.
Before World War II, Canada had diplomatic
representatives in the United Kingdom, the United
States, France, Japan, Belgium, and the Netherlands.
Today, Canada is represented in almost every recognized
nation in the world.

At times in the past, Canadian foreign
policymaking was apparently a fairly informal process,
as illustrated by the following story told by a
Dr. Gibson and involving former Canadian Prime Minister
W. L. MacKenzie King:

I remember one Saturday afternoon in
August, 1940, when in company with the then
United States Minister at Ottawa, Mr. King
drove at high speed from Ottawa to Prescott,
passed over the St. Lawrence by a special
trip of the Prescott-Ogdensburg ferry, and
met President Roosevelt and Mr. Henry L.
Stimson. Out of their discussions came the
Ogdensburg agreement, foreshadowing the
appointment of the Canadian-United States

201

permanent Joint Board of Defence. The first copy of the agreement which I saw was the single paragraph, mimeographed on plain paper aboard the President's special train. Some days later when I asked for an official copy which might be placed in the Departmental archives, I was told I already had it. So it was that a plain sheet, with Mr. King's notes in pencil, passed into foreign policy.[1]

The day-to-day conduct of foreign policy has now become much more complicated and much of the routine business is left in the hands of specialized personnel in the Department of External Affairs. On the other hand, prime ministers such as Diefenbaker, Pearson, and Trudeau have periodically functioned as their own "unofficial" External Affairs ministers and have been particularly assertive during crisis situations.[2]

The Cuban missile crisis provides us with some very good background information on how Canadian foreign policy has been handled during tense situations.[3] Whereas the United States had broken off diplomatic relations with Cuba and had imposed a trade embargo after Fidel Castro's takeover, Canada had continued to maintain relations with the Cuban regime and was not totally in agreement with Washington's antagonistic stance toward Castro. Following John F. Kennedy's famous 1962 speech announcing the placement of Russian missiles in Cuba and America's intention to force their withdrawal, Prime Minister John Diefenbaker decided not to support Kennedy's position immediately. Instead, Diefenbaker hoped that the problem could be resolved through the efforts of the United Nations.

Diefenbaker's dilemma was further complicated when Kennedy placed American forces in NORAD on alert. The United States and Canada are the two members of NORAD (the North American Air Defense Command), and the Americans expected that the Canadians would automatically join them on alert status. Diefenbaker, however, refused to issue a formal order placing his forces on alert until after he had thoroughly discussed the issue with his cabinet. But even after the cabinet had met, Diefenbaker delayed his decision, perhaps believing that Canadian public opinion was opposed to such a military escalation and that Washington had not provided Ottawa with sufficient information about the Cuban state of affairs.

202

The Canadian defense minister was not in agreement with Diefenbaker's stance and firmly believed that Canada was defaulting on its NORAD commitments. Acting on his own accord, the defense minister asked the Canadian forces to assume at least a semi-alert status. It has also been rumored that the Royal Canadian Air Force put itself into the same state of readiness as its American counterparts in NORAD "without waiting for orders."[4] Some critics who claim that Canada has been too subservient to the interests of the American superpower have seized upon this incident as support for their argument. In essence, they assert that when the chips were down, the Canadian defense establishment knew which voice to heed, the voice which came from south of the border.

Diefenbaker finally ordered Canadian troops on formal alert two days after American forces had assumed that status. Nonetheless, the incident indicates that Prime Minister Diefenbaker was much less supportive of American actions during the Cuban crisis than several other Western leaders. The incident also illustrates the difficulty in trying to conduct an independent foreign policy in the shadow of a superpower. In addition, the Cuban crisis shows that Diefenbaker was fairly dominant in determining Canada's role during the tense situation, even though he had received some noticeable resistance from his defense minister and a few other officials. Likewise, Kennedy was the forceful architect of America's strategy during the crisis, in spite of receiving some static from the navy concerning the deployment of the Cuban blockade.

Canada's expanded role in foreign affairs has largely been carried out under the direction of federal officials. Canada has been particularly active in Commonwealth and Third World activities and has provided peacekeeping missions in the post-World War II era to Kashmir, Palestine, Cyprus, the Sinai, Lebanon, West New Guinea, Yemen, Pakistan, and a few other regions of the world. The major thrust for Canada's "world presence" has undoubtedly come from the prime minister and the cabinet with the Department of External Affairs providing some of the necessary expertise and much of the logistical support.

In a major reorganization of the Department of External Affairs announced in 1982, trade and commercial activities were brought into the department and given a status equal to that of the diplomatic functions. This was done in recognition of the importance which international trade plays in Canada's economic growth. Canadian exports have grown from nearly 20 percent of Canada's total gross national product in 1970 to more than 25 percent in the early 1980s. Canada now ranks eighth in the world in terms of the total value of its exports and Canadian prosperity at home is increasingly linked to its ability to sell products in the United States and overseas. Indeed, an astounding 85 percent of Canada's total production of goods winds up in foreign markets.

Provincial "Foreign Relations"

An area of study which deserves further development by scholars is the foreign policy role played by the Canadian provinces. In the United States, the individual states must receive permission from Congress to enter into agreements with other state governments, let alone foreign countries. With rare exceptions, the American federal government has virtually monopolized the conduct of diplomatic relations with foreign nations, although state governments are increasingly involved in efforts to attract foreign investment and international trade opportunities. In comparison, the Länder in Western Germany may conclude treaties with other countries, but these agreements are subject to examination by federal authorities. In Switzerland, the cantons may negotiate foreign agreements if these pacts are not injurious to the integrity of the Swiss confederation. Only two such agreements have been made in recent years and the cantons have usually been content to allow the federal government in Bern to handle foreign affairs.

In Canada, however, the provincial governments have a much greater policy latitude than their American counterparts and some of the provinces have been actively involved in certain foreign policy spheres. In the 1960s, Quebec signed a series of educational and cultural agreements with the French government and certain other French-speaking countries. Ottawa was not particularly pleased with some of Quebec's initiatives and the Secretary of State for External Affairs finally conceded that direct negotiations between the provinces and foreign nations were constitutionally permissible but that the federal

204

government rejected the notion that the provinces could sign international agreements without Ottawa's approval.[5] A compromise between Ottawa and Quebec was finally reached and most of Quebec's international agreements were allowed to stand.

The powers of the provinces in foreign affairs have not as yet been clearly delineated, in spite of the uneasy truce which was worked out between the federal government and Quebec. Some critics, in fact, contend that if the provinces become too active in the foreign realm, the provincial-federal balance of power will be greatly jeopardized.[6] Nevertheless, Quebec, Ontario, Alberta, and British Columbia have established more than 40 liaison offices around the world for the purposes of attracting tourists and foreign investment and cultivating markets for the export of natural resources and manufactured products. Quebec, for example, has opened 22 offices outside of Canada, and the French government has accorded Quebec's delegations in Paris a status just below that of an embassy (see Table VII:1 for a list of the Quebec government's overseas offices). In addition, most of the provinces have entered into cooperative agreements with various American states, and Quebec has signed multi-billion dollar pacts with New York and the New England states for the sale by Hydro-Quebec of hydroelectric energy.[7] In recognition of the importance of economic ties with the United States and other countries, Quebec and Alberta have recently created Ministries of International Trade and it is to be expected that some of the other provinces will soon follow suit.

Thus, the problem of the degree to which the provinces should be involved in foreign affairs remains to be resolved. Section 132 of the constitution stipulates that "the Parliament and Government of Canada shall have all powers necessary or proper for performing the obligations of Canada or any province thereof, as part of the British empire, towards foreign countries, arising under treaties between the empire and such foreign countries." These guidelines worked quite well as long as Canada was part of the British empire, but due to the dismantlement of the empire, this provision has been rendered obsolete. Perhaps the best solution thus far presented to rectify the uncertainty of this situation is found in the recommendations made by a joint House of Commons-Senate committee, even though these recommendations fail to

205

TABLE VII:1

QUEBEC IN THE WORLD:
A LIST OF QUEBEC OFFICES OVERSEAS

Argentina
  Buenos Aires

Belgium
  Brussels

France
  Paris

Germany
  Dusseldorf

Haiti
  Port-au-Prince

Hong Kong
  Hong Kong

Italy
  Milan
  Rome

Ivory Coast
  Abidjan

Japan
  Tokyo

Mexico
  Mexico City

Portugal
  Lisbon

United Kingdom
  London

United States
  Atlanta
  Boston
  Chicago
  Dallas
  Lafayette, LA
  Los Angeles
  New York City
  Washington, D.C.

Venezuela
  Caracas

consider the special status of Quebec within the confederation.

1. Section 132 of the British North America Act should be replaced.
2. The Constitution should make it clear that the Federal Government has exclusive jurisdiction over foreign policy, the making of treaties, and the exchange of diplomatic and consular representatives.
3. All formal treaties should be ratified by Parliament rather than by the Executive Branch of Government.
4. The Government of Canada should, before binding itself to perform under a treaty an obligation that deals with a matter falling within the legislative competence of the Provinces, consult with the Government of each Province that may be affected by the obligation.
5. The Government of a Province should remain free not to take any action with respect to an obligation undertaken by the Government of Canada under a treaty unless it has agreed to do so.
6. Subject to a veto power in the Government of Canada in the exercise of its exclusive power with respect to foreign policy, the Provincial Governments should have the right to enter into contracts, and administrative, reciprocal and other arrangements with foreign states, or constituent parts of foreign states, to maintain offices abroad for the conduct of Provincial business, and generally to cooperate with the Government of Canada in its international activities.[8]

For the moment, however, these provisions have not been included in Canada's constitution and much uncertainty continues to exist concerning provincial activities overseas.

The Commonwealth Connection

In the pre-World War II period, Canada was much more involved in certain foreign activities than the isolationist-oriented United States, mainly because of its Commonwealth attachments. For example, Canada entered both world conflicts long before the United States in order to fight alongside the British. In 1939, Quebec Premier Maurice Duplessis denounced Canada's participation in an "imperialist war" and threatened to seek autonomy for his province. Nonetheless, Canada became Great Britain's senior ally during the crucial early war period and supplied the British with badly needed manufactured equipment. In order to placate the demands of the Quebec residents, the Canadian government pledged not to order conscription during the war, instead relying totally on volunteers. In a plebiscite held in April 1942, 80 percent of the voters in English Canada favored releasing the prime minister from his pledge not to order conscription, whereas 78 percent in Quebec voted against releasing him from his promise. The plebiscite vote aptly illustrates some of the internal divisions fomented by Canada's persistent British links.

Some French Canadians were also irritated by the continued use of British symbols in the modern era. For example, Canadians used British passports until World War II and, as mentioned previously, the British flag and national anthem were not dropped until the 1960s. Some Quebec residents also resented having Queen Elizabeth open the festivities for the 1976 Summer Olympic Games, an extravaganza which was held in the predominately French-speaking province of Quebec.

In spite of the lingering irritation felt by some because of the continuing reminders of the "British connection," Canada has undoubtedly played a major role in contemporary Commonwealth relations. Since the mid-1960s, the British have reassessed their own world commitments and have reluctantly resigned themselves to playing the role of a European regional power. Canada has helped fill the void caused by Great Britain's reassessment and has generally maintained very cordial relations with the developing nations within the Commonwealth structure. Even though it is numbered among the advanced industrial nations, Canada enjoys ready access to many Asian and African nations because of its traditional non-nuclear, middle power stance, its major role in world peacekeeping operations, and its commitment to international economic development. On a per capita basis, Canada's economic assistance to Third World nations is among the highest in the advanced industrial world, and Canadian leaders have been in the forefront in efforts to improve the so-called North-South dialogue between industrialized and developing nations. In 1981, Canada earmarked 0.42 percent of its gross national product for development assistance to Third World countries and multilateral agencies. This percentage is appreciably below that of the Netherlands (0.99 percent), Norway (0.82 percent), and Sweden (0.76 percent), but well above the 0.27 percent provided by the United States.[9] As a consequence, Canada's Commonwealth ties can no longer be construed as being simply a London-Ottawa linkage.

Canadian-American Relations: The Background

Canadian-American relations have usually been very friendly, but Pierre Trudeau was correct when he once stated that Canada faces special difficulties in sharing a continent with a superpower, as was aptly illustrated by the Cuban crisis. To paraphrase Trudeau, the mouse must always be much more careful than the elephant when they are sharing the same bed.

Relations have not always been particularly cordial between the two North American nations. American revolutionaries invaded Canada in 1775 and captured Montreal. These revolutionaries were disappointed, however, when Canadians did not flock to their cause and the forces were soon withdrawn from Canadian soil.[10]

Frankly, many Americans continued to yearn for expansion northward and public pressure undoubtedly helped to precipitate an American declaration of war against British Canada in 1812. But even as far back as 1778, John Adams warned in a letter to his cousin Samuel that "as long as Great Britain shall have Canada, Nova Scotia, and the Floridas, or any of them, so long will Great Britain be the enemy of the United States."[11] In a speech to Congress in 1810, Henry Clay of Kentucky insisted that "the conquest of Canada is in your power. I trust I shall not be deemed presumptuous when I state that the militia of Kentucky are alone competent to place Montreal and Upper Canada at your

feet."[12]   Felix Grundy, another Western congressman
from Tennessee, promised on the eve of the 1812 War
that:

> We shall drive the British from our
> continent--they will no longer have an
> opportunity of intriguing with our Indian
> neighbors, and setting on the ruthless savage
> to tomahawk our women and children.   That
> nation will lose her Canadian trade, and, by
> having no resting place in this country, her
> means of annoying us will be diminished.[13]

The opinions of these two notable congressmen were
indicative of the feelings of many who felt that God's
manifest destiny for the United States was expansion
from the Atlantic to the Pacific and from Panama to the
North Pole.   The United States, however, was very
fortunate to emerge from the War of 1812 with its own
territory intact.   The Americans did manage to burn
down York (now Toronto), but the war went miserably for
the Americans and the British finally reciprocated by
burning down Washington, D.C.

In 1818, the United States and Great Britain
finally agreed that the 49th parallel from Lake
Superior to the Rockies would serve as the permanent
boundary between the two North American neighbors.
James Polk later warned that the boundary running from
the Rockies to the Pacific would have to be extended
northward to the 54th parallel or America might have to
resort to warfare.   However, the American chief
executive eventually cast aside his pugnacious attitude
and agreed to a British offer in 1846 to extend the
boundary along the 49th parallel all the way to the
Pacific.

The next serious period of potential confrontation
between the two neighbors occurred during the American
Civil War.   Great Britain's tacit support of the
Confederacy proved to be a very unwise move and rumors
were rampant that the Union forces would seize Canada
as an act of reprisal.[14]   America was literally an
armed camp at the time and, most likely, Canada could
have been seized from the British.   The founders of the
confederation were quite aware of this and pushed for
Canadian independence from Great Britain as a way of
softening the American resolve to take over Canada.   In
fact, Lord Durham had suggested 20 years prior to the

Civil War that a Canadian confederation "might in some measure counterbalance the preponderant and increasing influence of the United States on the American continent."[15]

Several raids were actually launched against Canada from American territory in the period 1864-1871. The Fenians were Irish extremists who had nothing but ill feelings for the British and believed that Canada should be forcefully removed from the British empire. Their raids caused some embarrassing exchanges between Ottawa and Washington, but Canada's territorial integrity was never seriously threatened.

A few decades later, Teddy Roosevelt had his own ideas about a proper boundary line which should be established between Alaska and Canada. Roosevelt's line of demarcation included a huge chunk of disputed territory, and many Canadians were opposed to his proposition. Nonetheless, the British were in charge of the negotiations with Washington and Roosevelt was granted pretty much what he had demanded. Some Canadians were quite irritated by the agreement, believing that Canadian interests had been sacrificed for the sake of more cordial Anglo-American relations.

There were few major squabbles between the two nations in the years following Roosevelt's power play, and Warren G. Harding eventually became the first American leader to visit Canada in 1923. In a speech before a Vancouver audience, Harding declared that "we profit both mentally and materially from the fact that we have no 'departed greatness' to recover, no 'lost provinces' to regain, no new territory to covet, no ancient grudges to gnaw eternally at the heart of our National consciousness."[16]

Harding was essentially correct in his assessment of the situation, although some minor "gnawing at the heart" has occurred since his presidency. For example, Canadians were especially irritated with the Smoot-Hawley Tariff of 1931 which precipitously raised tariff rates on the import of Canadian raw materials. In addition, Canadians were less than ecstatic 40 years later when Richard Nixon placed a surcharge on Canadian and other foreign products. On the whole, however, friendly interactions have long typified Canadian-American relations.

Contemporary Canadian-American Relations

Foreign Policy Differences

Although relations are indeed solid between the two North American neighbors, Canada understandably has foreign policy goals which are distinct from those of the United States. Unfortunately, many Americans believe that American-Canadian interests in world affairs are synonymous and what the United States espouses in foreign affairs will ultimately prove to be beneficial for Canada. Thus when Canada seems to differ with the United States on certain policy goals, some Americans are keenly disappointed.

Canada and the United States do share memberships in such organizations as the North Atlantic Treaty Organization (NATO) and NORAD and have both favored strong cooperation among the Western nations in defense arrangements. On the other hand, Prime Minister Trudeau decided several years ago that it was in Canada's best interests to reduce its troop commitments in Europe and to cut down on defense allocations in general. Although pledging continued membership in NATO, Trudeau's withdrawal of Canadian troops displeased the United States and most of the Western European allies as well.

Moreover, many Canadians were not in agreement with the U.S. Indochinese policy of the 1960s and early 1970s and the Canadian government allowed draft resisters to seek asylum north of the border. Canada also maintained good relations with Havana and had fairly cordial ties with Peking during a period when the United States had no formal diplomatic ties with either capital. The U.S. Congress eventually passed legislation which forbade American-based companies and their foreign affiliates from trading with these nations. Many of America's multinational corporations have subsidiaries in Canada and most Canadians were infuriated when the U.S. government sought compliance from these businesses located on Canadian soil.

The Cultural Challenge

Aside from the differences in foreign policy priorities, Canadians have also become increasingly concerned with the American cultural influence on

212

Canadian society. In 1971, Prime Minister Trudeau received a petition containing 175,000 signatures which called for a governmental commitment to decrease American influence in Canada. In addition, a Committee for an Independent Canada was established and claimed a membership of 250,000 in 1973.

As a Canadian Senate committee report indicates, the United States has ten times the population and ten times the gross national product (GNP) of Canada and "because of this disparity, Canada is more dependent, more sensitive, and more vulnerable to the state of the relationship than is the United States. For Canada, it is by far the most important of all its external relationships."[17] America's cultural influence is much greater than Canada's, and when one takes into account that a vast majority of all Canadians live within 100 miles of the American border, it is not too surprising that Canadians are inundated with American television programs. For example, only 20 percent of the television programming available in Vancouver in 1983 was of Canadian origin and it was about the same in most other parts of Canada. Even a good share of the programs appearing on Quebec television is comprised of American productions which had been dubbed into French.

In addition, an overwhelming percentage of films shown in Canadian movie houses are from Hollywood. In recent years, foreign films have accounted for more than 90 percent of all box office receipts, foreign magazines for more than 80 percent of the total magazine circulation, and foreign books for more than 80 percent of the total book sales in Canada. Most of these foreign-made items were produced in the United States.

Some Canadians have complained that Canadian cultural values are rapidly being submerged by the American cultural onslaught. As the head of the Canadian Broadcasting Corporation (CBC) once asserted:

> Official public policies have had the effect of increasing the viewing of American programs and thus we have invited into Canada the American value system, American heroes, American institutions and American touchstones. . . .

213

No country in the world allows or
encourages the massive intrusion of foreign
culture that Canada does.
We have what amounts to governmental and
public indifference to invasion by a foreign
culture. . . .
This has led to, among other things, the
importation of massive doses of U.S.
programming with its frequent emphasis on
violence and materialism through the
scheduling of fast-paced, action-oriented,
maximum 'jolts-per-minute' American
entertainment programming. . . .[18]

The CBC has pledged to dramatically increase
Canadian content on its network and official
encouragement has been given by the government for the
production of more Canadian programs. However,
progress has been slow and Canadian viewers have shown
a preference for American programs, largely because
these programs have much larger production budgets than
their Canadian counterparts. Ottawa has also moved to
penalize Canadian companies which place advertisements
on American television stations transmitting signals
into Canada. This Canadian government action, which
eliminates tax advantages for such advertising, was
prompted by the loss of revenues experienced by
Canadian-based stations because of the placement of
advertisements on stations south of the border.
However, Canada actually lost more revenue than it
gained from this policy because the U.S. Congress
retaliated by not allowing Americans to write off
expenses for conventions held in Canada.

The Canadian government also demanded in the
mid-1970s that two of the most popular magazines sold
in Canada, the Reader's Digest and Time Canada,
increase their Canadian content or Canadian advertisers
in these magazines would be penalized through tax
legislation. The Canadian edition of Reader's Digest
has been allowed to continue publication because the
owners pledged to improve that magazine's Canadian
content. But in March 1976, Time Canada ceased
publication altogether. Nonetheless, the regular
edition of Time prepared for the U.S. market continues
to be sold in Canada and is a financial success.
Canadian publishers definitely continue to face many
problems in trying to compete with the larger American
enterprises. As a special Canadian Senate report on

214

the mass media has noted, "we spend more money buying American comic books than we do on seventeen leading Canadian-owned magazines."[19]

The government has also taken an active role in encouraging the production of movies in Canada. A Film Development Corporation has been established to provide some financial assistance for the private production of feature films. Generous tax incentives are also being extended to investors who put up money for the production of films in Canada and several major movies have been made in Canada during the past few years. In the literary field, some Canadian authors have also been accorded government assistance for the publication of their materials.

The Canadian government has thus been quite involved in trying to "repatriate" the Canadian culture, and more Canadians than ever before are now sensitized to the need to foster a distinctive Canadian identity. On the other hand, economy of scale and a consumer preference for many American products have combined to make the government's goal difficult to achieve. Moreover, it is fairly easy to pinpoint the major characteristics of the French Canadian culture, but Canadians are still befuddled concerning what are the distinctive ingredients of the English Canadian culture and how should these cultural characteristics be protected from the dominant English language culture south of the border.

The Economic and Environmental Challenges

As Table VII:2 clearly illustrates, the United States and Canada far outdistance all of the other nations in the world in terms of the percentage of trade with each other. Moreover, a large segment of Canada's manufacturing sphere is owned by foreign investors, mainly Americans (see Table VII:3 for Canadian-American foreign direct investment). To be more precise, more than 50 percent of the Canadian manufacturing sector is foreign controlled, as are more than 50 of the 100 largest corporations in the manufacturing, resources, and utilities fields. Over 60 percent of Canada's pivotal oil and natural gas industry is also foreign-controlled and American-controlled companies produce and refine more than 70 percent of Canadian petroleum products (see

215

TABLE VII:2
TRADING STATISTICS

Nation	Exports as % Gross Domestic Product[1]	Imports as % Gross Domestic Product[1]	Trading Nation Providing Largest % of Imports[2]	Trading Nation Receiving Largest % of Exports[2]
Canada	25.6%	23.3%	USA - 67.4%	USA - 66.5%
Australia[2]	15.8	14.4	USA - 20.8	Japan - 28.8
France	17.1	20.7	W. Germany - 19.5	W. Germany - 17.5
Ireland	47.8	62.7	U.K. - 50.7	U.K. - 54.7
Japan	12.5	13.6	USA - 20.4	USA - 23.3
New Zealand	23.3	23.5	Australia - 24.6	U.K. - 24.5
Poland	N.A.	N.A.	USSR - 24.4	USSR - 32.4
USSR	N.A.	N.A.	E. Germany - 11.4	E. Germany - 10.4
U.K.	22.0	23.0	USA - 9.5	USA - 10.6
USA	8.5	9.3	Canada - 22.1	Canada - 20.2
West Germany	23.4	22.7	Netherlands - 14.2	France - 11.9

[1]Goods only using 1980 statistics at current prices
[2]Based on 1973-1974 statistics

Sources: U.N. International Trade Statistics, 1974, Vol. 1, and OECD Observer, March 1982.

TABLE VII:3

CANADIAN-AMERICAN
FOREIGN DIRECT INVESTMENT

Foreign Direct Investment ($ millions U.S.)

1970

Can
In US   3,117

US In   21,015
Can

1975

Can
In US   5,352

US In   31,038
Can

1980

Can
In US   9,810

US In   44,640
Can

Source: Statistical Abstract of the United States,
         1981.

Table VII:4 for foreign direct investment by industry and country). In addition, about 50 percent of the trade union members in Canada belong to American-based "international organizations."

Some Canadians worry that Canada is being mortgaged to the hilt to American investors who in the process acquire a disproportionate influence over Canadian economic development. Others point out that many companies now situated in Canada are "truncated" branch plants of American firms with money for vital research and development normally remaining at the firms' headquarters in the United States. In response to some of these complaints, the Canadian government has vetoed a few proposed American takeovers of Canadian firms. For example, the cabinet met in special session in 1970 and decided to disallow an American offer to buy the Denison Mines. In 1973, a law was passed which established the Foreign Investment Review Agency (FIRA), an organization which screens proposed foreign investments and recommends to the federal cabinet the denial of investment proposals which might be detrimental to Canadian interests. Some critics of this board claim that the FIRA standards are so lax that "the only U.S. business which wouldn't be cordially welcomed to Canada is Murder, Inc."[20] On the other hand, FIRA has turned down some proposals and has made all potential investors aware that compliance with certain standards is expected before foreign investment in Canada will be permitted.

American officials have bitterly complained that FIRA uses arbitrary and secretive methods for determining the acceptability of investment proposals and violates free trade and investment provisions accepted by members of the General Agreement on Tariffs and Trade (GATT) and the Organization for Economic Cooperation and Development (OECD). Both the United States and Canada are active members of GATT and the OECD.

Washington's ire was rekindled even further when Ottawa introduced in 1981 the National Energy Program (NEP). The NEP is designed to reduce foreign ownership of Canada's oil and natural gas industry to no greater than 50 percent by 1990. This goal is to be achieved by providing Canadian-controlled companies with lucrative government incentives for oil and natural gas exploration and development, while denying many of

TABLE VII:4

FOREIGN DIRECT INVESTMENT
IN CANADA, 1978

By Industry Group
1. Manufacturing
2. Petroleum and
   natural gas
3. Financial
4. Mining and
   smelting
5. Merchandising
6. Utilities
7. Other

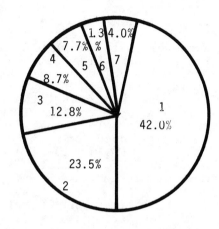

By area of ownership
1. United States
2. United Kingdom
3. All other
   countries

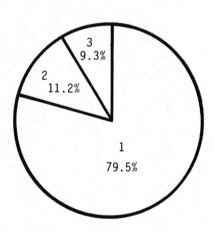

Source: Statistics Canada, Canada's International
Investment Position, 1971-1973.

219

these same incentives to companies which are controlled by foreign owners.[21] Because of these discriminatory practices, a few American and other foreign firms have abandoned the Canadian market. The U.S. government has denounced the NEP for its alleged anti-free market and anti-free trade provisions and several members of Congress have threatened retaliation. However, such threats are rarely transformed into actual laws. Moreover, with the deep recession of the late 1970s and early 1980s which left the Canadian economy in much poorer shape than the American, some of the more strident FIRA and NEP policies and procedures have been toned down. Eight of the ten provincial premiers also voted in 1982 to ask Ottawa either to temporarily or permanently close down FIRA because Canada was in desperate need of job-creating investments and the image of FIRA in the United States and elsewhere was hindering provincial efforts to attract this much-needed investment.

Washington and Ottawa have also been at odds over environmental issues. Because pollution is no respecter of borders, contaminants which adversely impact the environment in one country may quickly spread to the neighboring nation. For example, the two nations share the Great Lakes which form the largest single fresh water system in the world and account for one-fifth of all of the fresh water in lakes around the globe. More than 20 million people depend on the Great Lakes for their drinking water. However, more than 400 different industrial chemicals have been identified in the lakes and regardless of whether the source of each contaminant was in the United States or Canada, people on both sides of the border are negatively affected. An agreement to begin cleaning up the Great Lakes was signed between the two North American governments in 1978, but many Canadians feel that Washington has been much too slow in implementing its part of the pact.

Tensions between the two capitals have also been fairly high as a result of the acid rain controversy. Acids do occur naturally in the atmosphere and have always fallen to earth in precipitation, but nature's own system was able to neutralize most of the negative consequences of acidity. However, sulfur dioxide and nitrogen oxide emitted from smokestacks combine with moisture in the air to create dangerous levels of sulfuric and nitric acids. Both types of acids destroy plant and animal cells on contact and have caused

220

tremendous environmental damage in various parts of North America. For example, fish and various types of vegetation are now extinct in hundreds of lakes in the Adirondack region of New York and the Sudbury region of Ontario.

These dangerous acids usually originate in the burning of fossil fuels for electricity and for the smelting of ore. Although the contamination almost invariably occurs in areas of heavy industrialization, acid rain is carried downwind and may travel several hundred miles in a day. The problem may be greatly reduced by installing efficient emission devices on the smokestacks, but this remedy is very expensive.

The Canadian government has taken a forceful stance on this issue and its policies have already reduced harmful stack emissions by 25 percent over the past decade with another 25 percent decrease promised over the next decade. However, it is estimated that 50 percent or more of Canada's acidic rainfall comes from U.S. sources, whereas only 15 percent of acid rain in the United States emanates from Canada. Ottawa has therefore urged Washington to join in a cooperative project to reduce acid rain by cracking down on polluters and mandating that emission control devices be installed. Coal-burning facilities operated by utilities in the American Midwest would be the main targets if Canadian officials had their way. For its part, Washington has dragged its feet on the issue, claiming that acid rain must be subjected to greater scientific study before American industries and utilities are asked to spend billions of dollars for clean-up operations. U.S. federal officials also warn that the Canadian plan would cost thousands of American jobs in an era of high unemployment.

Canadian officials reject this line of argumentation and claim that increasing environmental damage on both sides of the border will be much more costly in the long run than the expense involved in cleaning up the sources of acid rain. Ottawa has spent hundreds of thousands of dollars in the United States on lobbying and advertising campaigns trying to convince Americans of the dangers of acid rain. In the summer of 1982, an environmental committee in the U.S. Senate voted 15 to 0 for a program which would order utility plants in 31 states east of the Mississippi River to gradually reduce emissions of sulphur dioxide.

221

However, as of mid-1983, this committee recommendation had not become law and little of substantive value has as yet been done by the U.S. government to combat acid rain.

Generally, Canadians perceive that relations between the United States and Canada have become somewhat less cordial in recent years and that the "special relationship" between the two countries has somewhat diminished. When asked in 1966 if they felt that Canada and the United States had been drawing closer together or getting further apart, 33 percent of those surveyed stated closer together, 8 percent further apart, and 59 percent no change or could not say. Ten years later, only 19 percent felt that the two nations had drawn closer together and 38 percent stated that they had moved further apart, with 43 percent not noticing any change or could not say.[22] Some Americans have also perceived that Canada and the United States have been drifting further apart. In an editorial which appeared in 1977, American publisher Walter Annenberg decried the fact that Time Canada had ceased publication and that the Canadian government was pushing for a much higher percentage of Canadian produced programs to be shown on Canadian television. In view of this turn of events and the earlier harboring of American "draft dodgers," Annenberg concluded that Canada was acting like an "unfriendly nation." As for plans to construct a pipeline through Canada in order to supply Canadian and American cities with oil and natural gas, Annenberg bluntly opposed the project. Instead, he recommended that the United States ship the oil from Alaska by freighter and not be dependent at all on Canadian goodwill.[23]

Most Americans would not share the intensity of Annenberg's feelings. In fact, the great majority of Americans has probably not taken the time to think one way or the other about the state of Canadian-American relations. Nonetheless, Canadian-American relations may well have entered a different phase in which "friendly" differences of opinion will persist. Just the same, solid relations still exist between Washington and Ottawa, and between the American and Canadian people. For example, it was personnel in the Canadian Embassy who offered shelter to Americans who escaped during the takeover of the U.S. Embassy in Iran and later helped them to flee from that country.

Canadians should rightfully consider that Americans would do the same if the circumstances were reversed.

Canada--The Middle Power

Canada is essentially a middle power which is capable of playing an extensive, nonmilitary role in world affairs. During the early years of Trudeau's administration, Canadian decision-makers considered that three major options were available to Canada in the field of foreign affairs. The first option was to continue existing policies which were closely identified with American foreign policy priorities. The second option was to move closer to the United States and perhaps establish a free trade area with the southern neighbor. The third option was to stress closer ties with other countries in the world and thus reduce Canada's vulnerability to developments which might occur in the United States.

Canadian officials opted for the third choice, which has tactfully been defined as a policy of "living distinct from but in harmony with the United States."[24] In 1969, Canada began extensive efforts to establish diplomatic relations with China during a period when Sino-American ties were almost nonexistent. Two years later, Trudeau became the first Canadian prime minister ever to visit Moscow. During the same year as the Russian trip, Trudeau unilaterally announced that Canada was reducing its NATO commitment by half. In addition, Canada initiated a strenuous policy of improving trade links with Western and Eastern Europe and Japan. Nonetheless, Canada's economic dependence on the United States remains as great today as it was when the Third Option was first introduced. Indeed, almost 70 percent of all Canadian imports and exports are linked directly to the United States.

Canada has also significantly decreased the size of its military forces and the percentage of GNP earmarked for defense purposes (see Tables VII:5 and VII:6 for a comparative look at the number of armed forces personnel and military expenditures). Indeed, of all of the NATO countries, only tiny Luxembourg spends less per capita on defense than Canada. Whereas Canada had 150,000 troops in uniform in the late 1940s, in 1983 its armed forces numbered 83,000. This troop strength is smaller than either the Netherland's or

TABLE VII:5

ARMED FORCES PERSONNEL PER 1,000
POPULATION, 1970-1978

Country	1970	1974	1978
Canada	4.5	3.6	3.4
Australia	6.8	5.0	4.9
France	11.2	11.0	9.4
Japan	2.3	2.2	2.1
Netherlands	8.8	7.8	7.2
South Africa	1.8	1.8	2.9
USSR	17.7	17.9	18.4
UK	6.8	6.3	5.7
USA	15.0	10.2	9.6
West Germany	8.4	8.1	8.0
World Total	6.9	6.8	6.2

Source: Statistical Abstract of the United States, 1981, p. 895, adapted from U.S. Arms Control and Disarmament Agency, World Military Expenditures and Arms Transfers, Annual.

TABLE VII:6

MILITARY EXPENDITURES, 1970-1978

Country	1970 % GNP	1970 Per Capita[1]	1978 % GNP	1978 Per Capita
Canada	2.4	161	2.0	174
Australia	3.4	208	2.6	189
France	4.2	238	3.9	289
Japan	0.8	37	0.9	57
Netherlands	3.4	218	3.3	250
South Africa	2.3	31	4.2	59
USSR	13.6	457	12.2	547
UK	4.7	185	4.8	215
USA	7.9	586	5.1	460
West Germany	3.3	245	3.3	302
World Total	6.3	105	5.4	103

[1]Expressed in constant (1977) US dollars

Source: Statistical Abstract of the United States, 1981, p. 894, adapted from U.S. Arms Control and Disarmament Agency, World Military Expenditures and Arms Transfers, Annual.

Belgium's, even though Canada is 155 times larger geographically than these two European nations combined and is strategically located from a polar vantage point between the United States and the Soviet Union. Canadian officials seem to be counting on Canada's geographical location and traditionally friendly ties with the United States as justification for slicing the military budget and diverting the money saved to the domestic social sector. In spite of deemphasizing its military role, Canada remains an active member of NATO and NORAD and apparently most Canadians have no desire to leave these defense organizations.[25]

As is the case with many people around the world, Canadians hope that the global economy will rebound because in an age of increasing economic interdependency, improved productivity and market conditions in the United States and elsewhere will help to brighten Canadian economic prospects. In the spring of 1983, the Canadian unemployment rate was well above 12 percent, the highest since the Great Depression, and its inflation rate was appreciably above that of the United States. Moreover, the value of the Canadian dollar stood close to an historical low vis-à-vis the American dollar and Canada faced the specter during the mid-1980s of annual federal government budget deficits of 30 billion dollars (Canadian) or more, an extremely high figure for a nation of 24 million people. High government deficits mean that an increasingly large chunk of government revenues will have to go to pay for the interest on the federal debt, which will be over 150 billion dollars (Canadian) by the end of the 1984 fiscal year. This debt represents about 36 percent of Canada's GNP, whereas the federal debt in 1973 amounted to only 21 percent of the GNP. In view of these major problem areas, economic issues will certainly dominate Canada's future agenda in both the domestic and international spheres.

Canada was once referred to in one of its leading newspapers as "a fat cat in a suffering world."[26] In spite of current economic woes, this statement is still essentially correct when one takes into account the high standard of living, democratic government, and rich mineral and food deposits to be found in this vast country. Nevertheless, Canada has assumed a very active role in many Third World regions as well as being a participant at major summit meetings of the other "fat cats." Canada has thus far shown quite clearly that it can exist next to the elephant pit and still pursue a distinctive foreign policy which is aimed at satisfying Canadian needs and at promoting a safer, more prosperous international society.

[1]Recounted in R. Barry Farrell, The Making of Canadian Foreign Policy (Scarborough: Prentice-Hall, 1969), p. 11.

[2]Diefenbaker, for example, twice held the portfolio for External Affairs in his own hands for 12-week periods.

[3]For a very good account of Canadian activities during the Cuban crisis, consult Peyton Lyon, Canada in World Affairs, 1961-1963 (Toronto: Oxford University Press, 1968).

[4]Ibid., p. 53. This incident was reported by Clive Baxter of the Financial Post.

[5]For an informative look at provincial foreign relations, see Howard A. Leeson and Wilfried Vanderelst, External Affairs and Canadian Federalism: The History of a Dilemma (Toronto: Holt, Rinehart and Winston, 1973).

[6]See, for example, Ronald G. Atkey, "The Role of the Provinces in International Affairs," International Journal, 26 (Winter 1970-71): 249-273.

[7]For state-provincial relations, consult Roger Frank Swanson, State/Provincial Interaction: A Study of Relations Between U.S. States and Canadian Provinces Prepared for the U.S. Department of State (Washington, D.C.: Canus Research Institute, 1974).

[8]Leeson and Vanderelst, External Affairs, pp. iv-v. For more information concerning provincial activities of an international nature, see Earl H. Fry, "Provincial Politics and Canadian Foreign Policy: The Transgovernmental Linkages of Quebec and Alberta," in Wayne G. Reilly, ed., Encounter with Canada: Essays in the Social Sciences (Durham, N.C.: Duke University Center for International Studies, 1980), pp. 102-120.

[9]OECD Observer, March 1982, p. 26.

[10]A few Canadians at one time or another flirted with joining the United States. For example, a group of English-speaking merchants from Montreal issued a manifesto in 1849 which argued that the best remedy for

Canada's economic problems was "a friendly and peaceful separation from British connection and a union upon equitable terms with the great North American confederacy of sovereign states." To say the least, this proposal did not elicit widespread support among other sectors of Canadian society. In the late 1970s, two members of the Saskatchewan legislature also called for unification with the United States. These two members failed to survive the next election.

[11]Robert H. Divine, ed., American Foreign Policy: A Documentary History (New York: Meridian Books, 1960), p. 29.

[12]Ibid., p. 50.

[13]Ibid., p. 53.

[14]Great Britain and the Union came close to going to war during the conflict. In November 1861, the U.S. warship San Jacinto stopped the British steamer Trent near the Bahamas and arrested two Confederate envoys to Great Britain. The British reacted by sending a regiment of troops to Canada. The envoys were eventually released.
Great Britain, which desired the South's cotton and other raw materials, allowed two warships to be built for the Confederacy in English shipyards. However, the British eventually saw the handwriting on the wall and gradually withdrew their commitments to the South.

[15]Janet Morchain, Sharing a Continent (Toronto: McGraw-Hill Ryerson, 1973), p. 120.

[16]Quoted in Roger Frank Swanson, ed., Canadian-American Summit Diplomacy, 1923-1973 (Ottawa: McClelland and Stewart, 1975), p. 313.

[17]Standing Senate Committee on Foreign Relations, Canada-United States Relations, vol. 1 (Ottawa: Queen's Printer, 1975), p. 7.

[18]This quote from CBC President Al Johnson appeared in the Vancouver Sun, 14 June 1977, p. 2.

[19]Special Senate Committee on the Mass Media, Report, vol. 1 (Ottawa: Queen's Printer, 1970), p. 156.

[20]See Abraham Rotstein, "Canada: The New Nationalism,," Foreign Affairs, 55 (October 1976):100. This quote originally appeared in a Barron's article.

[21]For an in-depth study of the National Energy Program, see Earl H. Fry, ed., Energy Development in Canada: The Political, Economic, and Continental Dimensions (Provo, Utah: Brigham Young University Center for International and Area Studies, 1981).

[22]Gallup Report, February 21, 1976.

[23]Annenberg's editorial originally appeared in the American edition of one of his own publications, TV Guide. The editorial was reprinted in the Vancouver Sun, 27 May 1977, p. 5.

[24]Standing Senate Committee on Foreign Relations, Canada-United States, p. 8.

[25]Canadians who were interviewed in a 1976 poll were asked the following question: "Some commentators have suggested that Canada withdraw from the North Atlantic Treaty Organization (NATO), cancel its joint defense agreement with the United States, and adopt a policy of neutrality. Would you agree or disagree with this proposal?" Twenty-three percent of the respondents agreed, 57 percent disagreed, and 20 percent had no opinion (see the Gallup Report, June 19, 1976).

[26]Toronto Globe and Mail, 30 September 1974, p. 7.

BIBLIOGRAPHY

I. Canada in Comparative Perspective

A. The Comparative Dimension

Albinski, Henry S. Canadian and Australian
Politics in Comparative Perspective. New
York: Oxford University Press, 1973.

Albinski, Henry S., ed. Perspectives on
Revolution and Evolution. Durham, N.C.:
Duke University Press, 1979.

Almond, Gabriel A. "Comparative Political
Systems." Journal of Politics 18 (August
1956): 391-409.

Blondel, J. Comparative Legislatures.
Englewood Cliffs: Prentice-Hall, 1973.

Hawkins, Freda. "Multiculturalism in Two
Countries: The Canadian and Australian
Experience." Journal of Canadian Studies
17 (Spring 1982):64-80.

Lammers, William W., and Nyomarkay, Joseph L.
"The Canadian Cabinet in Comparative
Perspective." Canadian Journal of
Political Science 15 (March 1982):29-46.

Lijphart, Arend. "Consociational Democracy."
World Politics 21 (January 1969):207-225.

Lipset, S. M. "Revolution and Counter-
Revolution: The United States and
Canada." The Canadian Political Process:
A Reader, 2nd ed. Edited by Orest
Kruhlak, Richard Schultz, and Sidney
Pobihuschchy. Toronto: Holt, Rinehart
and Winston, 1973, pp. 3-29.

McAllister, Ian. Regional Development and
the European Community: A Canadian
Perspective. Montreal: Institute for
Research on Public Policy, 1982.

231

Michalos, Alex C. North American Social Report: A Comparative Study of the Quality of Life in Canada and the USA from 1964 to 1974. Dordrecht, Netherlands: D. Reidel, 1980.

Teichman, Judith. "Businessmen and Politics in the Process of Economic Development: Argentina and Canada." Canadian Journal of Political Science 15 (March 1982):47-66.

B. A General Overview of Canadian Politics and Government

Beaujot, Roderic P. Growth and Dualism: The Demographic Development of Canadian Society. Toronto: Gage, 1982.

Butler, Eric D. The Battle for Canada. Flesherton, Ont.: Canadian League of Rights, 1981.

Cairns, Alan C. "Alternative Styles in the Study of Canadian Politics." Canadian Journal of Political Science 7 (1974):101-128.

Creighton, Donald. The Story of Canada. Toronto: Macmillan, 1971.

Dreijmanis, John. Canadian Politics, 1950-1975: A Selected Research Bibliography. Monticello, Ill: Council of Planning Librarians, 1976.

Fawcett, Margot J., and Malmo, Gail L., eds. Corpus Almanac of Canada. Toronto: Corpus, yearly.

Fox, Paul W. Politics: Canada, 5th ed. Toronto: McGraw-Hill Ryerson, 1982.

Hockin, Thomas A. Government in Canada. New York: Norton, 1975.

McFadden, Fred. _Canada, the 20th Century_. Don Mills, Ont.: Fitzhenry & Whiteside, 1982.

McInnes, Edgar. _Canada: A Political and Social History_, 4th ed. Toronto: Holt, Rinehart and Winston, 1982.

Redekop, John. _Approaches to Canadian Politics_. Scarborough: Prentice-Hall, 1978.

Reilly, Wayne G., ed. _Encounter with Canada: Essays in the Social Sciences_. Durham, N.C.: Duke University Center for International Studies, 1980.

Ricker, John, and Saywell, John. _How Are We Governed?_ Toronto: Clarke, Irwin, 1977.

Saywell, John., ed. _Canadian Annual Review of Politics and Public Affairs_. Toronto: University of Toronto Press, yearly.

Schlesinger, Benjamin. _What about Poverty in Canada?_ Toronto: University of Toronto Press, 1982.

Schultz, Richard; Kruhlak, Orest M.; and Terry, John C. _The Canadian Political Process_, 3rd ed. Toronto: Holt, Rinehart, and Winston of Canada, 1979.

Van Loon, Richard J., and Whittington, Michael S. _The Canadian Political System: Environment, Structure, and Process_, 3rd ed. Toronto: McGraw-Hill Ryerson, 1981.

II. The Canadian Heritage

Bothwell, Robert; Drummond, Ian; and English, John. _Canada Since 1945: Power, Politics, and Provincialism_. Toronto: University of Toronto Press, 1981.

Brown, Graham L. _Pioneer Settlement in Canada, 1763-1895_. Scarborough, Ont.: Prentice-Hall, 1981.

Bumsted, J. M. A Flannel Shirt and Liberty: British Emigrant Gentlewomen in the Canadian West, 1880-1914. Vancouver: University of British Columbia Press, 1982.

Bumsted, J. M. The People's Clearance: Highland Emigration to British North America, 1770-1815. Winnipeg: University of Manitoba Press, 1982.

Callwood, June. Portrait of Canada. Garden City, N.Y.: Doubleday, 1981.

Careless, J. M. S., and Brown, R. Craig, eds. The Canadians, 1867-1967. Toronto: Macmillan, 1967.

Careless, J. M. S., ed. Colonists and Canadians, 1760-1867. Toronto: Macmillan, 1971.

Clark, S. D. Canadian Society in Historical Perspective. Toronto: McGraw-Hill Ryerson, 1976.

Clark, S. D. Colonists and Canadians 1760-1867. Toronto: Macmillan, 1971.

Clark, S. D. The Developing Canadian Community, 2nd. ed. Toronto: University of Toronto Press, 1968.

Cook, Sharon A. The Confident Years: Canada in the 20's. Scarborough, Ont.: Prentice-Hall, 1981.

Cook, Sharon A. The Depression Years: Canada in the 30's. Scarborough, Ont.: Prentice-Hall, 1981.

Creighton, Donald. The Road to Confederation. Toronto: Macmillan, 1964.

Dicks, Stewart K. A Nation Launched: MacDonald's Dominion, 1867-1896. Scarborough, Ont.: Prentice-Hall, 1978.

Dicks, Stewart K. Les Canadiens: The French
in Canada, 1600-1867. Scarborough, Ont.:
Prentice-Hall, 1981.

Duane, Patrick A. Gentlemen Immigrants:
From the British Public Schools to the
Canadian Frontier. Vancouver: Douglas &
McIntyre, 1981.

Hamelin, Louis-Edmond. Canada: A Geograph-
ical Perspective. Translated by M. C.
Storrie and C. I. Jackson. Toronto:
Wiley, 1973.

Hartz, Louis, ed. The Founding of New
Societies. New York: Harcourt, Brace and
World, 1964.

Hill, Douglas. The Opening of the Canadian
West. New York: John Day, 1976.

Lanctot, Gustave. A History of Canada, 3
vols. Translated by Margaret Cameron.
Toronto: Clarke, Irwin, 1964.

Lower, Arthur R. M. Colony to Nation: A
History of Canada, 5th ed. Toronto:
McClelland and Stewart, 1977.

Lower, J. A. Canada: An Outline History.
Toronto: McGraw-Hill Ryerson, 1973.

McNaught, Kenneth. The Pelican History of
Canada. London: Penguin, 1976.

Mansfield, Nick. Introduction to Sociology:
Canadian Perspectives. Toronto: Collier
Macmillan, 1982.

Martin, Chester. Foundations of Canadian
Nationhood. Toronto: University of
Toronto Press, 1955.

Martin, Ged. The Durham Report and British
Policy. Cambridge: Cambridge University
Press, 1973.

Patterson, E. Palmer. The Canadian Indian:
A History since 1500. Don Mills, Ont.:
Collier Macmillan, 1972.

Reid, J. H. Stewart; McNaught, Kenneth; and
Crowe, Harry, eds. A Source Book of
Canadian History. Toronto: Longmans,
Green, 1959.

Stanley, George F. G. New France: The Last
Phase. Toronto: McClelland and Stewart,
1968.

Surtees, Robert J. Canadian Indian Policy:
A Critical Bibliography. Bloomington:
University of Indiana Press, 1982.

Taylor, George Rogers, ed. The War of 1812.
Boston: Heath, 1963.

Thompson, Robert N. Canadians Face Facts.
Quebec: Editions 'Alerte', 1980.

Trudel, Marcel. Introduction to New France.
Toronto: Holt, Rinehart, and Winston,
1968.

Warkentin, John, ed. The Western Interior of
Canada. Toronto: McClelland and Stewart,
1964.

III. Constitutionalism

Cheffins, R. I., and Tucker, R. N. The
Constitutional Process in Canada, 2nd ed.
Toronto: McGraw-Hill, 1976.

Creighton, D. G. British North America at
Confederation. Ottawa: Queen's Printer,
1963.

Dawson, Robert MacGregor, ed. Constitutional
Issues in Canada, 1900-1931. London:
Oxford University Press, 1933.

Faribault, Marcel. La révision constitu-
tionnelle. Montreal: Fides, 1970.

Favreau, Guy. The Amendment of the Constitution of Canada. Ottawa: Queen's Printer, 1965.

Hodgins, Barbara. Where the Economy and the Constitution Meet in Canada. Montreal: C. D. Howe Institute, 1981.

McConnell, William H. A Commentary on the British North American Act. Toronto: Macmillan, 1977.

McCormick, Peter. Regional Representation: The Canadian Partnership. Calgary: Canada West Foundation, 1981.

McInnes, Simon. "The Inuit and the Constitutional Process." Journal of Canadian Studies 16 (Summer 1981):53-68.

McWhinney, Edward. Canada and the Constitution, 1979-1982. Toronto: University of Toronto Press, 1982.

Mallory, J. R. The Structure of Canadian Government. Toronto: Gage, 1980.

Mécanismes pour une nouvelle constitution. Ottawa: Editions de l'Université d'Ottawa, 1981.

Moss, John E. "Native Proposals for Constitutional Reform." Journal of Canadian Studies (Winter 1980-81):85-92.

Stanley, George F. G. A Short History of the Canadian Constitution. Toronto: Ryerson, 1969.

Thomas, Paul G. "Theories of Parliament and Parliamentary Reform." Journal of Canadian Studies 14 (Summer 1979):57-66.

IV. Federalism

A. Federal-Provincial Relations

Armour, Leslie. *The Idea of Canada and the Crisis of Community*. Ottawa: Steel Rail, 1981.

Banting, Keith G. *The Welfare State and Canadian Federalism*. Kingston, Ont.: McGill-Queen's University Press, 1982.

Beck, J. M., ed. *The Shaping of Canadian Federalism: Central Authority or Provincial Right?* Toronto: Copp Clark, 1971.

Bellamy, David J.; Pammett, Jon H.; and Rowat, Donald C., eds. *The Provincial Political Systems*. Toronto: Methuen, 1976.

Blank, Edwin R. *Divided Loyalties: Canadian Concepts of Federalism*. Montreal: McGill-Queen's University Press, 1975.

Careless, Anthony. *Initiative and Response: The Adaptation of Canadian Federalism to Regional Economic Development*. Montreal: McGill University Press, 1977.

Chandler, Marsha A., and Chandler, William M. *Public Policy and Provincial Politics*. Toronto: McGraw-Hill Ryerson, 1979.

Cook, Ramsay. *The Maple Leaf Forever: Essays on Nationalism and Politics in Canada*. Toronto: Macmillan, 1971.

Feldman, Elliot J., and Milch, Jerome. *The Politics of Canadian Airport Development: Lessons for Federalism*. Durham, N.C.: Duke University Press, 1983.

Gibbins, Roger. *Regionalism: Territorial Politics in Canada and the United States*. Toronto: Butterworths, 1982.

Hodgetts, J. E., and Dwivedi, O. P. Provincial Governments as Employers. Montreal: McGill-Queen's University Press, 1974.

Kornberg, Allan; Mishler, William; and Clarke, Harold D. Representative Democracy in the Canadian Provinces. Scarborough, Ont.: Prentice-Hall, 1982.

Lithwick, N. H. "Is Federalism Good for Regionalism?" Journal of Canadian Studies 15 (Summer 1980):62-73.

Mallory, J. R. "Confederation: The Ambiguous Bargain." Journal of Canadian Studies 12 (July 1977):18-23.

Meekison, J. Peter, ed. Canadian Federalism: Myth or Reality? 3rd ed. Toronto: Methuen, 1977.

Melnyk, George. Radical Regionalism. Edmonton: NeWest, 1981.

Phillips, Paul. Regional Disparities: Why Ontario Has So Much and the Others Can't Catch Up. Toronto: Lorimer, 1982.

Robin, Martin, ed. Canadian Provincial Politics. 2nd ed. Scarborough, Ont.: Prentice-Hall, 1978.

Rowell-Sirois Commission. Report of the Royal Commission on Dominion-Provincial Relations. 3 vols. Ottawa: Queen's Printer, 1940.

Sabourin, Louis, ed. Le système politique du Canada. Ottawa: L'Université d'Ottawa, 1970.

Simeon, Richard. Federal-Provincial Diplomacy. 3rd ed. Toronto: University of Toronto Press, 1977.

Smiley, D. V. Canada in Question: Federalism in the Seventies. 2nd ed. Toronto: McGraw-Hill Ryerson, 1976.

239

Stevenson, Garth. "Canadian Regionalism in Continental Perspective." Journal of Canadian Studies 15 (Summer 1980):16-28.

Stevenson, Garth. Unfulfilled Union. Toronto: Gage, 1979.

Veilleux, Gérard. Les relations inter-gouvernementales au Canada, 1867-1967. Montreal: Les Presses de l'Université du Québec, 1971.

B. Provincial-Municipal Relations

Axworthy, L., and Gillies, James M. The City: Canada's Prospects, Canada's Problems. Toronto: Butterworth, 1973.

Bourne, Larry S.; MacKinnon, Ross D.; Siegel, Jay; and Simmons, James W., eds. Urban Futures for Central Canada: Perspectives on Forecasting Urban Growth and Form. Toronto: University of Toronto Press, 1974.

Federation of Canadian Municipalities. Summary Proceedings of the Federation of Canadian Municipalities Annual Conference. Ottawa: Federation of Canadian Municipalities, 1980.

Feldman, Lionel D., and Goldrick, Michael E., eds. Politics and Government of Urban Canada, 3rd ed. Toronto: Methuen, 1976.

Johnson, J. A. "Provincial-Municipal Intergovernmental Fiscal Relations." Canadian Public Administration 12 (No. 2, 1969):-166-180.

Kay, Barry J. "Urban Decision-Making and the Legislative Environment: Toronto Council Re-Examined." Canadian Journal of Political Science 15 (September 1982):553-574.

Krueger, Ralph R., and Bryfogle, R. Charles, eds. Urban Problems: A Canadian Reader.

Toronto: Holt,   Rinehart   and   Winston,
1971.

Magnusson, Warren. "Metropolitan Reform in
the Capitalist City." Canadian Journal of
Political Science 14 (September 1981):557-
586.

Nadar, George A. Cities of Canada. 2 vols.
Toronto: Macmillan, 1976.

Powell,   Alan,   ed.   The   City.   Toronto:
McClelland and Stewart, 1972.

Richardson, Boyce. The Future of Canadian
Cities. Toronto: New Press, 1972.

Rowat, Donald C. The Canadian Municipal
System. Toronto: McClelland and Stewart,
1969.

Rowat, Donald C. Your Local Government, 2nd
ed. Toronto: Macmillan, 1975.

Simmons, James, and Simmons, Robert. Urban
Canada. Canada: Copp Clark, 1969.

Taylor, John. "'Relief from Relief': The
Cities' Answer to Depression Dependency."
Journal of Canadian Studies 14 (Spring
1979):16-23.

Yeates, Maurice, and Garner, Barry. The
North American City. 2nd ed. New York:
Harper and Row, 1976.

C. Regionalism

1. Quebec

Bergeron,   Gérard.   Du   Duplessisme   au
Johnsonisme, 1956-1966. Montreal: Parti
Pris, 1967.

Bergeron, Léandre. The History of Quebec: A
Patriote's Handbook. Toronto: NC Press,
1975.

Beriault, Jean. Anti-Québec: Les réactions du Canada anglais face au French-power. Montreal: Quinze, 1977.

Bernard, André. La Politique au Canada et au Québec. 2nd ed. Montreal: Presses de l'Université du Québec, 1977.

Bernard, André. What Does Québec Want? Toronto: James Lorimer, 1978.

Bourgault, Pierre. Oui à l'indépendance du Québec. Montreal: Quinze, 1977.

Cappon, Paul. Conflit entre les néo-Canadiens et les francophones de Montréal. Quebec: Les Presses de l'Université Laval, 1974.

Clift, Dominique. Quebec Nationalism in Crisis. Montreal: McGill-Queen's University Press, 1982.

Coleman, William D. "From Bill 22 to Bill 101: The Politics of Language Under the Parti Québécois." Canadian Journal of Political Science 14 (September 1981):459-86.

Cook, Ramsay, ed. French-Canadian Nationalism. Toronto: Macmillan, 1969.

Desbarats, Peter. René: A Canadian in Search of a Country. Toronto: McClelland and Stewart, 1976.

Dion, Léon. Quebec: The Unfinished Revolution. Montreal: McGill-Queen's University Press, 1976.

Gagnon, Alain, and Montcalm, Mary Beth. "Economic Peripheralization and Quebec Unrest." Journal of Canadian Studies 17 (Summer 1982):32-42.

Gold, Gerald L., and Tremblay, Marc-Adélard. Communities and Culture in French Canada. Toronto: Holt, Rinehart and Winston, 1973.

242

Gonick, C. W. "Is Canada Falling Apart?" Current, March 1977, pp. 38-47.

Grow, Stewart L. The Murky Future of Canadian Federalism. Provo: Brigham Young University, 1978.

Hamelin, Jean, ed. Histoire du Québec. St. Hyacinthe: Edisem, 1977.

Harvey, Fernand. "La question régionale au Québec." Journal of Canadian Studies 15 (Summer 1980):74-87.

Heintzman, Ralph. "The Political Culture of Quebec, 1840-1960." Canadian Journal of Political Science 16 (March 1983):3-59.

Hodgins, B. W.; Bowles, R. P.; Hanley, J. L.; and Rawlyk, G. A., eds. Canadiens, Canadians and Québécois. Scarborough: Prentice-Hall, 1974.

Latouche, Daniel, ed. Premier mandat: une prospective à court terme du gouvernement péquiste. 2 vols. Montreal: Aurore, 1977.

Mallea, John R., ed. Québec's Language Policies: Background and Response. Québec: Les Presses de l'Université Laval, 1977.

Monet, Jacques. La première Révolution Tranquille: Le nationalisme Canadien-Francais, 1837-1850. Montreal: Fides, 1981.

Morin, Claude. Quebec Versus Ottawa. Toronto: University of Toronto Press, 1976.

Orban, Edmund, ed. La modernisation politique du Québec. Sillery, Québec: Boréal, 1976.

Ornstein, Michael D., and Stevenson, Michael H. "Elite and Public Opinion Before the Québec Referendum: A Commentary on the

State in Canada." <u>Canadian Journal of Political Science</u> 14 (December 1981):745-774.

Plasse, Micheline. "Les Chefs de cabinets ministériels au Québec: la transition du Gouvernement Libéral au Gouvernement Péquiste (1976-1977)." <u>Canadian Journal of Political Science</u> 14 (June 1981):309-336.

Posgate, Dale, and McRoberts, Kenneth. <u>Quebec: Social Change and Political Crisis</u>. Toronto: McClelland and Stewart, 1976.

Rioux, Marcel. <u>Quebec in Question</u>. Translated by James Boake. Toronto: James Lewis and Samuel. 1971.

Rioux, Marcel, and Martin, Yves, eds. <u>La société canadienne-francaise</u>. Montreal: Hurtubise, 1971.

Saywell, John. <u>Quebec 70</u>. Toronto: University of Toronto Press, 1971.

Shere, Waris, ed. <u>Miracles of Survival: Canada and French Canada</u>. Smithtown, NY: Exposition Press, 1981.

Simeon, Richard, ed. <u>Must Canada Fail?</u> Montreal: McGill-Queen's University Press, 1977.

Tellier, Luc-Normand. <u>Le Québec, état nordique</u>. Montreal: Quinze, 1977.

Trudeau, Pierre Elliott, ed. <u>The Asbestos Strike</u>. Translated by James Boake. Toronto: James Lewis and Samuel, 1974.

Trudeau, Pierre Elliott. <u>Federalism and the French Canadians</u>. Toronto: Macmillan, 1968.

Vallières, Pierre. <u>Choose!</u> Translated by Penelope Williams. Toronto: New Press, 1972.

Vallières, Pierre. White Niggers of America. Translated by Joan Pinkham. Toronto: McClelland and Stewart, 1971.

Veltman, Calvin. Contemporary Quebec. Montreal: Université du Québec à Montréal Département d'Études Urbaines, 1981.

Wade, Mason. The French Canadians, 1760-1945. Toronto: Macmillan, 1955.

Wade, Mason. "Québécois and Acadien." Journal of Canadian Studies 9 (May 1974): 47-53.

Young, R. A. "National Identification in English Canada: Implications for Québec Independence." Journal of Canadian Studies 12 (July 1977):53-68.

2. Other Regions

Alexander, David. "New Notions of Happiness: Nationalism, Regionalism and Atlantic Canada." Journal of Canadian Studies 15 (Summer 1980):29-42.

Armstrong, Christopher. The Politics of Federalism: Ontario's Relations with the Federal Government, 1867-1942. Toronto: University of Toronto Press, 1981.

Barr, John J., and Anderson, Owen, eds. The Unfinished Revolt: Some Views on Western Independence. Toronto: McClelland and Stewart, 1971.

Beck, J. Murray. The Government of Nova Scotia. Toronto: University of Toronto Press, 1957.

Bercuson, David Jay, ed. Canada and the Burden of Unity. Toronto: MacMillan of Canada, 1977.

Bercuson, David Jay, ed. Eastern and Western Perspectives. Toronto: University of Toronto Press, 1981.

Bercuson, David Jay. "Regionalism and 'Unlimited Identity' in Western Canada." Journal of Canadian Studies 15 (Summer 1980):121-126.

Bolger, Francis W. P., ed. Canada's Smallest Province: A History of P.E.I. Canada: John Deyell, 1973.

Byers, R. B., and Reford, Robert W., eds. Canada Challenged: The Viability of Confederation. Toronto: Canadian Institute of International Affairs, 1979.

Caldarola, Carlo. Society and Politics in Alberta. Toronto: Methuen, 1979.

Chadwick, St. John. Newfoundland. Cambridge: Cambridge University Press, 1967.

Conway, J. F. "The Prairie Populist Resistance to the National Policy: Some Reconsiderations." Journal of Canadian Studies 14 (Fall 1979):77-91.

Dacks, Gurston. A Choice of Futures: Politics in the Canadian North. Toronto: Methuen, 1981.

Donnelly, M. S. The Government of Manitoba. Toronto: University of Toronto Press, 1963.

Elliott, Jean Leonard, ed. Native Peoples. Scarborough: Prentice-Hall, 1971.

Elton, David K., ed. Proceedings of One Prairie Province? A Question for Canada. Lethbridge: Lethbridge Herald, 1970.

Francis, R. Douglas. "Changing Images of the West." Journal of Canadian Studies 17 (Fall 1982):5-19.

Garreau, Joel. The Nine Nations of North America. Boston: Houghton Mifflin, 1981.

246

Hanson, Eric J. "The Future of Western Canada: Economic, Social, and Political." Canadian Public Administration, 18 (Spring 1974):104-120.

Jull, Peter. "Aboriginal Peoples and Political Change in the North Atlantic Area." Journal of Canadian Studies 16 (Summer 1981):41-52.

MacDonald, Darald C., ed. Government and Politics of Ontario. Toronto: Macmillan, 1975.

McInnes, Simon. "The Inuit and the Constitutional Process." Journal of Canadian Studies 16 (Summer 1981):53-68.

Macpherson, Alan, ed. The Atlantic Provinces. Toronto: University of Toronto Press, 1972.

Macpherson, C. B. Democracy in Alberta. 2nd ed. Toronto: University of Toronto Press, 1962.

Manuel, George. "An Appeal from the Fourth World: The Dene Nation and Aboriginal Rights." Canadian Forum, November 1976, pp. 8-12.

Mardiros, Anthony. William Irvine: The Life of a Prairie Radical. Toronto: J. Lorimer, 1979.

Mowat, Farley. Canada North Now: The Great Betrayal. Toronto: McClelland & Stewart, 1976.

Noel, S. J. R. Politics in Newfoundland. Toronto: University of Toronto Press, 1971.

Owram, Douglas. "The Myth of Louis Riel." Canadian Historical Review 63 (September 1982):315-336.

247

Palmer, Howard, and Palmer, Tamara. "The Alberta Experience." Journal of Canadian Studies 17 (Fall 1982):20-34.

Pratt, Larry, and Stevenson, Garth, eds. Western Separatism: The Myths, Realities and Dangers. Edmonton: Hurtig, 1981.

Robinson, J. Lewis, ed. British Columbia. Toronto: University of Toronto Press, 1972.

Rutan, Gerard F. "Western Canada: The Winds of Alienation." American Review of Canadian Studies 12 (Spring 1982):74-97.

Schwartz, Mildred A. Politics and Territory: The Sociology of Regional Persistence in Canada. Montreal: McGill-Queen's University Press, 1974.

Simeon, Richard. "Regionalism and Canadian Political Institutions." Queen's Quarterly, 82 (Winter 1975):499-511.

Smith, Allan. "Quiet Revolution in the West." Canadian Forum, June-July, 1978, pp. 12-15.

Smith, P. J., ed. The Prairie Provinces. Toronto: University of Toronto Press, 1972.

Thorburn, Hugh G. Politics in New Brunswick. Toronto: University of Toronto Press, 1961.

Ward, Norman; and Spafford, Duff, eds. Politics in Saskatchewan. Don Mills: Longmans, 1968.

Watkins, Mel., ed. Dene Nation: The Colony Within. Toronto: University of Toronto Press, 1977.

Weaver, Sally M. Making Canadian Indian Policy: The Hidden Agenda, 1968-1970. Toronto: University of Toronto Press, 1981.

248

Wonders, William C., ed. The North. Toronto: University of Toronto Press, 1972.

Wood, John R. "Secession: A Comparative Analytical Framework." Canadian Journal of Political Science 14 (March 1981):107-134.

V. The Electoral System and the Polity

A. Political Socialization

Adachi, Ken. The Enemy that Never Was: A History of the Japanese Canadians. Toronto: McClelland and Stewart, 1976.

Bell, David V. J., and Tepperman, Lorne. The Roots of Disunity: A Look at Canadian Political Culture. Toronto: McClelland and Stewart, 1979.

Campbell, Colin. Canadian Political Facts, 1945-1976. Toronto: Methuen, 1977.

Cleverdon, Catherine L. The Woman Suffrage Movement in Canada. Toronto: University of Toronto Press, 1974.

Desbarats, Peter. Canada Lost, Canada Found: The Search for a New Nation. Toronto: McClelland and Stewart, 1981.

Kalbach, Warren E., and McVey, Wayne W. The Demographic Bases of Canadian Society. Toronto: McGraw-Hill, 1971.

McMenemy, John. The Language of Canadian Politics: A Guide to Important Terms and Concepts. Toronto: John Wiley and Sons, 1980.

Manzer, Ronald. Canada: A Socio-Political Report. Toronto: McGraw-Hill Ryerson, 1974.

Martin, Wilfred B. W., and Macdonell, Allan J. Canadian Education: A Sociological

249

Analysis. Scarborough, Ont.: Prentice-Hall Canada, 1982.

Pammett, Jon H.; Le Duc, Lawrence; Jenson, Jane; and Clarke, Harold D. "The Perception and Impact of Issues in the 1974 Federal Election." Canadian Journal of Political Science 10 (March 1977):93-126.

Pammett, Jon H., and Whittington, Michael S., eds. Foundations of Political Culture: Political Socialization in Canada. Toronto: Macmillan, 1976.

Porter, John. The Vertical Mosaic. Toronto: University of Toronto Press, 1965.

Ramu, G. N., and Johnson, Stuart, D., eds. Introduction to Canadian Society. Toronto: Macmillan, 1976.

Reid, Raymond, ed. The Canadian Style: Yesterday and Today in Love, Work, Play, and Politics. New York: P. S. Eriksson, 1973.

Roussopoulos, Dimitrios, I., ed. Canada and Radical Social Change. Montreal: Black Rose, 1973.

Stephenson, Marylee, ed. Women in Canada. Toronto: New Press, 1973.

Willcox, Paul. The Capital Crisis and Labour: Perspectives on the Dynamics of Working-Class Consciousness in Canada. Uppsala, Sweden: Uppsala University Press, 1980.

Winks, Robin W. The Blacks in Canada. Montreal: McGill-Queen's University Press, 1971.

Wiseman, Nelson. "An Historical Note on Religion and Parties on the Prairies." Journal of Canadian Studies 16 (Summer 1981):109-112.

Young, Walter. "The Voices of Democracy: Politics and Communication in Canada." Canadian Journal of Political Science 14 (December 1981):683-700.

B. Elections and the Electorate

Bernard, André. Québec-élections 1981. La Salle, Québec: Hurtubise, 1981.

Courtney, John C. "The Defeat of the Clark Government: The Dissolution of Parliament, Leadership Conventions, and the Calling of Elections in Canada." Journal of Canadian Studies 17 (Summer 1982):82-90.

Hibbard, Dale. Hibbard's 1980 Federal Election Handbook. Ottawa: D. Hibbard, 1980.

Penniman, Howard R., ed. Canada at the Polls, 1979 and 1980: A Study of the General Election. Washington, D.C.: American Enterprise Institution, 1981.

Penniman, Howard R., ed. Canada at the Polls: The General Election of 1974. Washington, D.C.: American Enterprise Institute for Public Policy Research, 1975.

Smiley, Donald. "As the Options Narrow: Notes on Post-November 15 Canada." Journal of Canadian Studies 12 (July 1977):3-7.

C. Political Parties

Avakumovic, Ivan. The Communist Party in Canada. Toronto: McClelland and Stewart, 1975.

Barr, John J. The Dynasty: The Rise and Fall of Social Credit in Alberta. Toronto: McClelland and Stewart, 1974.

251

Betcherman, Lita-Rose. The Swastika and the Maple Leaf: Fascist Movements in Canada in the Thirties. Toronto: Fitzhenry & Whiteside, 1975.

Brodie, M. Janine, and Jenson, Jane. Crisis, Challenge, and Change: Party and Class in Canada. Toronto: Methuen, 1980.

Cairns, Alan C. "The Electoral System and the Party System in Canada, 1921-1965." Canadian Journal of Political Science 1 (March 1968):55-80.

Caplan, Gerald L. The Dilemma of Canadian Socialism: The CCF in Ontario. Toronto: McClelland and Stewart, 1973.

Carrigan, D. Owen, ed. Canadian Party Platforms, 1867-1968. Canada: Copp Clark, 1968.

Christian, William, and Campbell, Colin. Political Parties and Ideologies in Canada: Liberals, Conservatives, Socialists, Nationalists. Toronto: McGraw-Hill Ryerson, 1974.

Courtney, John C. The Selection of National Party Leaders in Canada. Toronto: Macmillan, 1973.

Engelmann, Frederick C., and Schwartz, Mildred A. Canadian Political Parties: Origin, Character, Impact. Scarborough: Prentice-Hall, 1975.

English, John. The Decline of Politics: The Conservatives and the Party System, 1901-1920. Toronto: University of Toronto Press, 1977.

Gibbons, Kenneth M., and Rowat, Donald C., eds. Political Corruption in Canada. Toronto: McClelland & Stewart, 1976.

Gwyn, Richard. Le Prince. Montreal: France-Amérique, 1981.

252

Heggie, Grace F. Canadian Political Parties, 1867-1968: A Historical Bibliography. Toronto: Macmillan Canada, 1977.

Kashtan, William. Toward Socialism. Toronto: Progress Books, 1976.

Laxer, James, and Laxer, Robert. The Liberal Idea of Canada. Toronto: Lorimer, 1977.

Lipset, S. M. Agrarian Socialism: The Cooperative Commonwealth Federation in Saskatchewan. Garden City, N.Y.: Doubleday, 1968.

Marchak, M. Patricia. Ideological Perspectives on Canada. Toronto: McGraw-Hill Ryerson, 1975.

Monière, Denis. Ideologies in Quebec: The Historical Development. Toronto: University of Toronto Press, 1981.

Morton, Desmond. Social Democracy in Canada: NDP. 2nd ed. Toronto: S. Stevens, 1977.

Perlin, George C. The Tory Syndrome: Leadership Politics in the Progressive Conservative Party. Montreal: McGill-Queen's University Press, 1980.

Pinard, Maurice. The Rise of a Third Party: A Study in Crisis Politics. Englewood Cliffs: Prentice-Hall, 1971.

Pothier, Diane. "Parties and Free Votes in the Canadian House of Commons." Journal of Canadian Studies 14 (Summer 1979): 80-96.

Smith, David E. The Regional Decline of a National Party: Liberals on the Prairies. Toronto: University of Toronto Press, 1981.

Thorburn, Hugh G., ed. Party Politics in Canada, 4th ed. Scarborough: Prentice-Hall, 1979.

Weinrich, Peter. *Social Protest from the Left in Canada, 1870-1970: A Bibliography*. Toronto: University of Toronto Press, 1982.

Whitaker, Reginald. *The Government Party: Organizing and Financing the Liberal Party of Canada, 1930-1958*. Toronto: University of Toronto Press, 1977.

Winn, Conrad, and McMenemy, John. *Political Parties in Canada*. Toronto: McGraw-Hill Ryerson, 1976.

Young, Walter D. *The Anatomy of a Party: The National CCF, 1932-1961*. Toronto: University of Toronto Press, 1969.

D. Pressure Groups

Kwavnick, David. *Organized Labour and Pressure Politics: The Canadian Labour Congress 1956-1968*. Montreal: McGill-Queen's University Press, 1972.

Presthus, Robert. *Elite Accommodation in Canadian Politics*. Toronto: Macmillan, 1973.

Presthus, Robert. "Interest Groups and the Canadian Parliament: Activities, Interaction, Legitimacy, and Influence." *Canadian Journal of Political Science* 4 (December 1971):444-460.

Pross, A. Paul. "Canadian Pressure Groups in the 1970s: Their Role and Their Relations with the Public Service." *Canadian Public Administration* 18 (Spring 1974):121-135.

Pross, A. Paul, ed. *Pressure Group Behavior in Canadian Politics*. Toronto: McGraw-Hill Ryerson, 1975.

VI.   Public Policymaking

   A.   The Executive

      D'Aquino, Thomas. "The Prime Minister's
         Office: Catalyst or Cabal?" Canadian
         Public Administration 17 (Spring 1974):55-
         79.

      French, Richard D. How Ottawa Decides:
         Planning and Industrial Policy-Making,
         1968-1980. Toronto: Lorimer, 1980.

      Gwyn, Richard. The Northern Magus: Pierre
         Trudeau and the Canadians. Markham, Ont.:
         Paper Jacks, 1981.

      Hockin, Thomas A., ed. Apex of Power: The
         Prime Minister and Political Leadership in
         Canada. Scarborough: Prentice-Hall,
         1971.

      Kirk-Greene, Anthony H. M. "The Governors
         General of Canada, 1867-1952: A Collec-
         tive Profile." Journal of Canadian
         Studies 12 (Summer 1977):35-57.

      MacKinnon, Frank. The Crown in Canada.
         Calgary: McClelland and Stewart West,
         1976.

      Matheson, W. A. The Prime Minister and the
         Cabinet. Toronto: Methuen, 1976.

      Simeon, Richard. "The 'Overload Thesis' and
         Canadian Government." Canadian Public
         Policy 2 (Autumn 1976):541-552.

      Ward, Norman. "Responsible Government: An
         Introduction." Journal of Canadian
         Studies (Summer 1979):3-7.

   B.   The Parliament

      Aiken, Gordon. The Backbencher. Toronto:
         McClelland and Stewart, 1974.

Bejermi, John Zeyad. Canadian Parliamentary
Handbook. Ottawa: Borealis, 1982.

Burns, R. M. "Second Chambers: German
Experience and Canadian Needs." Canadian
Public Administration 18 (Winter 1975):
541-568.

Campbell, Colin. The Canadian Senate: A
Lobby from Within. Toronto: Macmillan of
Canada, 1978.

Gaboury, Jean Pierre, and Hurley, James Ross,
eds. The Canadian House of Commons
Observed: Parliamentary Internship
Papers. Ottawa: University of Ottawa
Press, 1979.

Hockin, Thomas. "Flexible and Structured
Parliamentarism: From 1848 to Contem-
porary Party Government." Journal of
Canadian Studies 14 (Summer 1979):8-17.

Jackson, Robert J., and Atkinson, Michael M.
The Canadian Legislative System: Politi-
cians and Policymaking. 2nd ed. Toronto:
Macmillan of Canada, 1980.

Kornberg, Allan, and Mishler, William.
Influence in Parliament: Canada. Durham,
N.C.: Duke University Press, 1976.

March, Roman R. The Myth of Parliament.
Scarborough: Prentice-Hall, 1974.

Schwarz, John E., and Shaw, L. Earl. The
United States Congress in Comparative
Perspective. Hinsdale, Ill.: Dryden,
1976.

Stewart, John B. The Canadian House of
Commons. Montreal: McGill-Queen's
University Press, 1977.

Van Loon, R. J. "The Frustrating Role of
Ottawa Backbenchers." Toronto Globe and
Mail, 5 April 1971, p. 7.

C. Public Administration

Adie, Robert F., and Thomas, Paul G. Canadian Public Administration: Problematical Perspectives. Scarborough, Ont.: Prentice-Hall Canada, 1982.

Beattie, Christopher. Minority Men in a Majority Setting: Middle-Level Francophones in the Canadian Public Service. Toronto: McClelland and Stewart, 1975.

Denham, Ross A. "The Canadian Auditors General--What Is Their Role?" Canadian Public Administration, 17 (Summer 1974): 259-273.

Doern, Bruce, and Aucoin, Peter. Public Policy in Canada: Organization, Process, and Management. Toronto: Macmillan, 1979.

Frederick, Jarman E., and Hux, Allan D. Political Decisions in Canada. Toronto: Wiley Publishers of Canada, 1980.

Garant, Patrice. La Fonction publique, canadienne et québécoise. Quebec: Les Presses de l'Université Laval, 1973.

Hodgetts, J. E.; McCloskey, William; Whitaker, Reginald; and Wilson, V. Seymour. The Biography of an Institution: The Civil Service Commission of Canada, 1908-1967. Montreal: McGill-Queen's University Press, 1972.

Hodgetts, J. E. The Canadian Public Service: A Physiology of Government, 1867-1970. Toronto: University of Toronto Press, 1973.

Kernaghan, W. D. K., ed. Bureaucracy in Canadian Government. 2nd ed. Toronto: Methuen, 1973.

Langford, John W. Transport in Transition: The Reorganization of the Federal Transport Portfolio. Montreal: McGill-Queen's University Press, 1976.

Lupul, Manoly R. "The Political Implementation of Multiculturalism." Journal of Canadian Studies 17 (Spring 1982):93-102.

Swanick, Eric L. Bilingualism in the Federal Canadian Public Service. Monticello, Ill.: Vance Bibliographies, 1980.

Walls, C. E. S. "Royal Commissions--Their Influence on Public Policy." Canadian Public Administration 12 (No. 3, 1969): 365-371.

Willms, A. M., and Kernaghan, W. D. K., eds. Public Administration in Canada: Selected Readings. 4th ed. Toronto: Methuen, 1982.

D. Judiciary

Cairns, Alan C. "The Judicial Committee and Its Critics." Canadian Journal of Political Science 4 (September 1971): 301-345.

Gall, Gerald L. The Canadian Legal System. Toronto: Carswell, 1977.

Linden, Allen M., ed. The Canadian Judiciary. Toronto: Osgood Hall Law School, 1976.

Reports of the Supreme Court 1876-. Ottawa: Registrar of the Court, various years.

Schubert, Glendon, and Danelski, David J., eds. Comparative Judicial Behavior. New York: Oxford University Press, 1969.

Smith, Jennifer. "The Origins of Judicial Review in Canada." Canadian Journal of Political Science 16 (March 1983):115-134.

VII. Canadian Foreign Policy

    A. Foreign Policymaking

Barrett, June R. A Bibliography of Works on Canadian Foreign Relations, 1976-1980. Toronto: Canadian Institute of International Affairs, 1982.

Berkowitz, S. D., and Logan, Robert K., eds. Canada's Third Option. Toronto: Macmillan of Canada, 1978.

Canadian Institute of International Affairs. Canada's Response to the Polish Crisis. Toronto, 1982.

Canadian-Soviet Relations 1936-1981. Oakville, Ont.: Mosaic Press, 1981.

Cox, David. "Leadership Change and Innovation in Canadian Foreign Policy: The 1979 Progressive Conservative Government." International Journal 37 (Autumn 1982): 555-583.

Dobell, W. M. "Interdepartmental Management in External Affairs." Canadian Public Administration 21 (Spring 1978):83-102.

Farrell, R. Barry. The Making of Canadian Foreign Policy. Scarborough: Prentice-Hall, 1969.

Leeson, Howard A., and Vanderelst, Wilfried. External Affairs and Canadian Federalism: The History of a Dilemma. Toronto: Holt, Rinehart and Winston, 1973.

Keenleyside, T. A. "Lament for a Foreign Service: The Decline of Canadian Idealism." Journal of Canadian Studies 15 (Winter 1980-81):75-84.

Osbaldeston, Gordon. "Reorganizing Canada's Department of External Affairs." International Journal 37 (Summer 1982):453-466.

Stacey, C. P. Canada and the Age of Conflict: A History of Canadian External Policies. Toronto: Macmillan, 1981.

Tucker, Michael. Canadian Foreign Policy: Contemporary Issues and Themes. Toronto: McGraw-Hill Ryerson, 1980.

B. The "Middle Power"

Byers, R. B. "The Canadian Military and the Use of Force: End of an Era?" International Journal 30 (Spring 1975):284-298.

Dauphin, Roma. "Une nouvelle politique économique canadienne." Journal of Canadian Studies 14 (Fall 1979):118-125.

Dolan, Michael B.; Towlin, Brian W.; and Von Riekhoff, Harald. "Integration and Autonomy in Canada-United States Relations, 1963-1972." Canadian Journal of Political Science 15 (June 1982):331-364.

Dosman, E. J., and Abele, Frances. "Offshore Diplomacy in the Canadian Arctic: The Beaufort Sea and Lancaster Sound." Journal of Canadian Studies (Summer 1981):3-15.

Eayrs, James. In Defense of Canada. 3 vols. Toronto: University of Toronto Press, 1972.

Fuhrman, Peter Harry. Business in the Canadian Environment. Scarborough, Ont.: Prentice-Hall, 1982.

Harbron, John D. "Our International Problems: What Will We Do?" Canadian Geographic, August/September, 1981, pp. 12-19.

Holmes, John W. "Divided We Stand." International Journal 31 (Summer 1976):385-398.

Hunter, W. T. "The Decline of the Tariff-- But Not of Protection." Journal of Canadian Studies 14 (Fall 1979):111-117.

260

Lyon, Peyton, and Ismal, Tareg Y., eds. Canada and the Third World. Toronto: Macmillan, 1976.

Lyon, Peyton V., and Tomlin, Brian W. Canada as an International Actor. Toronto: Macmillan of Canada, 1979.

Ogelsby, J. C. M. Gringos from the Far North. Toronto: Macmillan, 1976.

Pelletier, Jean. The Canadian Caper. Markham, Ont.: Paper Jacks, 1981.

Thomson, D. C., and Swanson, R. F. Canadian Foreign Policy: Options and Perspectives. Toronto: McGraw-Hill Ryerson, 1971.

C. Canadian-U.S. Relations

Axline, Andrew; Hyndman, James E.; Lyon, Peyton V.; and Molot, Maureen A., eds. Continental Community? Independence and Integration in North America. Toronto: McClelland and Stewart, 1974.

Berton, Pierre. Hollywood's Canada: The Americanization of Our National Image. Toronto: McClelland and Stewart, 1975.

Burley, Tony. Neighbors: The United States and Canada. Toronto: Globe/Modern Curriculum Press, 1982.

Byers, R. B., and Leyton-Brown, David. "The Strategic and Economic Implications for the United States of a Sovereign Quebec." Canadian Public Policy 6 (Spring 1980): 325-341.

Clarkson, Stephen. Canada and the Reagan Challenge. Toronto: Lorimer, 1982.

Dickey, John Sloan. Canada and the American Presence. New York: New York University Press, 1975.

Donnelly, Daniel K. Can-American Union Now! Toronto: Griffin House, 1978.

English, H. Edward, ed. Canada-U.S. Relations. New York: The Academy of Political Science, 1976.

Fox, Annette Baker; Hero, Alfred O., Jr.; and Nye, Joseph S., Jr., eds. Canada and the United States: Transnational and Transgovernmental Relations. New York: Columbia University Press, 1976.

Grey, Rodney de C. Trade Policy in the 1980s: An Agenda for Canadian-U.S. Relations. Montreal: C. D. Howe Institute, 1981.

Hatch, Robert McConnell. Thrust for Canada: The American Attempt on Quebec in 1775-1776. Boston: Houghton Mifflin, 1979.

Holmes, John W. Life With Uncle: The Canadian-American Relationship. Toronto: University of Toronto Press, 1981.

Innis, Hugh., ed. Americanization. Toronto: McGraw-Hill Ryerson, 1972.

Keohane, Robert O., and Nye, Joseph S. Power and Interdependence. Boston: Little, Brown, 1977.

Lumsden, Ian, ed. Close the 49th Parallel, Etc.: The Americanization of Canada. Toronto: University of Toronto Press, 1970.

Morchain, Janet. Sharing a Continent. Toronto: McGraw-Hill Ryerson, 1973.

Munton, Don, and Swanson, Dean. Forecasting the Political Economy of Canadian-American Relations, 1976-1986: Report on a Delphi Exercise. Halifax: Centre for Foreign Policy Studies of Dalhousie University, 1976.

Murray, Janice L. The Fourth Lester B. Pearson Conference on the Canada-United States Relationship. New York: New York University Press, 1977.

Preston, Richard A. "Two Centuries in the Shadow of Behemoth: The Effect on the Canadian Psyche." International Journal 31 (Summer 1976):413-433.

Redekop, John H. "A Reinterpretation of Canadian-American Relations." Canadian Journal of Political Science 9 (June 1976):227-243.

Rotstein, Abraham. "Canada: The New Nationalism." Foreign Affairs 55 (October 1976):97-118.

Schwartz, Mildred A. The Environment for Policy-Making in Canada and the United States. Montreal: C. D. Howe Institute, 1981.

Swanson, Roger Frank, ed. Canadian-American Summit Diplomacy 1923-1973. Ottawa: McClelland and Stewart, 1975.

Swanson, Roger Frank. State/Provincial Interaction: A Study of Relations Between U.S. States and Canadian Provinces Prepared for the U.S. Department of State. Washington, D.C.: Canus Research Institute, 1974.

Von Riekoff, Harald. Canadian-U.S. Relations: Policy Environments, Issues, and Prospects. Montreal: C. D. Howe Research Institute, 1979.

D. The Economic and Environmental Challenges

Armstrong, Muriel. The Canadian Economy and Its Problems, 3rd ed. Scarborough, Ont.: Prentice-Hall Canada, 1982.

263

Easterbrook, W. T., and Aitken, Hugh G. J.
Canadian Economic History. Toronto:
Gage, 1980.

Fry, Earl H., ed. Energy Development in
Canada: The Political, Economic, and
Continental Dimensions. Provo, UT:
Brigham Young University Center for
International and Area Studies, 1981.

Gold, Peter S., ed. Acid Rain. Buffalo:
Canadian-American Center, State University
of New York at Buffalo, 1982.

Lazar, Fred. The New Protectionism: Non-
Tariff Barriers and Their Effects on
Canada. Toronto: Lorimer, 1981.

Marr, William L., and Paterson, Donald G.
Canada: An Economic History. Toronto:
Gage, 1980.

Reuber, Grant L. Canada's Political Economy:
Current Issues. Toronto: McGraw-Hill
Ryerson, 1980.

Robinson, H. Lukin. Canada's Crippled
Dollar: An Analysis of International
Trade and Our Troubled Balance of Pay-
ments. Toronto: Lormier, 1980.

Ruggeri, G. C., ed. The Canadian Economy:
Problems and Policies. Toronto: Gage,
1981.

INDEX

266

269

National Energy Program (NEP) 220, 222
Native population (See also Dene nation, Métis) 39,
    72-73, 84, 121, 125-129
Netherlands, 3, 203, 211, 226, 227
New Brunswick, 17, 30, 33, 98, 120, 124, 161, 163
New Democratic Party (NDP), 47, 143, 147, 152, 156-159,
    161-163
New England, 117, 207
Newfoundland, 17, 34, 98, 120, 124, 125, 161, 163, 180
New France, 21-24, 28, 39
New Jersey, 18, 117
New York, state of, 6, 18, 117, 130, 207
New York City, 10, 18, 106, 130, 135, 139, 208
New York Times, 6
New Zealand, 3, 218
Nixon, Richard, 150, 175, 213
North American Air Defense Command (NORAD) 110, 204,
    214, 228
North Atlantic Treaty Organization (NATO), 110, 214,
    225
Northern Ireland, 6
Northwest Territories, 37, 120, 126, 129, 161
Norway, 211
Nova Francia (See New France)
Nova Scotia, 17, 28, 30, 33, 39, 41, 44, 98, 117, 120,
    124, 161, 163, 211

O'Connor, Sandra Day, 197
Ohio, 18, 117
Ombudsmen, 178
Ontario, 17, 29, 33, 43, 86, 98, 103, 130, 142, 154,
    161, 163, 180, 182, 195
Organization for Economic Cooperation and Development
    (OECD), 218
Ottawa, 16, 27, 44, 48, 53, 61, 96, 100, 101, 103, 105,
    109, 123, 124, 130, 155, 203, 204, 222

Papineau, Louis 30, 42
Parliament, federal, 8, 56-58, 97, 111, 153-161, 171,
    178-191, 207
Parliament of Canada Act of 1875, 53
Parti Québécois (PQ), 27, 28, 38, 49, 60, 84, 109-122,
    158, 162, 163
Party discipline, 100, 158-160, 164, 165, 175
Party system, 16, 118, 153-168
Pennsylvania, 18, 117
Plains of Abraham, 24, 41
Poland, 218